A CATALOGUE OF THE MANUSCRIPTS IN THE IRVING LAYTON COLLECTION

A CATALOGUE OF THE MANUSCRIPTS IN THE IRVING LAYTON COLLECTION

Compiled by
Joy Bennett

The University of Calgary Press

© 1988 Joy Bennett. All rights reserved

ISBN 0-919813-88-7

The University of Calgary Press
2500 University Drive N.W.
Calgary, Alberta, Canada T2N 1N4

Canadian Cataloguing in Publication Data

Concordia University. Libraries. Special Collections
    Division
    A catalogue of the manuscripts in the Irving Layton
Collection

   Includes index.
   ISBN 0-919813-88-7

   1. Layton, Irving, 1912– – Manuscripts – Catalogs.
2. Manuscripts, Canadian – Quebec (Province)
– Montreal – Catalogs. 3. Concordia University.
Libraries. Special Collections Division – Catalogs.
I. Bennett, Joy, 1946– II. Title
PS8523.A97Z991 1989   016.811'54   C88-091644-3
Z8492.4.C65 1989

No part of this book may be stored in a retrieval system, translated or reproduced in any form, by print, photoprint, microfilm, microfiche, or any other means, without permission from the publisher.

Printed in Canada

Table of Contents

	Page
Acknowledgements	ix
How to Use the Catalogue	x
Technical Notes	xi
Abbreviations Used	xv
Introduction	xvii
Balls for a One-armed Juggler	1
The Cold Green Element	6
The Covenant	7
Droppings from Heaven	9
Europe and Other Bad News	15
For My Brother Jesus	22
For My Neighbours in Hell	36
Final Reckoning: Poems 1982-1986	43
The Gucci Bag	67
The Gucci Bag (2nd ed.)	85
The Improved Binoculars	97
The Improved Binoculars (2nd ed.)	98
In the Midst of My Fever	99
A Laughter in Mind	99
A Laughter in Mind (2nd ed.)	100
Lovers and Lesser Men	102
The Long Pea-shooter	104
The Love Poems of Irving Layton	104
The Laughing Rooster	105
Music in Kazoo	106
The Gucci Bag (McClelland and Steward ed.)	106
Nail Polish	109
Periods of the Mood	120
The Pole-vaulter	126
The Swinging Flesh	146
The Shattered Plinths	147

The Tightrope Dancer	157
Unpublished	170
The Whole Bloody Bird	179
Essays	181
Miscellaneous	183
Manuscripts	184
Notebooks	188
Prose	192
The Index	195
Title Index	196
Other Items	211
Chronological Index	213

FOR GARY,
WITHOUT WHOSE LOVE AND SUPPORT
NOTHING WOULD BE POSSIBLE

ACKNOWLEDGMENTS

This work has been made possible by a generous grant from the Social Science and Humanities Research Council of Canada under the auspices of the Canadian Studies Research Tools Programme. The encouragement and support of the Concordia University Library is also acknowledged.

I am particularly indebted to my Research Assistant Ms. Jacqueline Dealy who has brought enthusiasm, meticulous attention to detail and a considerable professional knowledge to this project. The credit for most of the work must be given to her. Ms. Elyse Greenberg was responsible for computer input and on-line editing of our data, and Ms. Anne Wade-Stephen has done the revisions and indexing. I am grateful to them for their expertise, patience and perseverance.

Finally special thanks are due to Irving Layton himself who provided us with the wealth of material to work with. He has been supportive and helpful throughout this project. In my 1981 bibliography of Irving Layton's published work, he wrote "immortality is the name of the game." It is our hope that this catalogue will help to ensure the immortality he seeks.

HOW TO USE THE CATALOGUE

The catalogue consists of three sections:

1. The catalogue proper
2. The alphabetical index
3. The chronological index

The catalogue

The catalogue proper has one entry for each manuscript in the Layton Collection at Concordia University. Many of the entries contain multiple titles, reflecting Mr. Layton's tendency to work on more than one poem at a time or to re-use pages that contained drafts of earlier poems. The reader **MUST** refer to the alphabetical index at the end of the catalogue for a complete listing of titles that are included in the catalogue. Each title in the index is followed by one or more location symbols directing the reader to the appropriate entry or entries in the catalogue.

The alphabetical index

An alphabetical index has been created to facilitate access to the catalogue. All manuscript titles and/or their published equivalents have been included in the index. The user is referred to the explanatory notes at the beginning of the index section for further details.

The chronological index

The chronological index consists of only those titles that are in the Layton Collection at Concordia University. It is not meant to be an inclusive chronology of Mr. Layton's work.

TECHNICAL NOTES

Standard archival cataloguing procedures (*AACR2*) have been followed wherever possible in this catalogue. However, due to the constraints imposed by the volume of the material and the repetitive nature of the entries, it was necessary to modify the rules to some extent. The following paragraphs explain our methods and formats.

Scope

There are 528 entries in the catalogue. Each entry represents an original manuscript held in the Layton Collection at Concordia University. A manuscript may consist of a single sheet of paper or of several sheets stapled or in some other way designated a unit by the author. For instance the manuscript of a poem encased in a file folder or in the cover of an examination booklet has been catalogued as a single item. A majority of the manuscripts consist of Layton's poetic works, but the catalogue also includes some essays, notebooks and miscellaneous writings, as well as several versions of the manuscript for his memoirs *Waiting for the Messiah*.

We removed the author's paper clips and staples from the manuscripts, but in all cases the original order of the pages, as they were received from the author, has been maintained.

Arrangement

The logical order of the catalogue parallels the physical arrangement of the manuscripts as they are stored in the files at Concordia University. Each item has been assigned a number derived from a combination of the title of the published volume in which the poem first appeared and the sequential order of the manuscript in the file. Multiple occurrences of the same title are given successive numbers. For example: BFOJ 3/2 which is the number assigned to "The gods speak out" means that "The gods speak out" is the third title in the *Balls For a One-Armed Juggler* manuscript file and that it is the second occurrence of "The gods speak out." More explicitly:

> **BFOJ** = Balls For a One-Armed Juggler
>
> **3** = Third title in the BFOJ file
>
> **2** = Second time this title has been catalogued as a separate manuscript.

A third occurrence of "The gods speak out" would be labeled BFOJ 3/3.

Main Entries

The most prominent title on each item, often holograph, or underlined, has been used as the main entry. If a title was not found on the manuscript, the item was identified from Irving Layton's published works and the title recorded in square brackets []. In many cases a group of stapled pages, or even a single page, may contain the manuscript of more than one poem. The titles of these poems are noted in the title section of the entry and their scope, (number of pages, etc.) is added to the note section. However, these poems are not "added entries" in the proper sense of the term as it is commonly used. That is to say, they do not have their own entry in the catalogue. They can, however, be found in alphabetical order in the index, which refers the reader to the main entry with which they have been catalogued.

Titles

Three kinds of titles need to be considered. They are:

1. The title that appears on the manuscript, which may or may not be the published title of the poem.

2. Variations of the title that appear on the manuscript while the work is in progress.

3. The published title of a poem, which may or may not appear on the manuscript.

Title variants (2 & 3) that do not represent a permanent change in the title have been mentioned in the note section as a means of identifying the individual pages of a manuscript. However, since they have not been permanently assigned to the poem they have not been included in the index.

Published titles that are not found on the manuscript (1 & 3) are mentioned in the note section and have been included in the index.

Publication

The first publication of each item is mentioned at the end of the note section. We also tried to identify subsequent publications in monograph and in most cases we were successful. The reader is encouraged to look at all published versions of the poems as some have been revised between publications, and unfortunately it was beyond the scope of this catalogue to detail such changes. It was also impossible, given the time frame, to check publication of the poems in the periodical literature.

Manuscripts for which we could find no evidence of publication are entered under the title found on the manuscript and have been noted as "not published to date."

We were fortunate to have the help of Mr. Layton in verifying these poems as not yet published.

Dates

At Mr. Layton's suggestion manuscripts that were not dated at time of writing have been dated one year prior to publication.

Description

Items that consist of both holograph and typescript drafts are recorded in terms of the portion that is holograph. For example, "in part holograph" means that a smaller portion of the item is in holograph, while "chiefly holograph" means that the larger portion is in holograph. Most revisions of the manuscripts have been done in holograph and have not been noted as such. However, when the revision is in a hand other than that of the author, it has been noted as "ms." revision. Likewise, notes or portions of the draft not in the author's hand are described as "ms. note."

The number of stanzas on any given page is noted only if the draft varies from the published version. The number of lines is noted when the poem only contains one stanza, the length of which differs from the published version. Numbering of lines is interpreted as follows: "lines 1-10" indicates the first ten lines of a poem; "10 lines" indicates any ten lines, that is to say the ten lines may occur anywhere in the poem.

AACR2

As mentioned above *AACR2*, with special reference to chapter 4, has been used as a standard in so far as was possible. To facilitate use of the catalogue some of the technical aspects are clarified below.

1. "Holograph" refers to an item written in the author's hand.

2. "Ms." refers to written items not in the author's hand.

3. "Typescript" refers to an item that has been produced by a typewriter or other mechanical device such as a word processor.

4. "Marginalia" refer to information that is extraneous to the poem being considered. This can be anything from an unidentified phone number to a grocery list or a tally of figures.

5. The manuscripts have been described in terms of "leaves" and "pages." A "page" is a sheet of paper that has writing on both sides. A "leaf" is a single sheet of paper that has writing on only one side. Sheets of paper that have significant material on both sides are considered, for descriptive

purposes, as two sides of a page and are numbered "page 1" and "page 2," etc. However, if the information on one side of a sheet of paper is fragmentary, or otherwise insignificant, such as marginalia, it is considered a single leaf and numbered accordingly and the information on the overleaf is recorded as being on the "verso."

6. Each page has been measured and the length of the page recorded in centimeters. In cases where the length is more than twice the width, both the length and width are recorded. Pages, which have material on both sides, are considered leaves for purposes of measurement.

7. Square brackets [] have been used to indicate information found in places other than on the item being catalogued, such as in a published monograph or another manuscript.

ABBREVIATIONS USED *

BFOJ	Balls for a one-armed juggler 1963
CGE	The cold green element 1955
COV	The covenant 1977
CP65	Collected poems 1965
CP71	The collected poems of Irving Layton 1971
DD	Dance with desire 1986
DF	Darkening fire 1975
DFH	Droppings from heaven 1979
E	Essays
EBN	Europe and other bad news 1981
FMBJ	For my brother Jesus 1976
FR	Final reckoning 1987
GB	The Gucci bag 1983
GB2	The Gucci bag, Mosaic Press, 2nd ed., 1983
GP	Seventy-five Greek poems 1974
IB	The improved binoculars 1956
IB2	The improved binoculars, 2nd state 1956
IMF	In the midst of my fever 1954
LIM	Laughter in the mind 1958
LIM2	Laughter in the mind, 2nd state 1959
LLM	Lovers and lesser men 1973
LP	The long pea shooter 1954
LPIL1	The love poems of Irving Layton 1980
LPIL2	The love poems of Irving Layton 1984
LR	The laughing rooster 1964
MISC	Miscellaneous
MOK	Music on a kazoo 1956
MS	Manuscripts
MSGB	The Gucci bag, McClelland & Stewart ed. 1983
NB	Notebooks
NP	Nail polish 1971
PIL	The poems of Irving Layton 1977
POM	Periods of the moon 1967
PR	Prose
PV	The pole-vaulter 1974
RC	A red carpet for the sun 1959
SEL	Selected poems 1969
SF	The swinging flesh 1961
SP	The shattered plinths 1968
TD	The tightrope dancer 1978

UE	The unwavering eye 1975
UN	Unpublished
UP	The uncollected poems 1976
WBB	The whole bloody bird 1969
WPJ	A wild peculiar joy 1982

* This list includes only those books in which manuscripts from the collection have been published.

INTRODUCTION

> They dance best who dance with desire,
> Who lifting feet of fire from fire
> Weave before they lie down
> A red carpet for the sun.
>
> > from For Mao Tse Tung:
> > A meditation on flies and
> > kings.

From his pen, the image the poet seeks to create becomes the image of the creator himself. Certainly few would dispute that Irving Layton has ever approached his work, or in fact his life, with anything less than "feet of fire." From the first publication of his poetry in the Macdonald College *Failt Ye-Times* in 1935, Layton has never failed to provoke, anger, dismay and disturb his readers.

Irving Layton was born in Romania in 1912, immigrating a year later with his parents to Montreal. He grew up on Elizabeth Street in Montreal's "Jewish Ghetto" surrounded by the sights, sounds and sensations of a deeply ethnic community. There, bearing the brunt of racial attacks from street gangs, Layton began to develop a sense of the world as a place of injustice, anger and inequality, of the "demons of the human soul" that would eventually take shape in his poetry. He attended Baron Bing High School and in 1930, his final year, he was introduced to A.M. Klein, the poet and teacher who was instrumental in shaping Layton's early years as a writer. Layton recalls in his memoirs, *Waiting for the Messiah*, that Klein was a man of "general kindness" and patience who spent hours talking to him about poetry, writing and politics. (It is perhaps a credit to Klein's generosity to the young poet that Layton himself became a generous and thoughtful teacher of aspiring writers.) After graduating from Macdonald College with a B.Sc. in agriculture, Layton enrolled at McGill University and did postgraduate work in economics and political science. He received an M.A. degree in 1946.

As a forerunner of the modernist movement, Layton is credited with jarring Canadian poetry out of the complacent aesthetic style it had adopted from British tradition into an identity of its own. He was a member of an elite group of young poets who contributed to *First Statement*, the literary publication founded by John Sutherland in 1942. He served as an editor with Contact Press in 1952 and one year later was instrumental in setting the editorial policy of *CIV/n*. During its two-year run *CIV/n* published the essays and poems of such writers as Leonard Cohen, Gael Turnbull, F.R. Scott and Patrick Anderson. A prolific writer, Layton has published more than forty volumes of poetry and essays. He has received honorary degrees from three Canadian universities, was writer-in-residence at Sir George Williams

University in 1965 and Guelph University in 1969, and in 1978 was appointed Professor of English at York University. Layton has received every major Canadian writing award, including the Governor General's Award for *A Red Carpet for the Sun*. In 1977 he became an officer of the Order of Canada and in 1987 was nominated for the Nobel Prize in literature.

The Layton Collection at Concordia University houses the most complete body of work by and about the poet that exists to date. Since its inception in 1969, the collection has grown from a few boxes of miscellaneous manuscripts and letters to a large and important collection of manuscripts, notebooks, letters, published material, tapes and photographs.

When we first approached the cataloguing of the Layton manuscripts, we had little idea of the enormity of the task ahead. More than 500 pre-publication manuscripts, including ten personal notebooks, were examined and analyzed. If at times the task of deciphering and ordering the material seemed daunting, it also served to better acquaint us with one of Canada's premier poets. Personal notations such as lists of people Layton had met at parties or poetry readings, telephone numbers and addresses, drafts of letters and notations of debts he owed and those owed to him, were scattered throughout the notebooks and drafts of his poems. They gave us the sense that we were actually looking over Layton's shoulder as he wrote, reading his thoughts and eavesdropping on his private conversations. As we worked, the image of Layton as a true craftsman emerged, gifted and hard-working, often seeming to be ruled by some invisible force that makes him write draft after draft of a single poem only to arrive at a final version that is only slightly changed from the original.

Layton has said that most people have the romantic idea that a poem just "gushes out." Although he admits that this has occasionally happened to him, most notably with the poems "The Swimmer" and "A Tall Man Executes a Jig," he contends that more often he keeps revising until the poem says what he wants it to say without losing any of its fervour. A poem, he says, has to "dance off the page into a life of its own." If it fails at that, it has no "poetic value" and should be consigned to "fire and flame."

From our examination of the manuscripts it became clear that very few poems do indeed write themselves. Although we found that only a minor number undergo significant change, it must be noted that even a slight change, a word or two or a phrase, may alter the very intent and tone of the poem. In many cases Layton clearly indicates the final version with a bold square drawn around the poem and the date and familiar signature written at the bottom of the page. Layton's mediums are pen or pencil and paper, and many of the drafts were scribbled on whatever paper he found readily at hand--restaurant place mats, brown paper bags, university examination booklets and odd scraps of paper. The only exception was a series of notebooks acquired so he could keep track of his ideas and thoughts while he was travelling.

This catalogue has taken more than a year to complete. We have studied each draft or group of drafts (always maintaining the provenance), and created a record for each unique title. In every case the poem has been identified in the catalogue by the title under which it was first published in a bound volume. Each item has been dated, either by the date Layton assigned it on the final draft or the date when the poem was first published. Where no date was indicated, we consulted Layton who assured us that most of the poems were published within one year of being written.

We used *Anglo-American Cataloguing Rules 2 (AACR2)* rules for the cataloguing of the manuscripts, providing as much physical detail as possible, and have adapted *AACR2* punctuation to render the information more publishable. The format was selected for facility of use and comprehension.

Poems noted as "not published to date" were designated as such only after every possible source, including Layton himself, was consulted. We decided to use that notation because Layton has suggested that the poems may yet be published.

Joy Bennett
Montreal, Quebec
January 1988

BFOJ - Balls for a One-armed Juggler

BFOJ 1/1
BAUDELAIRE IN A SUMMER COTTAGE
[1962].
[1] leaf; 28 cm.
Typescript with holograph revisions.
Poem.
Thirty lines beginning "He sports his son's peaked cap...."
Published with further revisions in: Balls for a one-armed juggler/Irving Layton.
Toronto: McClelland and Stewart, 1963, (also in CP65, CP71).

BFOJ 1/2
BAUDELAIRE IN A SUMMER COTTAGE
[1962].
[1] leaf; 28 cm.
Typescript with holograph revisions.
Poem.
Thirty lines beginning "He sports his son's peaked cap...."
Published with further revisions in: Balls for a one-armed juggler/Irving Layton.
Toronto: McClelland and Stewart, 1963, (also in CP65, CP71).

BFOJ 1/3
BAUDELAIRE IN A SUMMER COTTAGE
[1962].
[1] leaf; 28 cm.
Typescript with holograph revisions.
Poem.
Thirty lines beginning "He sports his son's peaked cap...."
Published with further revisions in: Balls for a one-armed juggler/Irving Layton.
Toronto: McClelland and Stewart, 1963, (also in CP65, CP71).

BFOJ 1/4
BAUDELAIRE IN A SUMMER COTTAGE
[1962].
[2] leaves; 28 cm.
Typescript.
Poem.
Published with revisions in: Balls for a one-armed juggler/ Irving Layton. Toronto: McClelland and Stewart, 1963.

BFOJ 2/1
FOR ALEXANDER TROCCHI [NOVELIST]; [PORTRAIT OF A GENIUS]
[1962].
[4] p., [1] leaf; 28 cm.
Holograph.
Two poems.
On p. [1,3]:2 drafts with revisions of "Alexander Trocchi" on pages torn from notebook.
On p. [2,4]:2 drafts of poem beginning "My friend Cohen, a yiddish Keats..."; mood and images used in "[Portrait of a genius]."
Recto of leaf[1] blank.
On verso of leaf [1]:draft of poem beginning "My friend Cohen, a yiddish Keats..."; lines 1-11 of "Alexander Trocchi."
Poems on leaf [1] and verso of leaves [2,3] crossed out.
"For Alexander Trocchi novelist" published with further revisions in: Balls for a one-armed juggler/Irving Layton. Toronto: McClelland and Stewart, 1963, (also in CP65, CP71, DF).
"[Portrait of a genius]" published in: The laughing rooster/ Irving Layton. Toronto: McClelland and Stewart, 1964.

BFOJ 2/2
FOR ALEXANDER TROCCHI [NOVELIST]; [PORTRAIT OF A GENIUS]
[1962].
[4]p.; 28 cm.
Holograph.
Two poems.
On p.[1,4]:draft with revisions of "For Alexander Trocchi" on pages torn from notebook.
On p.[2,3]:2 drafts of poem beginning "My friend Cohen, a yiddish Keats..."; mood and images used in "Portrait of a genius"; 2 lines of "Alexander Trocchi" at bottom of p.[3].
"For Alexander Trocchi" published with further revisions in: Balls for a one-armed juggler/Irving Layton. Toronto: McClelland and Stewart, 1963, (also in CP65, CP71, DF).
"[Portrait of a genius]" published in: The laughing rooster/ Irving Layton. Toronto: McClelland and Stewart, 1964.

BFOJ 2/3
FOR ALEXANDER TROCCHI [NOVELIST]
[1962].
[1] leaf; 28 cm.

...con't

BFOJ 2/3...con't

Typescript with holograph revisions.
Poem.
Published with further revisions in: Balls for a one-armed juggler/Irving Layton. Toronto: McClelland and Stewart, 1963, (also in CP65, CP71, DF).

BFOJ 2/4
FOR ALEXANDER TROCCHI [NOVELIST]
[1962].
[1] leaf; 28 cm.
Typescript with holograph revisions.
Poem.
Published with further revisions in: Balls for a one-armed juggler/Irving Layton. Toronto: McClelland and Stewart, 1963, (also in CP65, CP71, DF).

BFOJ 2/5
FOR ALEXANDER TROCCHI [NOVELIST]
[1962].
[1] leaf; 28 cm.
Typescript.
Poem.
Published with revisions in: Balls for a one-armed juggler/ Irving Layton. Toronto: McClelland and Stewart, 1963, (also in CP65, CP71, DF).

BFOJ 2/6
FOR ALEXANDER TROCCHI [NOVELIST]
[1962].
[1] leaf; 28 cm.
Typescript.
Poem.
Published with revisions in: Balls for a one-armed juggler/ Irving Layton. Toronto: McClelland and Stewart, 1963, (also in CP65, CP71, DF).

BFOJ 2/7
[FOR ALEXANDER TROCCHI, NOVELIST]; [PORTRAIT OF A GENIUS]
[1962].
[6]p., [5] leaves; 28 cm.
Holograph.
Two poems.
On p.[1]:draft beginning "Each night from the paved streets of Montreal...";
 holograph note explaining poem was never completed but words and images used in "Portrait of a genius."

...con't

BFOJ 2/7...con't
On p.[2] and leaf [1]:2 drafts beginning "My friend Cohen, a yiddish Keats...."
On p.[3]:draft beginning "My friend Cohen..."; lines 1-10 of "Alexander Trocchi."
On p.[4]:draft of 16 lines beginning "My young friend..." crossed out.
On leaves [1-2]:2 drafts beginning "My friend Cohen..." crossed out.
On p.[5]:draft of 19 lines beginning "My friend Cohen..." crossed out; marginalia.
On p.[6]:draft of 23 lines beginning "Cohen can't write..."; lines 1-15 crossed out.
On leaves [3-5] and verso of leaves [3-4]:3 drafts of "My friend Cohen" crossed out.
"[For Alexander Trocchi, novelist]" published in: Balls for a one-armed juggler/Irving Layton. Toronto: McClelland and Stewart,
1963, (also in CP65, CP71, DF).
"[Portrait of a genius]" published in: The laughing rooster/ Irving Layton. Toronto: McClelland and Stewart, 1964.

BFOJ 3/1
THE GODS SPEAK OUT
[1962].
[2] leaves; 28 cm.
Typescript with holograph revisions.
Poem.
Published with further revisions in: Balls for a one-armed juggler/Irving Layton. Toronto: McClelland and Stewart, 1963.

BFOJ 3/2
THE GODS SPEAK OUT
[1962].
[2] leaves; 28 cm.
Typescript with holograph revisions.
Poem.
Published with further revisions in: Balls for a one-armed juggler/Irving Layton. Toronto: McClelland and Stewart, 1963.

BFOJ 4/1
THE HAG
[1962].
[1] leaf; 28 cm.
Typescript with holograph revisions.
Poem.
On recto:stanzas 1-8 of "The hag."

BFOJ 4/1...con't

On verso:10 lines beginning "Those whom woman or opinion made comfortable rejecting...."
Published with further revisions in: Balls for a one-armed juggler/Irving Layton. Toronto: McClelland and Stewart, 1963.

BFOJ 5/1
MAN GOING UP AND DOWN
[1962].
[2]p.; 28 cm.
Holograph.
Poem.
Draft with revisions on verso of typescript personal letter to Irving [Layton].
Published with further revisions in: Balls for a one-armed juggler/Irving Layton. Toronto: McClelland and Stewart, 1963. (also in CP65, CP71).

BFOJ 6/1
[A TALL MAN EXECUTES A JIG]; [THIS MACHINE AGE]
[1962].
[6]p., [3] leaves; 28 cm.
Chiefly holograph.
Two poems.
On p.[1]:holograph draft of 5 lines and list of words on theme of "[A tall man executes a jig]."
On p.[2]:holograph draft of 14 lines on theme of "[A tall man executes a jig]."
On p.[3]:holograph draft of 6 lines on theme of "[A tall man executes a jig]"; list of titles of 20 poems by [Irving Layton] with heading "15 poems."
On p.[4,6]:typescript draft of "[This machine age]."
On p.[5] and leaves [1-3]:4 holograph drafts with revisions of stanza 7 of "[A tall man executes a jig]."
"[A tall man executes a jig]," published with further revisions in: Balls for a one-armed juggler/Irving Layton. Toronto: McClelland & Stewart, 1963, (also in CP65, CP71, DF, PIL, SEL).
"[This machine age]," ibid., (also in CP65, CP71, SEL).

BFOJ 6/2
[A TALL MAN EXECUTES A JIG]
[1962].
[2]p., [1] leaf; 21 cm.
Holograph.
Poem.

...con't

BFOJ 6/2...con't
On p.[1]:draft of stanzas 1-2.
On p.[2]:draft with revisions of stanzas 3-4; 2 lines of typescript beginning "I'll split the ground beneath your feet...."
On leaf [1]:draft with revisions of stanzas 3.
Published with further revisions in: Balls for a one-armed juggler/Irving Layton. Toronto: McClelland and Stewart, 1963, (also in CP65, CP71, DF, PIL, SEL, WPJ).

BFOJ 7/1
EPIGRAM FOR ROY DANIELLS
[1962].
[1] leaf; 28 cm.
Holograph.
Poem.
Two drafts with revisions on verso of letter from McClelland and Stewart dated June 11, 1962. Published in: Balls for a one-armed juggler/Irving Layton. Toronto: McClelland and Stewart, 1963.

CGE - The Cold Green Element

CGE 1/1
THE BOYS
[1954].
[2]p.; 20 cm.
Holograph.
Poem.
Draft on lined yellow page of daily journal dated April 11, 1953.
Notes on p.[2] concerning percentage of mentally ill in population at large.
"The boys" published with revisions as "[Boys in October]."
Published in: The cold green element/Irving Layton. [S.l.]: Contact Press, 1955, (also in CP65, CP71, IB, IB2, RC).

CGE 2/1
ENEMIES
[1954].
[2] leaves; 20 cm.
Holograph.
Poem.
Draft of 15 stanzas on yellow lined pages from daily journal dated August 14,15, 1953.
Published with revisions in: The cold green element/Irving Layton. [S.l.]: Contact Press, 1955, (also in CP65, CP71, DF, IB, IB2, RC, SEL).

CGE 3/1
SARATOGA BEACH
1954.
[2]p., [2] leaves; 20 cm.
Holograph.
Poem.
Two drafts with revisions on yellow lined pages from daily journal dated July 27,28,29, August 1, 1953.
Draft dated June 21, 1954.
Published with further revisions in: The cold green element/ Irving Layton. Toronto: Contact Press, 1956, (also in CP65, CP71, IB, IB2, RC).

COV - The Covenant

COV 1/1
BACILLUS PRODIGIOSUS
1976.
[1] leaf; 28 cm.
Holograph signed.
Poem.
Draft with revisions.
Words from text printed in margin.
Dated Brussels, February 8, 1976.
Published with further revisions in: The covenant/Irving Layton. Toronto: McClelland and Stewart, 1977.

COV 2/1
THOUGHTS ON TITLING MY NEXT BOOK "BRAVO LAYTON"
[1976].
[2] leaves; 28 cm.
Typescript with holograph revisions.
Poem.
Published with further revisions in: The covenant/Irving Layton. Toronto: McClelland and Stewart, 1977.

COV 3/1
LIKE ONCE I LOST
[1976].
[1] leaf; 28 cm.
Typescript with holograph revisions signed.
Poem.
Published with further revisions in: The covenant/Irving Layton. Toronto: McClelland and Stewart, 1977, (also in LPIL1).

COV 4/1
MEDITATIONS OF AN AGING LEBANESE POET; BACILLUS PRODIGIOSUS
[1976].
[2]p.; 28 cm.
Holograph signed.
Two poems.
On p.[1]:draft of "Meditations of an aging Lebanese poet"; draft of "Bacillus prodigiosus" crossed out.
On p.[2]:photocopy of published unidentified essay on Canadian poetry.
"Meditations of an aging Lebanese poet" published in: The covenant/Irving Layton. Toronto: McClelland and Stewart, 1974, (also in WPJ).
"Bacillus prodigiosus," ibid., (with revisions).

COV 5/1
AVIVA
[1976].
[6] leaves; 28 cm.
Chiefly holograph.
Poem.
On leaves [1-4]:4 holograph drafts with revisions; leaf [3] titled "Musia."
On leaves [5-6]:2 typescript drafts.
Drafts 1-4 numbered.
Published with further revisions in: The covenant/Irving Layton. Toronto: McClelland and Stewart, 1977, (also in LPIL1, LPIL2).

COV 6/1
THE GLASS DANCER
1975.
[12] leaves; 28 cm.
Holograph.
Poem.
On leaves [1-2]:2 drafts of 6 stanzas with revisions.
On leaves [3,11-12]:3 drafts of 2 stanzas with revisions.
On leaves [4-10]:7 drafts of 3 stanzas with revisions.
Leaves [2-8] titled "Bool."
Dated Oracabesa, December 23, 1975.
Drafts numbered 1-12.
Published with further revisions in: The covenant/Irving Layton. Toronto: McClelland and Stewart, 1977.

DFH - Droppings From Heaven

DFH 1/1
AUTUMN SEEN AS MY LADY; CUISINE CANADIENNE THE REAL THING
[1978].
[2]p., [4] leaves; 28 cm.
Typescript with holograph revisions.
Two poems.
On p.[1] and leaves [1-4]:5 drafts with revisions of "Autumn seen as my lady"; p.[1] and leaf [1] titled "Autumn seen as a woman."
On p.[2]:draft with revisions of "Cuisine canadienne the real thing."
"Cuisine canadienne the real thing" published as "[Cuisine canadienne]."
"Autumn seen as my lady" published in: Droppings from heaven/ Irving Layton. Toronto: McClelland and Stewart, 1979.
"[Cuisine canadienne]," ibid., (with revisions).

DFH 2/1
CALIBRATIONS
[1978].
[4] leaves; [2] leaves 21 cm., 2 leaves 28 cm.
In part holograph.
Poem.
On leaf [1]:draft with revisions and reworking of stanza 1.
On verso of leaf [1]:draft of stanza 3.
On leaf [2]:draft with revisions and reworking of stanza 2.
On leaves [3-4]:2 typescript drafts.
Drafts 1-2 numbered.
Published with further revisions in: Droppings from heaven/ Irving Layton. Toronto: McClelland and Stewart, 1979.

DFH 3/1
FATA MORGANA; SHIT; THE LAST SURVIVOR; MAN AND WOMAN; ACQUIRED COURAGE; WASP SONG
1978.
[20]p., [2] leaves; 28 cm.
Chiefly holograph.
Six poems.
On p.[1]:holograph draft of 24 lines with theme and images of "Fata Morgana."
On p.[2,6]:typescript draft of "Shit."
On p.[3,5,7,9] and leaves [1-2]:3 holograph drafts with revisions of "Fata Morgana."
On p.[11,13,15]:3 crossed out drafts of stanza 1 of "Fata Morgana."

...con't

DFH 3/1...con't

On p.[17,19]:typescript draft with revisions of "Fata Morgana."
On p.[4,12]:2 typescript drafts of "The last survivor."
On p.[8,10]:2 typescript fragments beginning "Thoughtless and primitive selling...."
On p.[14]:typescript draft of "Acquired courage."
On p.[16]:typescript draft of "Man and woman."
On p.[18,20]:2 typescript drafts of "Wasp song"; draft on p.[18] crossed out.
"Fata Morgana" dated Toronto, Ontario, June 2, 1978.
"Man and woman" published as "[The hex]."
"Acquired courage" published as "[Two solitudes]."
"[Two solitudes]" published as 2 titled stanzas of "The mildewed maple."
"Fata Morgana" published with further revisions in: Droppings from heaven/Irving Layton. Toronto: McClelland and Stewart,
1979.
"Shit," ibid., (with revisions).
"The last survivor" published with revisions in: For my neighbours in hell/Irving Layton. Oakville, Ont.: Mosaic Press/ Valley Editions, [1980].
"The mildewed maple," ibid., (with revisions).
"Wasp song" not published to date.

DFH 3/2
FATA MORGANA; [THE LAST SURVIVOR]
1978.
[2]p., [1] leaf; 28 cm.
Typescript with holograph revisions.
Two poems.
On p.[1] and leaf [1]:draft with revisions of "Fata Morgana."
On p.[2]:draft of "[The last survivor]."
"Fata Morgana" published with further revisions in: Droppings from heaven/Irving Layton. Toronto: McClelland and Stewart, 1979, (also in LPIL1, LPIL2, DD).
"[The last survivor]" published with revisions in: For my neighbours in Hell/Irving Layton. Oakville, Ont.: Mosaic Press/Valley Editions, [1980].

DFH 4/1
THE HAPPY HOOKER
1979.
[3] leaves; 28 cm.
Typescript with holograph revisions.
Poem.

...con't

DFH 4/1...con't

On leaf [1]:draft with revisions.
On leaf [2]:draft with revisions and reworking of stanzas 2,3.
On leaf [3]:draft of 5 stanzas.
Lower edge of leaf [3] missing.
Dated West Palm Beach, Florida, March 8, 1979.
Published with further revisions in: Droppings from heaven/ Irving Layton. Toronto: McClelland and Stewart, 1979.

DFH 5/1
LETTER TO A LOST LOVE; QUIDNUNC
1978.
[2]p., [3] leaves; 28 cm.
In part holograph.
Two poems.
On p.[1]:holograph draft with revisions of "Letter to a lost love."
On p.[2]:typescript draft of "Quidnunc."
On leaves [1-2]:2 typescript drafts of "Letter to a lost love"; leaf [2] titled "Letter to Aviva."
On leaf [3]:typescript draft with holograph revisions of "Letter to a lost love."
"Letter to a lost love" dated July 23, 1978.
"Letter to a lost love" published with further revisions in: Droppings from heaven/Irving Layton. Toronto: McClelland and Stewart, 1979, (also in LPIL1, LPIL2, DD).
"Quidnunc" not published to date.

DFH 6/1
NOT ALL CANUCKS ARE SHMUCKS
[1978].
[1] leaf; 28 cm.
Typescript.
Poem.
Published with revisions in: Droppings from heaven/Irving Layton. Toronto: McClelland and Stewart, 1979.

DFH 7/1
SHLEMIHL
1978.
[1] leaf; 28 cm.
Photocopy of typescript.
Poem.

...con't

DFH 7/1...con't

Draft with revisions.
Dated Montreal, Que[bec], November 8, 1978.
Published in: Droppings from heaven/Irving Layton. Toronto: McClelland and Stewart, 1979.

DFH 8/1
WHERE WAS YOUR SHIT DETECTOR, PABLO?; PRAYER FOR MY OLD AGE
[1978].
[4]p., [1] leaf; 28 cm.
In part holograph.
Two poems.
On leaf [1]:holograph draft with revisions of stanzas 1-2 and lines 1-22 of stanza 3 of "Where was your shit detector, Pablo?"
On p.[1,3]:typescript draft with revisions of stanzas 1-2 and lines 1-21 of stanza 3 of "Where was your shit detector, Pablo?"
On p.[2]:typescript draft with revisions of 25 lines of "Prayer for my old age."
On p.[4]:typescript draft of "Prayer for my old age" with reworking of lines 1-12.
Brown stains on leaf [1].
"Where was your shit detector, Pablo?" published with further revisions in: Droppings from heaven/Irving Layton. Toronto: McClelland and Stewart, 1979, (also WPJ).
"Prayer for my old age," ibid., (with revisions).

DFH 9/1
DIVORCE; WHAT CRAZY JENNY SINGS IN HER GOLDEN GHETTO; QUEER MAMMAL; WASP SONG
1978.
[10]p.; 28 cm.
In part holograph.
Four poems.
On p.[1]:2 holograph drafts with revisions of stanza 2 of "Divorce."
On p.[2,6]:2 typescript drafts of "Wasp song."
On p.[3]:holograph draft with revisions of "Divorce"; fragment beginning "In an afterlife, if there is an afterlife...."
On p.[4,10]:2 typescript drafts of "What crazy Jenny sings in her golden ghetto."
On p.[5]:holograph draft with revisions of stanza 2 of "Divorce."
On p.[7,9]:2 typescript drafts of "Divorce."
On p.[8]:typescript draft of "Queer mammal."
"Queer mammal" published as "[The absurd animal]."

...con't

DFH 9/1...con't

"Divorce" dated July 29, 1978.
"Divorce" published with further revisions in: Droppings from heaven/Irving Layton. Toronto: McClelland and Stewart, 1979.
"What crazy Jenny sings in her golden ghetto," ibid., (with revisions), (also in LPIL1, LPIL2, DD).
"[The absurd animal]," ibid., (with revisions).
"Wasp song" not published to date.

DFH 10/1
PRAYER FOR MY OLD AGE; MITT A BANG; WHAT AN OLD POET TOLD ME; THE MOMENT; WHAT ANOTHER OLD POET TOLD ME
[1978].
[8]p., [1] leaf; 28 cm.
In part holograph.
Five poems.
On p.[1]:typescript draft of "Prayer for my old age"; includes 1 unpublished stanza.
On p.[2]:holograph draft of "What an old poet told me"; holograph draft of "What another old poet told me" crossed out.
On p.[3]:holograph draft of "Mitt a bang."
On p.[4]:holograph draft of "Prayer for my old age"; includes 1 unpublished stanza
On p.[2]:holograph draft of "What an old poet told me"; holograph draft of "What another old poet told me" crossed out.
On p.[3]:holograph draft of "Mitt a bant."
On p.[4]:holograph draft of "Prayer for my old age"; includes 1 unpublished stanza.
On p.[5]:typescript draft of "Mitt a bang."
On p.[6]:typescript draft of "What an old poet told me" with reworking of lines 1-3.
On p.[7]:typescript draft of "Mitt a bant"; lines 1-13 crossed out.
On p.[8]:typescript draft of "The moment"; typescript draft of "What an old poet told me."
On leaf [1]:typescript draft of "Mitt a bang."
"Mitt a bang" published with revisions as "[Not with a whimper]."
"What an old poet told me" published as "[Words from an old Greek poet]."
"Prayer for my old age" published in: Droppings from heaven/ Irving Layton. Toronto: McClelland and Stewart, 1979.
"[Not with a whimper]" published in: For my neighbours in hell/ Irving Layton. Oakville, Ont.: Mosaic Press/Valley Editions, [1980].
"[Words from an old Greek poet]," ibid.
"The moment" not published to date.
"What another old poet told me" not published to date.

DFH 11/1
COMB AND BIRD
1978.
1 paper bag 11 cm x 30 cm.
Holograph.
Poem.
Draft with revisions and reworking of stanzas 2-3.
Published with further revisions as "[Stillness]."
Dated July, 1978.
Published in: Droppings from heaven/Irving Layton. Toronto: McClelland and Stewart, 1979.

DFH 12/1
FOR SANDRA
[1978].
1 envelope; 30 cm.
Holograph signed.
Poem.
Draft with revisions on back of brown manila envelope addressed to Dr. Layton.
Published with further revisions in: Droppings from heaven/ Irving Layton. Toronto: McClelland, 1979, (also in LPIL1, LPIL2, DD).

DFH 13/1
MOLIBOS
1977.
[9] leaves; 5 leaves 21 cm., 4 leaves 30 cm.
In part holograph.
Poem.
On leaf [1]:2 holograph drafts of stanzas 1-2 with revisions.
On leaves [2-5]:4 holograph drafts with revisions.
On leaves [6-7]:2 typescript drafts with revisions.
On leaves [8-9]:2 typescript drafts.
Dated Molibos, July 23, 1977.
Published in: Droppings from heaven/Irving Layton. Toronto: McClelland and Stewart, 1979.

EBN - Europe and Other Bad News

EBN 1/1
BEING THERE
1980.
[7] leaves; 28 cm.
In part holograph.
Poem.
On leaves [1-2]:2 holograph drafts with revisions.
On leaves [3-7]:4 signed typescript drafts with revisions and 1 photocopy.
Drafts numbered 1-6.
Marginalia on leaf [6] and verso of leaf [7].
Dated Niagara-on-the-Lake, March 27, 1980.
Published in: Europe and other bad news/Irving Layton. Toronto: McClelland and Stewart, 1981.

EBN 2/1
JUNK
[1980].
1 leaf; 28 cm.
Typescript.
Poem.
Number "62" in upper right corner, "65" in lower right corner.
"Junk" published with revisions as "[Being]."
Published in: Europe and other bad news/Irving Layton. Toronto: McClelland and Stewart, 1981.

EBN 3/1
THE BALLOON
[1980].
[1] leaf; 28 cm.
Typescript with holograph revisions.
Poem.
Draft.
Published in: Europe and other bad news/Irving Layton. Toronto: McClelland and Stewart, 1981.

EBN 4/1
DEFINITIONS
[1980].
[1] leaf; 28 cm.
Holograph.

...con't

EBN 4/1...con't

Poem.
Draft with revisions and reworking of stanza 1 on lined paper torn from notebook.
Published with further revisions in: Europe and other bad news/ Irving Layton.
Toronto: McClelland and Stewart, 1981.

EBN 5/1
EINE KLEINE NACHTMUSIK; FOR HANS MAYBE KLAUS OR TADEUSZ
1980.
[14] leaves; 28 cm.
In part holograph.
Two poems.
On leaf [1]:holograph draft with revisions of "Eine kleine Nachtmusik" on lined paper torn from notebook.
On leaves [2-3]:2 typescript drafts with revisions of "Eine kleine Nachtmusik"; includes fragments and stanzas 6-8 of "For Hans maybe Klaus or Tadeusz" and 1 unpublished stanza.
On leaf [4]:typescript draft of lines 1-8 of "Eine kleine Nachtmusik."
On leaves [5-6]:2 typescript drafts of "Eine kleine Nachtmusik."
On leaf [7]:typescript draft with revisions of "Eine kleine Nachtmusik"; includes stanzas 6-7 of "For Hans maybe Klaus or Tadeusz."
On leaves [8-14]:7 typescript drafts of "Eine kleine Nachtmusik" with revisions.
Leaves [2-3,6-9] titled "I was not there"; leaf [10] titled "No witness."
Ms. title "Eine kleine Nachtmusik" on verso of leaf [3].
Dated June 1960.
"Eine kleine Nachtmusik" published in: Europe and other bad news/Irving Layton. Toronto: McClelland and Stewart, 1981, (also in WPJ).
"For Hans maybe Klaus or Tadeusz," ibid.

EBN 6/1
FOR HANS, MAYBE KLAUS OR PYOTYR; I WAS NOT THERE
1980.
[2]p., [5] leaves; 28 cm.
In part holograph.
Two poems.
On leaves [1-2]:holograph draft with revisions of "For Hans, maybe Klaus or Pyotyr" on page torn from Concordia University examination booklet; leaf [1] titled "For Hans, maybe Vladimir or Pyotyr."
On leaf [3]]:typescript draft with revisions of lines 1-32 of "For Hans, maybe Klaus or Pyotyr."
On p.[1]:typescript draft of "For Hans, maybe Klaus or Pyotyr titled "For Hans,

...con't

EBN 6/1...con't

maybe Klaus or Thaddeus."
On p.[2]:typescript draft of "I was not there."
On leaf [4] and verso:typescript draft with holograph revisions of "For Hans, maybe Klaus or Pyotyr."
On leaf [5]:typescript draft with holograph revisions of "For Hans, maybe Klaus or Pyotyr."
"For Hans, maybe Klaus or Pyotyr" published as "[For Hans, maybe Klaus or Tadeusz]."
"I was not there" published as "[Eine Kleine Nachtmusik]."
"[For Hans, maybe Klaus or Tadeusz]" published with further revisions in: Europe and other bad news/Irving Layton. Toronto: McClelland and Stewart, 1981.
"[Eine Kleine Nachtmusik]," ibid. (with revisions), (also in WPJ).

EBN 7/1
GULAG
[1980].
[1] leaf; 28 cm.
Holograph.
Poem.
Draft of 7 lines.
Marginalia crossed out.
Published with revisions in: Europe and other bad news/Irving Layton. Toronto: McClelland and Stewart, 1981.

EBN 8/1
IN AN ICE AGE
[1980].
1 leaf; 28 cm.
Poem.
Typescript.
Published in: Europe and other bad news/Irving Layton. Toronto: McClelland and Stewart, 1981.

EBN 9/1
HERZL
1980.
[2]p., [11] leaves; 1 leaf 20 cm., 11 leaves 28 cm.
Chiefly holograph.
Poem.
On p.[1] and leaf [1]:holograph draft of 5 stanzas with revisions.

...con't

EBN 9/1...con't

On p.[2]: carbon copy of letter to the editor of the Globe and Mail from Irving Layton, dated April 30, 1980.
On leaves [2-3]:2 holograph drafts of 5 stanzas with revisions.
On leaves [4-8]:5 holograph drafts with revisions.
On leaves [9-11]:3 typescript drafts with revisions.
Drafts numbered 1-11.
Dated May 1, 1980.
Published with further revisions in: Europe and other bad news/ Irving Layton. Toronto, Ont.: McClelland and Stewart, 1981.

EBN 10/1
ISLA MUJERES; IN AN ICE AGE
[1980].
[1] leaf; 28 cm.
In part holograph.
Two poems.
Typescript draft with revisions of "Isla Mujeres."
Holograph draft of 13 lines with theme and images of "In an ice age."
"Isla Mujeres" published with further revisions in: Europe and other bad news/Irving Layton. Toronto: McClelland and Stewart, 1981.
"In an ice age," ibid.

EBN 11/1
RUINA MAYA
[1980].
[3] leaves; 28 cm.
Typescript with holograph revisions.
Poem.
On leaf [1]:typescript draft with revisions and reworking of lines 20-27.
On leaves [2-3]:2 typescript drafts.
Published with further revisions in: Europe and other bad news/ Irving Layton. Toronto: McClelland and Stewart, 1981.

EBN 12/1
THE SCRIPT
[1980].
[1] leaf; 28 cm.
Typescript.
Poem.

...con't

EBN 12/1...con't

Draft of 28 lines.
"The script" published with revisions as "[To a shmuck with talent]."
Published in: Europe and other bad news/Irving Layton. Toronto: McClelland and Stewart, 1981.

EBN 13/1
TEN YEAR OLD CYNIC; THOU SHALT NOT KILL
[1980].
[2]p., [2] leaves; 2 leaves 21 cm., 1 leaf 29 cm.
Chiefly holograph.
Two poems.
On p.[1]:2 holograph drafts with revisions of "Thou shalt not kill."
On p.[2]:1 holograph draft with revisions of "Ten year old cynic"; 1 holograph draft of "Thou shalt not kill."
On leaf [1]:2 holograph drafts with revisions of "Ten year old cynic."
On leaf [2]:typescript draft of "Ten year old cynic."
On verso of leaf [2]:typescript draft of line 1 of "Ten year old cynic."
"Ten year old cynic" published as "[Death where is your sting-a-ling]."
"[Death where is your sting-a-ling]" published with further revisions in: Europe and other bad news/Irving Layton. Toronto: McClelland and Stewart, 1981.
"Thou shalt not kill" not published to date.

EBN 14/1
JEREMIAH
[1980].
[5] leaves; 28 cm.
In part holograph.
Poem.
On leaves [1-2]:2 holograph drafts with revisions; "Nietzsche is Pietzche" on verso of leaf [2].
On leaves [3-4]:2 typescript drafts with revisions.
On leaf [5]:typescript draft.
Published with further revisions as "[Poet]."
Published in: Europe and other bad news/Irving Layton. Toronto: McClelland and Stewart, 1981.

EBN 15/1
THE QUEEN OF HEARTS
[1980].
[3] leaves; 28 cm.

...con't

EBN 15/1...con't

Typescript.
Poem.
Three drafts with revisions.
Published in: Europe and other bad news/Irving Layton. Toronto: McClelland and Stewart, 1981.

EBN 16/1
ENDANGERED SPECIES
[1980].
[4] leaves; 2 leaves 20 cm., 2 leaves 28 cm.
In part holograph.
Poem.
On leaves [1-2]:2 holograph drafts with revisions; marginalia on leaf [1].
On leaves [3-4]:2 typescript drafts.
Number "62" in upper right corner of leaf [3].
Published with further revisions in: Europe and other bad news/ Irving Layton. Toronto: McClelland and Stewart, 1981.

EBN 17/1
ARMAGEDDON
[1980].
[1] leaf; 28 cm.
Holograph.
Poem.
Draft with revisions.
"Armageddon" published with further revisions as "[Eternal recurrence]."
Published in: Europe and other bad news/Irving Layton. Toronto: McClelland and Stewart, 1981, (also in UE, LPIL1, LPIL2).

EBN 18/1
OF FLIES AND MORNING GLORIES
1980.
[9] leaves; 28 cm.
Typescript with holograph revisions.
Poem.
On leaf [1]:draft of 38 lines with revisions.
On leaves [2,7-8]:3 drafts of 7 stanzas.
On leaf [3]:draft of 7 stanzas with revisions and reworking of stanza [1].
On leaves [4-6]:3 drafts of 7 stanzas with revisions.
On leaf [9]:draft of 7 stanzas with stanza 1 crossed out.

...con't

EBN 18/1...con't

On verso of leaf [1]:fragment beginning "After I've discussed life and love...."
On verso of leaf [3]:draft of lines 1-4.
On verso of leaf [4]:draft of lines 1-15.
Dated Niagara-on-the-Lake, September, 1980.
"Of flies and morning glories" published with further revisions as "[Early morning sounds]."
Published in: Europe and other bad news/Irving Layton. Toronto: McClelland and Stewart, 1981, (also in WPJ).

EBN 19/1
SUNFLOWERS
[1980].
[4] leaves; 28 cm.
In part holograph.
Poem.
On leaves [1-3]:3 typescript drafts with revisions.
On leaf [4]:typescript draft.
On verso of leaf [1]:typescript draft of lines 1-4.
On verso of leaf [2]:holograph draft of lines 1-5.
On verso of leaf [4]:typescript draft of 19 lines beginning "Despite warnings from giant dwarfs...."
Published with further revisions in: Europe and other bad news/ Irving Layton. Toronto: McClelland and Stewart, 1981, (also in WPJ).

EBN 20/1
MICHAL
[1980].
[2] leaves; 28 cm.
Typescript with holograph revisions.
Poem.
Two drafts.
Published with further revisions in: Europe and other bad news/ Irving Layton. Toronto: McClelland and Stewart, 1981.

EBN 21/1
GAY SUNSHINE ANTHOLOGY
1977.
[6]p., [5] leaves; 4 leaves 21 cm., 4 leaves 29 cm.
In part holograph.
Poem.

...con't

EBN 21/1...con't

On p.[1-6] and leaf [1]:4 holograph drafts with revisions; p.[3] titled "Narcissi."
On leaves [2-5]:4 typescript drafts with revisions.
Dated Molibos, June 7, 1977.
Published with further revisions in: Europe and other bad news/ Irving Layton. Toronto: McClelland and Stewart, 1981.

FMBJ - For My Brother Jesus

FMBJ 1/1
ADAM
1974.
[6] leaves; 28 cm.
Chiefly holograph.
Poem.
Five drafts with revisions on stationery from Excelsior Hotel, Gallia, Milano, Italy.
One photocopy of typescript.
Title on leaves [4-6] "Genesis."
Drafts 1-4 numbered.
Cigarette burn on right edge of leaf [6].
Dated Milano, November 25,26,27, 1974.
Published in: For my brother Jesus/Irving Layton. Toronto: McClelland and Stewart, 1976.

FMBJ 2/1
FOR EDDA; A WORD FROM DIOGENES
1974.
[3] leaves; 2 leaves 28 cm., 1 leaf 40 cm. x 30 cm.
Chiefly holograph signed.
Two poems.
On leaf [1]:holograph draft of "For Edda."
On verso of leaf [1]:typescript draft of "A word from Diogenes."
On leaf [2]:typescript draft of "For Edda" with revisions; marginalia.
On leaf [3]:holograph draft on 40x30 sheet with printed heading "2 Liceo Scientifico Statale-Vicenza"; "Poetry" in black lettering on verso.
Dated Milano, December 1, 1974.
"For Edda" published with further revisions in: For my brother Jesus/Irving Layton. Toronto: McClelland and Stewart, 1976, (also in DD).
"A word from Diogenes" published in: A laughter in the mind/ Irving Layton. 2nd ed. Montreal: Editions Orphée, 1959.

FMBJ 3/1
HYDRA; RUNTS; ISLAND CIRCE
1975.
[6]p., [5] leaves; 28 cm.
In part holograph.
Three poems.
On p.[1,3,5] and leaves [1-5]:2 holograph, 6 typescript drafts with revisions of "Hydra."
On p.[2,4]:2 holograph drafts with revisions of "Runts."
On p.[6]:holograph draft of "Island circe."
Drafts of "Hydra" numbered 1-8.
"Island circe" dated Poros, July 15, 1975.
"Hydra" published with further revisions as "[Act of creation]."
"[Act of creation]" published in: For my brother Jesus/Irving Layton. Toronto: McClelland and Stewart, 1976.
"Runts," ibid., (with revisions).
"Island circe," ibid., (with revisions).

FMBJ 4/1
THE ARCH; JEWISH DITTY; SOME OF MY BEST FRIENDS ARE GOYIM; JESUS AND ST PAUL; [JUNE BUG]
[1975].
[10]p.; 28 cm.
In part holograph.
Five poems.
On p.[1]:holograph draft of 32 lines with theme and images of "The arch."
On p.[2]:typescript draft of "Jewish ditty."
On p.[3,5]:holograph draft of "The arch."
On p.[4]:typescript draft of "Some of my best friends are goyim"; stanzas 3-5 crossed out.
On p.[6]:typescript draft with holograph revisions of "Jesus and Saint Paul."
On p.[7,9]:typescript draft with holograph revisions of "The arch."
On p.[8,10]:2 typescript drafts with holograph revisions of "[June bug]."
"Jewish ditty" published as "[C'est fini]."
"Some of my best friends are goyim" published as "[For some of my best friends]."
"The arch" published with further revisions in: For my brother Jesus/Irving Layton. Toronto: McClelland and Stewart, 1976, (also in WPJ).
"[C'est fini]," ibid., (with revisions).
"[For some of my best friends]," ibid., (with revisions).
"Jesus and St Paul," ibid., (with revisions).
"[June bug]," ibid., (with revisions).

FMBJ 5/1
AT THE BARCELONA ZOO
[1975].
[3] leaves; 28 cm.
Chiefly holograph.
Poem.
On leaves [1-2]:2 holograph drafts with revisions.
On leaf [3]:typescript draft.
On verso of leaf [1]:list of 22 titles of poems by [Irving Layton]; rough hand drawn map of Madrid and surroundings.
Published with further revisions in: For my brother Jesus/ Irving Layton. Toronto: McClelland and Stewart, 1976.

FMBJ 6/1
LA BELLE FRANCE
[1975].
[4] leaves; 28 cm.
In part holograph.
Poem.
Two holograph, 2 typescript drafts with revisions.
Title on leaf [3] "Eutope" i.e. [Europe].
Published with further revisions in: For my brother Jesus/ Irving Layton. Toronto: McClelland and Stewart, 1976.

FMBJ 7/1
DAPHNIS AND CHLOE; [THE] NEOLITHIC [BRAIN]; GREEKS
[1975].
[9] leaves; 2 leaves 20 cm., 7 leaves 28 cm.
In part holograph.
Three poems.
On leaf [1]:holograph draft of "Daphnis and Chloe" with revisions; stanzas 1,3 inverted; page torn from coil binder notebook.
On leaf [2]:holograph draft of "Daphnis and Chloe" with revisions; page torn from coil binder notebook.
Leaves [3-4]:blank.
On verso of leaf [4]:holograph draft of "Daphnis and Chloe."
On leaf [5]:holograph draft of "Daphnis and Chloe" titled "Mammon and Eros."
On leaves [6,9]:2 typescript drafts of "Daphnis and Chloe."
On leaf [7]:typescript draft of "Greeks"; typescript draft of "Daphnis and Chloe."
On leaf [8]:typescript draft of "Daphnis and Chloe"; 3 holograph drafts of "[The] neolithic [brain]" titled "Neolithic"; 1 holograph draft of "Greeks."

...con't

FMBJ 7/1...con't
"Daphnis and Chloe" published in: For my brother Jesus/Irving Layton. Toronto: McClelland and Stewart, 1976.
"[The] neolithic [brain]," ibid.
"Greeks" not published to date.

FMBJ 8/1
FLORENCE
1975.
[3] leaves; 28 cm.
Typescript with holograph corrections.
Poem.
Three drafts.
Dated Florence, June 6, 1975.
Published in: For my brother Jesus/Irving Layton. Toronto: McClelland and Stewart, 1976.

FMBJ 8/2 FLORENCE
[1975].
[2]p., [2] leaves; 20 cm.
Holograph.
Poem.
On p.[1-2]:draft with reworking of stanzas 1,3-4.
On leaf [1]:draft of stanzas 2-3 with reworking of stanza 2; first 8 lines crossed out.
On leaf [2]:draft with revisions; stanzas 1,3 reversed.
Drafts on paper torn from spiral note book.
Published with further revisions in: For my brother Jesus/ Irving Layton. Toronto: McClelland and Stewart, 1976.

FMBJ 8/3
[FLORENCE]
1975.
[4] leaves; 28 cm.
Holograph.
Poem.
Four drafts with revisions on paper torn from examination booklet.
Yellow stains at top of leaves [1-3].
"L'ammore de un Vecchio" next to title on leaf [3].
Dated June 7, 1975.
Published with further revisions in: For my brother Jesus/ Irving Layton. Toronto: McClelland and Stewart, 1976.

FMBJ 9/1
FOR FRANCESCA
1974.
[2] leaves; 1 leaf 30 cm., 1 leaf 34 cm.
Holograph signed.
Poem.
On leaf [1]:draft with revisions on stationery from Excelsior Hotel, Gallia, Milano Italy; fragment beginning "My pillow is a loudspeaker...."
On leaf [2]:photocopy of draft with revisions on stationery from Excelsior Hotel, Gallia, Milano, Italy.
Dated Milano, November 28, 1974.
Published in: For my brother Jesus/Irving Layton. Toronto: McClelland and Stewart, 1976, (also in LPIL1, LPIL2, DD).

FMBJ 10/1
FOR JESUS CHRIST
[1975].
[4]p., [7] leaves; 28 cm.
In part holograph.
Poem.
On leaf [1]:holograph draft with revisions.
On p.[1]:holograph draft with images and themes of "For Jesus Christ."
On p.[2]:holograph draft of stanzas 1-2 with reworking of stanza 2; stanza 2 crossed out.
On leaf [2]:holograph draft of stanzas 1-2 with reworking of stanza 2; 2 stanzas reversed.
On p.[3]:holograph draft with revisions titled "The holocaust."
On p.[4]:holograph draft.
On leaves [3-7]:5 typescript drafts titled "The holocaust."
Published with further revisions in: For my brother Jesus/ Irving Layton. Toronto: McClelland and Stewart, 1976.

FMBJ 11/1
FOR MY BROTHER JESUS
[1975].
[2]p., [9] leaves; 28 cm.
Chiefly holograph.
Poem.
On p.[1-2]:draft with revisions of stanzas 1-4; fragment of 6 lines beginning "What's the use Jeshua..."; marginalia.
On leaf [1]: draft with revisions of stanzas 1-4.

...con't

FMBJ 11/1...con't

On leaves [2-4]: draft of entire poem with reworking of stanza 6.
On leaf [5]: typescript draft of stanzas 1-6.
On leaf [6]: typescript draft of lines 1-4 of stanza 6.
On leaves [7-8]: typescript draft with revisions.
On leaf [9]: typescript draft of stanzas 6-7.
Published with further revisions in: For my brother Jesus/ Irving Layton. Toronto: McClelland and Stewart, 1976, (also in PIL, WPJ).

FMBJ 12/1
GALIM; [SAINT PINCHAS]
[1975].
[2]p., 3 leaves; 28 cm.
In part holograph.
Two poems.
On p.[1]:holograph draft of "Galim" with revisions and reworking of last 2 stanzas.
On p.[2]:typescript draft of lines 1-12 of "[Saint Pinchas]."
On leaves [1-3]:3 typescript drafts of "Galim."
"Galim" published with further revisions in: For my brother Jesus/Irving Layton. Toronto: McClelland and Stewart, 1976.
"[Saint Pinchas]," ibid.

FMBJ 13/1
THE HAEMORRHAGE
[1975].
[8] leaves; 28 cm.
In part holograph.
Poem.
On leaves [1-2]:2 holograph drafts with revisions.
On leaves [3-7]:5 typescript drafts with revisions.
On leaf [8]:photocopy of typescript draft.
Published in: For my brother Jesus/Irving Layton. Toronto: McClelland and Stewart, 1976, (also in WPJ).

FMBJ 14/1
THE HALLOWING; [EXCELSIOR]
[1975].
[2]p., [2] leaves; 28 cm.
In part holograph.
Two poems.
On p.[1]:2 holograph drafts of "The hallowing" with reworking of stanza 1; 1 draft

...con't

FMBJ 14/1...con't
titled "The benediction"; marginalia.
On p.[2]:holograph draft of "[Excelsior]."
On leaves [1-2]:2 typescript drafts of "The hallowing" with revisions.
"The hallowing" published with further revisions in: For my brother Jesus/Irving Layton. Toronto: McClelland and Stewart, 1976.
"[Excelsior]," ibid., (with revisions).

FMBJ 15/1
HOW MANY DAYS; [RELEASE]
1975.
[2]p., [5] leaves; 28 cm.
Chiefly holograph.
Two poems.
On p.[1]:draft with revisions of 12 lines of "How many days"; draft of 9 lines of "[Release]" at top of page; draft of 5 lines of "[Release]" at bottom of page.
On p.[2]:draft with revisions of "How many days."
On leaves [1-2]:2 holograph drafts with revisions of "How many days."
On leaves [3-5]:3 typescript drafts of "How many days."
Dated Paxos, Greece, June 15, 1975.
"How many days" published with further revisions in: For my brother Jesus/Irving Layton. Toronto: McClelland & Stewart, 1976.
"[Release]," ibid.

FMBJ 16/1
IN PRAISE OF OLDER MEN
[1975].
[1] leaf; 35 cm. folded to 24 cm.
Holograph.
Poem.
Draft with revisions in green ink on paper place mat.
Published with further revisions in: For my brother Jesus/ Irving Layton. Toronto: McClelland and Stewart, 1976, (also in LPIL1, LPIL2).

FMBJ 16/2
IN PRAISE OF OLDER MEN
[1975].
[2]p., [1] leaf; 23 cm.
Holograph.
Poem.

...con't

FMBJ 16/2...con't
Three drafts with revisions on lined paper torn from notebook.
Published with further revisions in: For my brother Jesus/ Irving Layton. Toronto: McClelland and Stewart, 1976, (also in LPIL1, LPIL2).

FMBJ 16/3
IN PRAISE OF OLDER MEN; [SAINT PINCHAS]
[1975].
[1] leaf; 28 cm.
Typescript.
Two poems.
On recto:draft of "In praise of older men."
On verso:draft of lines 1-6 of "[Saint Pinchas]."
"In praise of older men" published with further revisions in: For my brother Jesus/Irving Layton. Toronto: McClelland and Stewart, 1976, (also in LPIL1, LPIL2).
"[Saint Pinchas]," ibid.

FMBJ 17/1
JUDEA ETERNA
[1975].
[1] leaf; 28 cm.
Typescript with holograph revisions.
Poem.
Published in: For my brother Jesus/Irving Layton. Toronto: McClelland and Stewart, 1976.

FMBJ 18/1
AN AGING POET REFLECTS; [DAPHNIS AND CHLOE]
[1975].
[2]p.; 28 cm.
Typescript.
Two poems.
On p.[1]:draft of "An aging poet reflects"; fragment of [2] lines beginning "They are cheerful, and above all kind...."
On p.[2]:draft of lines 1-8 of "[Daphnis and Chloe]."
"An aging poet reflects" published as "[The neolithic brain]."
"[The neolithic brain]" published in: For my brother Jesus/ Irving Layton. Toronto: McClelland and Stewart, 1976.
"[Daphnis and Chloe]," ibid.

FMBJ 19/1
O JERUSALEM
1974.
[2]p., [16] leaves; 2p. 18cm., 15p. 28 cm.
In part holograph signed.
Poem.
On p.[1]:holograph draft with revisions on verso of page torn from unidentified published monograph.
On leaves [1-16]:16 typescript drafts with revisions.
Signed note to editor at bottom of leaves [14-16].
Dated Athens, August 2, 1974.
Published with further revisions in: For my brother Jesus/ Irving Layton. Toronto: McClelland & Stewart, 1976, (also in PIL, UE, WPJ).

FMBJ 20/1
OF THE MAN WHO SITS IN THE GARDEN; RELEASE; HOW MANY DAYS; [THE ARCH]; BEAUTY AND GENIUS; DAPHNIS AND CHLOE
1975.
[12]p., [5] leaves; 28 cm.
In part holograph.
Six poems.
On leaf [1] and p.[1,3]: holograph draft of "Of the man who sits in the garden" with revisions and reworking of stanza 3.
On verso of leaf [1]:lines 1-2 of "[The arch]."
On p.[2,6]:2 typescript drafts of "How many days."
On p.[4,8]:2 typescript drafts of "Release."
On p.[5,7,9,11,] and leaves [2-5]:1 holograph and 3 typescript drafts of "Of the man who sits in the garden."
On p.[10]:typescript draft of "Beauty and genius."
On p.[12]:typescript draft of "Daphnis and Chloe."
Drafts 1-2 of "Of the man who sits in the garden" numbered.
"Of the man who sits in the garden" dated Hydra, July 9, 1975.
"How many days" dated Paxos, Greece, June 15, 1975.
"Of the man who sits in the garden" published with further revisions in: For my brother Jesus/Irving Layton. Toronto: McClelland and Stewart, 1976, (also in LPIL1, LPIL2, DD).
"Release," ibid.
"How many days," ibid.
"[The arch]," ibid., (also in WPJ).
"Beauty and genius," ibid.
"Daphnis and Chloe," ibid.

FMBJ 21/1
PARQUE DE MONTJUICH; AT THE BARCELONA ZOO
1975.
[2]p., 3 leaves; 28 cm.
Holograph.
Two poems.
On p.[1]:draft of stanzas [1-3] of part II of "Parque de Montjuich";hand drawn map of section of [Barcelona?].
On p.[2]:draft with revisions of "At the Barcelona Zoo"; marginalia.
On leaves [1-3]:3 drafts with revisions of part II of "Parque de Montjuich"; leaves [2-3] titled "Above Jardines de Miramar."
Drafts 1-3 numbered.
"Parque de Montjuich" dated Barcelona, August 6, 1975.
"Parque de Montjuich" published with further revisions in: For my brother Jesus/Irving Layton. Toronto: McClelland and Stewart, 1976, (also in P1L, WPJ).
"At the Barcelona Zoo," ibid., (with revisions).

FMBJ 21/2
PARQUE DE MONTJUICH; ASYLUMS
1975.
[2]p., [2] leaves; 28 cm.
Chiefly holograph.
Two poems.
On p.[1]:holograph draft with revisions of part III of "Parque de Montjuich"; marginalia on verso.
On p.[2]:typescript draft with revisions of "Asylums."
On leaf [1]:holograph draft of stanza 2 of part III of "Parque de Montjuich"; marginalia on verso.
On leaf [2]:holograph draft with revisions of part III of "Parque de Montjuich."
"Asylums" dated Barcelona, August 4, 1975.
"Parque de Montjuich" published with further revisions in: For my brother Jesus/Irving Layton. Toronto: McClelland and Stewart, 1976, (also in PIL, WPJ).
"Asylums," ibid.

FMBJ 21/3
PARQUE DE MONTJUICH
1975.
[2]p., [2] leaves; 28 cm.
In part holograph.

...con't

FMBJ 21/3...con't

Poem.
On p.[1-2]:holograph draft of part III of "Parque de Montjuich" with reworking of stanza 1; marginalia on p.[1].
On leaf [1]:typescript draft of part II of "Parque de Montjuich" titled "Above Jardines de Miramar."
On leaf [2]:typescript draft of part I of "Parque de Montjuich."
Dated Barcelona, August 2,5, 1975.
Published with further revisions in: For my brother Jesus/ Irving Layton. Toronto: McClelland and Stewart, 1976, (also in PIL, WPJ).

FMBJ 21/4
PARQUE DE MONTJUICH
1975.
[2] leaves; 29 cm.
Typescript.
Poem.
Dated Barcelona August 6, 1975.
Published with revisions in: For my brother Jesus/Irving Layton. Toronto: McClelland and Stewart, 1976, (also in PIL).

FMBJ 22/1
THE PLAKA; JUDEA ETERNA; [GALIM]; GREEKS; SAVED
[1975].
[8]p., [2] leaves; 28 cm.
Chiefly holograph.
Five poems.
On p.[1,3]:2 drafts of 22 lines with theme and images of "The Plaka"; marginalia on p.[1].
On p.[5,7] and leaves [1-2]:2 holograph and 2 typescript drafts with revisions of "The Plaka."
On p.[2]:typescript draft of "Judea eterna"; typescript signature.
On p.[4]:typescript draft of "Saved."
On p.[6]:typescript draft of stanzas 1-4 of "[Galim]."
On p.[8]:typescript draft of "Greeks."
Drafts of "The Plaka" numbered 1-8.
"The Plaka" published with further revisions in: For my brother Jesus/Irving Layton. Toronto: McClelland and Stewart, 1976.
"Judea eterna," ibid.
"[Galim]," ibid.
"Saved," ibid.
"Greeks" not published to date.

FMBJ 23/1
THE RED GERANIUM; DISCOTHEQUE; THE HALLOWING; FOR MY OLD FOREST HILL GYPSY; HOW MANY DAYS; AN AGING POET REFLECTS
1975.
[14]p., [2] leaves; 28 cm.
In part holograph.
Six poems.
On p.[1,3,5-6,7,9,11] and leaves [1-2]:2 holograph and 2 typescript drafts with revisions of "The red geranium."
On p.[2,4]:2 typescript drafts with revisions of "Discothque."
On p.[6]:typescript draft of "The hallowing" crossed out.
On p.[8]:typescript draft of stanzas 1-2 of "For my old Forest Hill gypsy."
On p.[10]:typescript draft of "For my old Forest Hill gypsy" crossed out.
On p.[12]:typescript draft with revisions of "How many days."
On p.[13]:typescript draft of stanzas 1-5 of "The red geranium."
On p.[14]:typescript draft of "An aging poet reflects."
"For my old Forest Hill gypsy" published with revisions as "[For my incomparable gypsy]."
"An aging poet reflects" published as "[Neolithic brain]."
"The red geranium" dated Hydra, July 5th, 1975.
"Discothque" dated Hydra, July 3rd, 1975.
"The red geranium" published in: For my brother Jesus/Irving Layton. Toronto: McClelland and Stewart, 1976.
"Discothque," ibid., (also in LPIL1, LPIL2, DD).
"The hallowing," ibid., (with revisions).
"[For my incomparable gypsy]," ibid., (with revisions), (also in LPIL1, LPIL2, DD).
 "How many days," ibid.
"[Neolithic brain]," ibid.

FMBJ 24/1
AT TANGIER - A MEDITATION UPON THE FUTURE
1975.
1 card; 10 cm x 14 cm.
Holograph draft on verso of postcard.
Poem.
Dated Madrid Airport, August 28, 1975.
"At Tangier - a meditation upon the future" published as "[Tabletalk]."
Published in: For my brother Jesus/Irving Layton. Toronto: McClelland and Stewart, 1976.

FMBJ 24/2
TANGIERS - A MEDITATION ON THE FUTURE
1975.
[1] leaf; 30 cm.
Holograph.
Poem.
Draft on stained wrinkled paper with frayed edges; upper right corner missing.
Dated Tangiers, August 27, 1975.
Published as "[Tabletalk]."
Published in: For my brother Jesus/Irving Layton. Toronto: McClelland and Stewart, 1976.

FMBJ 25/1
SAINT PINCHAS; BEAUTY AND GENIUS; JUDEA ETERNA; QUO VADIS
1975.
[6]p., [3] leaves; 1 leaf 23 cm., 5 leaves 28 cm.
In part holograph.
Four poems.
On p.[1,3,5] and leaf [1]:1 holograph draft, 3 typescript drafts with revisions of "Saint Pinchas."
On leaves [2-3]:2 typescript drafts of "Saint Pinchas."
On p.[2]:2 holograph drafts of "Beauty and genius."
On p.[4]:2 typescript drafts of "Judea eterna"; 1 typescript draft of "Beauty and genius."
On p.[6]:typescript draft of "Quo vadis."
Pages [3-5] and leaves [1-2] titled "Saint Peter."
"Quo vadis" published as "[Saved]."
"Saint Pinchas" dated St. Peter's Basilica, June 4, 1975.
"Beauty and genius" dated Rome, Florence, June 4, 1975.
"Saint Pinchas" published with further revisions in: For my brother Jesus/Irving Layton. Toronto: McClelland and Stewart, 1976.
"Beauty and genius," ibid.
"Judea eterna," ibid.
"[Saved]," ibid.

FMBJ 26/1
THE BLOOD OF CHRIST
1975.
[3] leaves; 2 leaves 19 cm., 1 leaf 28 cm.
Chiefly holograph.
Poem.

...con't

FMBJ 26/1...con't

On leaves [1-2]:3 holograph drafts with revisions; marginalia on leaf [1].
On leaf [3]:typescript draft.
Dated Florence, June 5, 1975.
Published with further revisions as "[Saved]."
Published in: For my brother Jesus/Irving Layton. Toronto: McClelland and Stewart, 1976.

FMBJ 27/1
THE VIOLENT LIFE
[1975].
[8] leaves; 28 cm.
In part holograph.
Poem.
On leaves [1-2,4]:5 holograph drafts with revisions.
On leaves [3,5-7]:5 typescript drafts.
On verso of leaf [7]:typescript draft of line 1.
On leaf [8]:typescript draft with revisions.
Leaves [2-3,5-6] titled "Sign of the times."
Published in: For my brother Jesus/Irving Layton. Toronto: McClelland and Stewart, 1976.

FMBJ 28/1
RELEASE; [EXCELSIOR]
[1975].
[4] leaves; 28 cm.
In part holograph.
Two poems.
On leaf [1]:holograph draft with revisions of "Release."
On leaf [2]:holograph draft with revisions of "Release"; draft of stanza 1 and line 1 of stanza 2 of "[Excelsior]."
On leaves [3-4]:2 typescript drafts with revisions of "Release."
"Release" published with further revisions in: For my brother Jesus/Irving Layton. Toronto: McClelland and Stewart, 1976.
"[Excelsior]," ibid., (with revisions).

FMBJ 29/1
KING DAVID
[1975].
1 card; 17 cm.
Holograph.

...con't

FMBJ 29/1...con't

Poem.
Draft with revisions and reworking of stanza [2] on verso of Alitalia Airline safety instruction card.
Titles of 3 poems by [Irving Layton] at bottom of card.
Published with further revisions as "[Warrior poet]."
Published in: For my brother Jesus/Irving Layton. Toronto: McClelland and Stewart, 1976.

FMBJ 30/1
JESHUA; ENVY; [HOW MANY DAYS]; [RELEASE]
1975.
[10] leaves; 28 cm.
Chiefly holograph.
Four poems.
On leaves [1-4]:2 holograph drafts with revisions of stanzas 1-5 of "Jeshua."
On leaves [5-10]:1 holograph, 2 typescript drafts with revisions of "Jeshua"; marginalia on leaf [5].
Drafts of "Jeshua" numbered 1-5.
On verso of leaf [1]:holograph draft of "Envy" with reworking of stanzas 1-2.
On verso of leaf [2]:typescript draft of "Envy" titled "Twinge by twinge."
On verso of leaf [5]:typescript draft of lines 1-11 of "[How many days]."
On verso of leaf [6]:typescript draft of lines 1-6 of "[Release]."
"Jeshua" dated Paxos, Greece, June 18, 1975.
"Envy" published as "[Excelsior]."
"Jeshua" published with further revisions in: For my brother Jesus/Irving Layton. Toronto: McClelland and Stewart, 1976.
"[Excelsior]," ibid.
"[How many days]," ibid.
"[Release]," ibid.

FMNH - For My Neighbours in Hell

FMNH 1/1
THE CHOSEN PEOPLE
1979.
[5] leaves; 28 cm.
In part holograph.
Poem.
On leaf [1]:2 holograph drafts with revisions.
On leaf [2]:typescript draft with reworking of lines 1-4.

...con't

FMNH 1/1...con't

On leaves [3-5]:3 typescript drafts.
Dated May 29, 1979.
Published with further revisions as "[The election]."
Published in: For my neighbours in hell/Irving Layton. Oakville, Ont.: Mosaic Press/Valley Editions, [1980].

FMNH 1/2
SCORECARD; CULTURE; THE CHOSEN PEOPLE
[1979].
[5] leaves; 28 cm.
Typescript.
Three poems.
On leaf [1]:draft of "The chosen people" and "Culture."
On leaf [2]:3 drafts of "Culture."
On verso of leaf [2]:draft of lines 1-7 of "The chosen people."
On leaf [3]:3 drafts of "Scorecard."
On leaf [4]:draft of "Scorecard" and "Culture."
On leaf [5]:draft of "Culture" and 2 drafts of "Scorecard."
"The chosen people" published as "[The election]."
"Culture" published with revisions as "[Southern comfort]."
"[Southern comfort]" published as one titled stanza of "The cracked mirror."
"Scorecard" published with revisions as one titled stanza of "The burning remnant."
"The burning remnant" published in: For my neighbours in hell/ Irving Layton. Oakville, Ont.: Mosaic Press/Valley Editions, 1980.
"The cracked mirror," ibid.
"The election," ibid.

FMNH 1/3
THE CHOSEN PEOPLE
[1979].
[1] leaf; 28 cm.
Typescript.
Poem.
Published with further revisions as "[The election]."
Published in: For my neighbours in hell/Irving Layton. Oakville, Ont.: Mosaic Press/Valley Editions, [1980].

FMNH 1/4
[THE ELECTION]
[1979].
[1] leaf; 28 cm.
Typescript.
Poem.
Published with revisions in: For my neighbours in hell/Irving Layton. Oakville, Ont.: Mosaic Press/Valley Editions, [1980].

FMNH 2/1
MOUNT ROYAL CEMETERY
[1979].
[5] leaves; 28 cm.
Typescript.
Poem.
Five drafts.
Published with further revisions in: For my neighbours in hell/ Irving Layton. Oakville, Ont.: Mosaic Press/Valley Editions, [1980].

FMNH 3/1
THE LAST SURVIVOR; SHIT; WASP SONG
[1979].
[2]p.,[3] leaves; 28 cm.
In part holograph.
Three poems.
On leaf [1]:typescript draft of "The last survivor" crossed out; holograph draft of "Shit."
On leaf [2]:2 typescript drafts of "Shit."
On leaf [3]:2 typescript drafts with revisions of "The last survivor."
On p.[1]:typescript draft of "The last survivor"; marginalia.
On p.[2]:4 typescript drafts of "Wasp song."
"The last survivor" published with further revisions in: For my neighbours in hell/Irving Layton. Oakville, Ont.: Mosaic Press/ Valley Editions, [1980].
"Shit" published with revisions in: Droppings from heaven/ Irving Layton. Toronto: McClelland and Stewart, 1979.
"Wasp song" not published to date.

FMNH 4/1
THE ABYSS; OLD AND YOUNG; RETRIBUTION FOR FERDINAND AND ISABELLA; DIRTY OLD MAN
1977.
[2]p., [5] leaves; 2 leaves 27 cm., 4 leaves 28 cm.
Chiefly holograph.

...con't

FMNH 4/1...con't

Four poems.
On p.[1]:holograph draft with revisions of "The abyss."
On p.[2]:typescript draft of "Dirty old man."
On leaf [1]:holograph draft of "The abyss"; holograph draft of "Old and young"; holograph draft of "Retribution"; on verso of lined paper torn from examination booklet.
On leaf [2]:holograph draft with revisions and reworking of stanzas 1-2 of "The abyss" on back cover of examination booklet; holograph draft of "Old and young."
On leaf [3]:holograph draft with revisions of "The abyss"; typescript draft of "Old and young"; typescript draft of "Retribution for Ferdinand and Isabella."
On leaf [4]:typescript draft of "Old and young."
On leaf [5]:typescript draft with revisions of "The abyss."
"The abyss" dated Molibos, Greece, July 11, 1977.
"The abyss" published with further revisions in: For my neighbours in hell/Irving Layton. Oakville, Ont.: Mosaic Press/ Valley Editions, 1980.
"Dirty old man," ibid.
"Old and Young" not published to date.
"Retribution for Ferdinand and Isabella" not published to date.

FMNH 5/1
PLATO WAS AN ASSHOLE; [OLD AND YOUNG]; SIR MORTIMER [1979].
[2]p., [5] leaves; 28 cm. + 1 envelope.
In part holograph.
Three poems.
On p.[1]:typescript draft of 14 lines with reworking of last 4 lines of "Plato was an asshole"; typescript draft of lines 1-7 of "[Old and young]."
On p.[2]:typescript draft of "Sir Mortimer"; typescript draft of "Plato was an asshole."
On leaf [1]:typescript draft of "Plato was an asshole."
On leaves [2-5]:4 typescript drafts with revisions of "Plato was an asshole."
Holograph draft of 9 lines of "Plato was an asshole" on back of envelope addressed to Irving Layton.
"Plato was an asshole" published with further revisions in: For my neighbours in hell/Irving Layton. Oakville, Ont.: Mosaic Press/Valley Editions, [1980].
"Sir Mortimer" published in: The tightrope dancer/Irving Layton. Toronto: McClelland and Stewart, 1978.
"[Old and young]" not published to date.

FMNH 6/1
GREEK FISHERMAN; BRIDEGROOM; THE SPECTER; O CANADA
1977.
[4]p., [1] leaf; 2 leaves 28 cm., 1 leaf 21 cm.
In part holograph.
Four poems.
On p.[1]:2 holograph drafts of "Bridegroom"; 1 typescript draft of "Greek fisherman"; 1 typescript draft of "O Canada."
On p.[2]:2 typescript drafts of "Bridegroom" with revisions and reworking of stanza 1.
On p.[3]:typescript draft of "The specter" (The spectre) crossed out; typescript draft of "Bridegroom" with reworking of stanza [3].
On p.[4]:typescript draft of "The specter" (The spectre); 2 typescript drafts of "Bridegroom."
On leaf [1]:typescript draft of "Bridegroom."
Dated July 12, 1977.
"Greek fisherman" published with further revisions in: For my neighbours in hell/Irving Layton. Oakville, Ont.: Mosaic Press/ Valley Editions, [1980].
"Bridegroom" published with further revisions in: The tightrope dancer/Irving Layton. Toronto: McClelland and Stewart, 1978.
"The specter" not published to date.
"O Canada" not published to date.

FMNH 7/1
HOMAGE TO SIR MORTIMER; TELL IT TO MAGGIE; THE SPECTRE
[1979].
[2]p., [2] leaves; 2 leaves 22 cm., 1 leaf 29 cm.
Chiefly holograph.
Three poems.
On leaves [1-2]:2 holograph drafts with revisions of "Homage to Sir Mortimer."
On p.[1]:typescript draft of "Homage to Sir Mortimer"; typescript draft of "Tell it to Maggie."
On p.[2]:typescript draft of "The spectre."
"Tell it to Maggie" published as "[Tell it to Peggy]."
"Homage to Sir Mortimer" published with further revisions in: For my neighbours in hell/Irving Layton. Oakville, Ont.: Mosaic Press/Valley Editions, [1980].
"[Tell it to Peggy]" published in: The tightrope dancer/Irving Layton. Toronto: McClelland and Stewart, 1978.
"The spectre" not published to date.

FMNH 8/1
SUNBATHER
[1979].
[4] leaves; [1] leaf 28 cm., [3] leaves 30 cm.
Typescript.
Poem.
On leaf [1]:typescript draft with revisions.
On leaves [2-4]:3 typescript drafts.
Published in: For my neighbours in hell/Irving Layton. Oakville, Ont.: Mosaic Press/Valley Editions, [1980].

FMNH 9/1
WHEN DEATH SAYS COME; [WATCH OUT FOR HIS LEFT]
[1979].
[4] leaves; 2 leaves 21 cm., 2 leaves 28 cm.
In part holograph.
Two poems.
On leaf [1]:holograph draft of 9 stanzas; stanzas 1-4 used in "[Watch out for his left]."
On leaf [2]:holograph draft with revisions of 4 stanzas of "When death says come."
On leaves [3-4]:2 typescript drafts of "When death says come."
"When death says come" published with further revisions in: For my neighbours in hell/Irving Layton. Oakville, Ont.: Mosaic Press/Valley Editions, [1980].
"[Watch out for his left]" published in: The tightrope dancer/ Irving Layton. Toronto: McClelland and Stewart, 1978.

FMNH 10/1
NOT ALL POETS ARE LIARS; ALIVE AND STILL KICKING; NO CYNIC
[1979].
[2]p., [2] leaves; 29 cm.
Typescript.
Three poems.
On leaf [1]:typescript draft of "Not all poets are liars."
On leaf [2]:typescript draft of "Alive and still kicking."
On p.[1]:2 typescript drafts of "Not all poets are liars."
On p.[2]:typescript draft of "Alive and still kicking"; 2 typescript drafts of "No cynic."
"Not all poets are liars" published with revisions as "[Egalitarian]."
"[Egalitarian]" published in: For my neighbours in hell/Irving Layton. Oakville, Ont.: Mosaic Press/Valley Editions, [1980].
"Alive and still kicking" not published to date.
"No cynic" not published to date.

FMNH 11/1
MOUNTAIN PLAYHOUSE; PASSING THROUGH THE ROCKIES; UNITED CHURCH SIGNBOARD; WHY THE AUSTRIANS OPTED FOR AUSCHWITZ; POETRY SEMINAR; BANFF POEM FOR HARRIET; THE GUARDRAIL [1979].
[12]p., [2] leaves; 4 leaves 28 cm., 1 leaf 27 cm., 1 leaf 36 cm. + 1 cardboard file folder.
Holograph.
Seven poems.
On p.[1]:2 drafts with revisions of "The guardrail"; draft of "Banff poem for Harriet"; marginalia.
On p.[2]:draft of "Poetry seminar"; draft of "Mountain playhouse."
On leaf [1] and p.[3,7]: 5 drafts with revisions of "Passing through the Rockies"; drafts on leaf [1] on verso of Lake Louise place mat.
On p.[4]:letter to Irving Layton from Adm. Assistant of The Banff Centre, dated May 29, 1979.
On p.[5]:draft of "The guardrail"; draft of "Why the Austrians opted for Auschwitz."
On p.[6]:letter to Irving Layton from Adm. Assistant of The Banff Centre, dated May 17, 1979.
On leaf [2]:draft with revisions of "Mountain playhouse" on program for The Banff Centre presentation of "Words and music."
On p.[8]:draft of "Mountain playhouse" crossed out; draft of "Why the Austrians opted for Auschwitz."
On p.[9]:draft of "Why the Austrians opted for Auschwitz"; draft of "United Church signboard."
On p.[10]:draft of "Mountain playhouse" crossed out.
On p.[11]:draft with revisions of "Mountain playhouse."
On p.[12]:3 drafts with revisions of "Why the Austrians opted for Auschwitz."
"Why the Austrians opted for Auschwitz" published as two titled stanzas of "The burning remnant."
"Mountain playhouse" published in: For my neighbours in hell/ Irving Layton. Oakville, Ont.: Mosaic Press/Valley Editions, [1980].
"Passing through the Rockies," ibid.
"United Church signboard," ibid.
"The burning remnant," ibid.
"Banff poem for Harriet" not published to date.
"The guardrail" not published to date.
"Poetry seminar" not published to date.

FMNH 12/1
FINALLY, THE FINAL SOLUTION; 2028
1979.
[2]p., [3] leaves; 28 cm.
In part holograph.
Two poems.
On p.[1] and leaf [1]:2 typescript drafts with revisions of "Finally, the final solution."
On p.[2]:typescript draft of "2028."
On leaf [2]:typescript draft with revisions of "Finally, the final solution."
On leaf [3]:typescript draft of "Finally, the final solution."
"Finally, the final solution" dated Montreal, Quebec, October 7- 8, 1979.
"Finally, the final solution" published with further revisions in: For my neighbours in hell/Irving Layton. Oakville, Ont.: Mosaic Press/Valley Editions, [1980].
"2028" published in: Droppings from heaven/Irving Layton. Toronto: McClelland and Stewart, 1979.

FMNH 13/1
THE CROSS
[1979].
[6]p.,[8] leaves; 6 leaves 21 cm., 5 leaves 29 cm.
Chiefly holograph.
Poem.
On p.[1-6] and leaves [1-3]:9 holograph drafts with revisions; drafts on p.[2,4] and leaf [1] titled "Prudence."
On leaf [4]:typescript draft with revisions.
On leaves [5-8]:4 typescript drafts.
Published with revisions as "The dysphasiac."
Published in: For my neighbours in Hell/Irving Layton. Toronto: McClelland and Stewart, [1980].

FR - Final Reckoning: Poems 1982-1986

FR 1/1
TWENTIETH CENTURY GOTHIC; SAY CHEESE PLEASE
1986.
[8]p., [26] leaves; 28 cm.
In part holograph signed.
2 poems.
On leaf [1]:holograph title "Twentieth century gothic."
On leaf [2]:3 holograph drafts with revisions of "Twentieth century gothic."

...con't

FR 1/1...con't

On verso of leaf [2]:2 lines of "Twentieth century gothic" and fragment beginning "As I sit in the corner armchair...."
On leaves [3-26]:14 holograph, 9 typescript (photocopies) drafts of "Twentieth century gothic" with revisions.
On p.[1-2]:2 holograph drafts of "Twentieth century gothic" with revisions.
On p.[3-4]:2 holograph drafts of "Twentieth century gothic" with revisions; 1 draft of "Say cheese please."
On p.[5-8]:2 holograph drafts with revisions.
Leaf [5] dated Rome, March 11, 1986.
Leaves [6-9,11] dated Rome, March 12, 1986.
Leaf 16 dated Montreal, March 26, 1986.
Leaf 17 dated March 28, 1986.
Leaves 5-9,11 titled "At the Albergo Esmerelda."
Leaves 13,15,16 titled "Gothic poem."
Leaves 16-25 titled "Twentieth century gothic."
Leaves [2-4] numbered 1-3; p.[1-2] numbered 4; leaves [5-12] numbered 5-11.
"Twentieth century gothic" published in: Final reckoning: poems 1982-1986/Irving Layton. Oakville, Ont.: Mosaic Press, 1987.
"Say cheese please" not published to date.

FR 2/1
THE INVESTITURE; BLACK TOURIST IN TINOS; THE THEATRE OF DIONYSOS; THE PADDLER
1985.
[12]p., [3] leaves; 28 cm.
Holograph.
4 poems.
On leaf [1]:holograph title on verso of leaf torn from Concordia University examination booklet.
On p.[1]:2 drafts with revisions of "The investiture."
On p.[2]:draft of "The investiture" titled "You and I"; 1 stanza of "Black tourist in Tinos" crossed out.
On p.[3]:draft of "The investiture" titled "You and I" dated Myconos, May 19, 1985.
On p.[4]:draft of "The investiture"; draft of 9 lines of "The theatre of Dionysos" crossed out.
On p.[5-9,11-12] and leaves [2-3]:9 drafts of "The investiture" with revisions.
On p.[10]:1 draft of "The investiture"; 1 stanza of "The paddler" crossed out.
On leaves [2-3]:2 holograph drafts with revisions of "The investiture."
Pages [3-6] dated Myconos, May 19, 1985; leaf [2] dated Poros, May 27, 1985.
"The investiture" published in: Final reckoning: poems 1982-1986/Irving

...con't

FR 2/1...con't

Layton. Oakville: Mosaic Press, 1987, (also in DD).
"Black tourist in Tinos," ibid., (also in DD).
"The theatre of Dionysos," ibid.
"The paddler," ibid.

FR 3/1
BLACK TOURIST IN TINOS; THE THEATRE OF DIONYSOS
1985.
[11] leaves; 28 cm.
Holograph signed.
2 poems.
On leaf [1]:holograph title.
On leaves [2-11]:10 drafts with revisions of "Black tourist in Tinos."
On verso of leaves [3-4]:3 lines of "The theatre of Dionysos."
Leaves [3-4] dated Tinos, May 12, 1985.
Leaf [6] dated Tinos, May 13, 1985.
Leaves [9-11] dated Tinos, May 14, 1985.
Marginalia on leaf [7].
Leaves [2-11] numbered 1-10.
"Black tourist in Tinos" published in: Final reckoning: poems 1982-1986/Irving Layton. Oakville, Ont.: Mosaic Press, 1987, (also in DD).
"The theatre of Dionysos," ibid.

FR 4/1
THE PADDLER
1985.
[5] leaves; 28 cm.
Holograph signed.
Poem.
On leaf [1]:draft with reworking of stanzas 1-3.
On leaf [2]:draft of stanza 1.
On leaves [3-5]:3 drafts with revisions.
Leaves [3,5] dated Myconos, May 19, 1985.
Published with further revisions in: Final reckoning: poems 1982-1986/Irving Layton. Oakville, Ont.: Mosaic Press, 1987.

FR 5/1
TRISTEZZA
1986.
[5] leaves; 28 cm.

...con't

FR 5/1...con't
In part holograph signed.
Poem.
On leaf [1]:holograph draft with reworking of last five lines.
On leaves [2-3]:2 typescript drafts with revisions and reworking of last five lines.
On leaf [4]:typescript draft with revisions; marginalia.
Typescript draft.
Leaves [1-4] titled, "Tristessa."
Leaves [2-3] dated August 4, 1986.
Published in: Final reckoning: poems 1982-1986/Irving Layton. Oakville, Ont.: Mosaic Press, 1987.

FR 6/1
OVERMAN
1986.
[4] leaves; 28 cm.
In part holograph.
Poem.
On leaf [1]:holograph draft with revisions and reworking of stanza 2.
On leaf [2]:1 typescript draft with revisions; 2 holograph drafts with reworking of stanza 2; dated December 4, 1986.
On leaf [3]:holograph draft with revisions; ms. interpretation at bottom of page.
On verso of leaf [3]:signed typescript (photocopy) draft crossed out.
On leaf [4]:typescript draft dated December 22, 1986.
Published in Final reckoning: poems 1982-1986/Irving Layton. Oakville, Ont.: Mosaic Press, 1987.

FR 7/1
HIGH FIDELITY
1986.
[3] leaves; 1 leaf 22 cm., 2 leaves 28 cm.
In part holograph.
Poem.
On leaf [1]:2 holograph drafts with revisions; marginalia.
On verso of leaf [1]: photocopy of German poem titled "Psalm."
On leaves [2-3]:2 typescript drafts; marginalia on leaf [2].
Leaves [1-2] dated December 20, 1986.
Published in: Final reckoning: poems 1982-1986/Irving Layton. Oakville, Ont.: Mosaic Press, 1987.

FR 8/1
POEM THAT SAYS IT ALL
1986.
[4] leaves; 28 cm.
In part holograph signed.
Poem.
On leaf [1]:holograph title.
On leaf [2]:2 holograph drafts with revisions.
On verso of leaf [2]:10 typescript lines of minutes of a meeting.
On leaf [3]:typescript draft with holograph revisions.
On leaf [4]:typescript (photocopy) draft with holograph revisions.
Leaves [2-3] dated Montreal, March 28, 1986.
Published in: Final reckoning: poems 1982-1986/Irving Layton. Oakville, Ont.: Mosaic Press, 1987.

FR 9/1
IMMORTELLES FOR A LITERARY STRUMPET; THE GELDED LION
1986.
[4] leaves; 28 cm.
In part holograph.
2 poems.
On leaf [1]:typescript draft of "Immortelles ..." with holograph revisions; 2 lines of "The Gelded Lion"; fragment beginning "La belle, corrupt France ..." dated July 24 and August 18, 1986; marginalia.
On leaves [2-4]:2 typescript drafts of "Immortelles ..." with holograph revisions; marginalia.
On leaf [3]: 1 typescript draft and 1 holograph draft with revisions of "Immortelles ..." dated October 3, 1986; marginalia.
Published with further revisions in: Final reckoning: poems 1982-1986/Irving Layton. Oakville, Ont.: Mosaic Press, 1987.
"The gelded lion," ibid.

FR 10/1
AND THEY ALL FALL DOWN; AESTHETIC CRUELTY
1986.
[2]p., [5] leaves; 28 cm.
In part holograph.
2 poems.
On leaf [1]:holograph title "And they all fall down."
On p.[1]:holograph draft of "And they all fall down" with revisions and reworking of stanza 3.

...con't

FR 10/1...con't

On p.[2]:typescript of "Aesthetic cruelty" dated July 12, 1986; titled "The Ascent of man."
On leaf [2]:typescript draft with revisions of "And they all fall down" dated August 2, 1986.
On leaf [3]:typescript draft with revisions of "And they all fall down" dated Newcastle-upon-Tyne, April 3, 1983 and August 3, 1983; marginalia.
On leaf [4]:typescript draft of "And they all fall down" with revisions dated Newcastle-upon-Tyne, April 1, 1983.
On leaf [5]:typescript draft of "And they all fall down" with revisions dated Newcastle-upon-Tyne, April 1, 1983 and October 3, 1986; marginalia.
Leaves [2-3]:titled "Bourgeois decadence"; leaf [4] titled "Newcastle-upon-Tyne."
"And they all fall down" published in: Final reckoning: poems 1982-1986/Irving Layton. Oakville, Ont.: Mosaic Press, 1987.
"Aesthetic cruelty," ibid.

FR 11/1
SOFT PORN; SOCRATES AT THE CENTAUR; MAIMONIDEAN PERPLEXITY
1986.
[2]p., [7] leaves; 1 leaf 34 cm., 6 leaves 28 cm.
In part holograph signed.
3 poems.
On p.[1]: typescript draft of "Socrates at the Centaur"; 2 holograph drafts with revisions of "Soft porn."
On p.[2]:4 holograph drafts with revisions of "Soft porn"; 2 holograph drafts with revisions of "Maimonidean perplexity"; marginalia.
On leaf [1];typescript draft of "Soft porn" with reworking of stanzas 1 and 3 dated June 27, 1986.
On leaf [2]:typescript draft with reworking of stanza 3 dated June 22, 1986.
On leaves [3-4]:2 typescript drafts of "Soft porn."
On leaf [6]:typescript draft with reworking of stanzas 1 and 3; marginalia.
"Soft porn" published in: Final reckoning: poems 1982-1986/ Irving Layton. Oakville, Ont.: Mosaic Press, 1987.
"Socrates at the Centaur," ibid.
"Maimonidean perplexity," ibid., (with revisions).

FR 12/1
OMNIPRESENCE
1985.
[4] leaves; 28 cm.
Typescript with holograph revisions.
Poem.
On leaf [1]:typescript draft with reworking of stanza [3]; marginalia; dated August 25, 1985.
On leaf [2]:typescript draft with revisions and reworking of stanza 3 dated June 27, 1986.
On leaf [4]:typescript draft with revisions dated December 23, 1986; marginalia.
Published with further revisions in: Final reckoning: poems 1982-1986/Irving Layton. Oakville, Ont.: Mosaic Press, 1987.

FR 13/1
ALISON PARROTT 1975-1986; SATURDAY NIGHT FARTICLE
1986.
[15] leaves; 28 cm.
In part holograph.
2 poems.
On leaf [1]:holograph draft of "Alison Parrott ..." with revisions dated August 8, 1986.
On leaves [2-4]:3 holograph drafts of "Alison Parrott ..." with revisions.
On verso of leaf [4]:3 lines of "Alison Parrott ..." crossed out.
On leaf [5]:typescript draft of "Alison Parrott ..." with reworking of stanza 6; marginalia.
On leaves [6-7,10-11]:4 typescript drafts of "Alison Parrott ..." with revisions.
On leaf [8]:1 typescript draft and 1 holograph draft of "Alison Parrott...."
On leaf [9]:1 holograph draft of "Alison Parrott ..." with reworking stanza 6; 4 typescript lines of "Saturday night farticle."
On verso of leaf [9]:ms. note.
On leaf [12]:1 typescript draft and 1 holograph draft of "Alison Parrott ..." with revisions.
On leaf [13]: holograph draft of "Alison Parrott ..." with revisions and reworking of stanza 6.
On leaf [14]: typescript draft of "Alison Parrott ..." with holograph and ms revisions dated August 9th.
On leaf [15]:typescript draft of "Alison Parrott ..." with revisions dated December 4, 1986; marginalia.

...con't

FR 13/1...con't

Published in: Final reckoning: poems 1982-1986/Irving Layton. Oakville, Ont.: Mosaic Press, 1987.
"Saturday night farticle," ibid.

FR 14/1
MUSTERING ALL HIS WIT
1986.
[2]p., [5] leaves; 28 cm.
In part holograph.
Poem.
On leaf [1]:holograph title.
On leaf [2]:2 holograph drafts with revisions.
On leaf [3]:3 holograph drafts with revisions.
On leaves [4-5]:2 holograph drafts with revisions; leaf [4] dated December 27, 1986; leaf [5] dated December 28, 1986.
On p.[1]:typescript draft with revisions and reworking of stanzas 2-3, dated December 27, 1986.
On p.[2]:3 holograph drafts with revisions; two drafts crossed out.
On leaf [7]:typescript draft dated December 29, 1986; marginalia.
Leaf [1] titled, "An obscenity."
Leaf [4] titled, "A Canadian obscenity."
Published in: Final reckoning: poems 1982-1986/Irving Layton. Oakville, Ont.: Mosaic Press, 1987.

FR 15/1
SOCRATES AT THE CENTAUR; TWENTIETH CENTURY GOTHIC
1986.
[2]p., [13] leaves; 28 cm.
In part holograph.
2 poems.
On leaf [1]:holograph title "Socrates at the Centaur."
On leaf [2]:holograph draft with revision of "Socrates at the Centaur."
On leaf [3] and p.[1]:holograph draft with revisions of "Socrates at the Centaur."
On p.[2]:signed typescript draft of "Twentieth century gothic."
On leaves [4-5]:holograph draft with revisions of "Socrates at the Centaur."
On leaves [6-7]:typescript draft of "Socrates at the Centaur" with revisions and reworking of last 7 lines dated June 3rd.
On leaves [8-9]:typescript draft with revisions of "Socrates at the Centaur" dated June 3, 1986; marginalia on leaf [8].
On leaves [10-13]:2 typescript drafts of "Socrates at the Centaur" with revisions

...con't

FR 15/1...con't

dated June 9, July 14, 1986; partial signature on leaf [10].
"Socrates at the Centaur" published with further revisions in: Final reckoning: poems 1982-1986/Irving Layton. Oakville, Ont.: Mosaic Press, 1987.
"Twentieth century gothic," ibid.

FR 16/1
THE GELDED LION
1986.
[5] leaves; 28 cm.
In part holograph.
Poem.
On leaf [1]:3 holograph drafts with revisions.
On leaf [2]:3 typescript drafts with revisions.
On leaf [3]:typescript draft with revisions, dated August 18, 1986.
On leaf [4]:typescript draft with revisions; marginalia.
On verso of leaf [4]: two typescript lines.
On leaf [5]:typescript draft.
Published in: Final reckoning: poems 1982-1986/Irving Layton. Oakville, Ont.: Mosaic Press, 1987.

FR 17/1
MAIMONIDEAN PERPLEXITY; SOFT PORN
1986.
[5] leaves; 28 cm.
In part holograph.
2 poems.
On leaf [1]:holograph draft of "Maimonidean perplexity"; 2 holograph drafts of "Soft porn" crossed out.
On leaf [2]:typescript draft of "Maimonidean perplexity" with revisions and reworking of stanza 1 and 2, dated June 22, 1986.
On leaf [3]:typescript draft of "Maimonidean perplexity" with revisions dated June 29, 1986.
On leaf [4]:typescript draft of "Maimonidean perplexity" with revisions dated July 25, 1986; marginalia.
On leaf [5]:typescript draft.
"Maimonidean perplexity" published in: Final reckoning: poems 1982-1986/Irving Layton. Oakville, Ont.: Mosaic Press, 1987.
"Soft porn," ibid.

FR 18/1
AESTHETIC CRUELTY; ASSHOLE IN RESIDENCE
1986.
[2]p.; [10] leaves; 28 cm.
In part holograph signed.
2 poems.
On p.[1]:holograph draft of "Aesthetic cruelty" with reworking of stanzas 2 and 3, dated July 8, 1986.
On p.[2]:2 holograph drafts with revisions of "Asshole in residence."
On leaf [2]:2 holograph drafts with revisions of "Aesthetic cruelty."
On leaf [3]:2 holograph drafts of "Aesthetic cruelty" with revisions and reworking of stanzas 2 and 3.
On leaf [4]:typescript draft of "Aesthetic cruelty" with holograph revisions dated July 9, 1986.
On leaves [5-7]:3 typescript drafts of "Aesthetic cruelty" with revisions.
On leaf [8]:typescript draft of "Aesthetic cruelty."
On leaf [9]:typescript draft of "Aesthetic cruelty" dated July 12, 1986.
On leaves [10-11]:2 typescript drafts of "Aesthetic cruelty" with revisions dated October 9 and December 4, 1986; marginalia.
Title on p.[1] and leaves [3-10]: "The ascent of man."
"Aesthetic cruelty" published in: Final reckoning: poems 1982-1986/Irving Layton. Oakville, Ont.: Mosaic Press, 1987.
"Asshole in residence" not published to date.

FR 19/1
NO BIRD BUT LIGHTER THAN ONE; AESTHETIC CRUELTY
1986.
[2]p., [6] leaves; 28 cm.
In part holograph.
2 poems.
On p.[1] and leaves [1-2]:3 holograph drafts with revisions of "No bird but lighter than one."
On p.[2]:typescript draft of "Aesthetic cruelty" crossed out.
On leaves [3-4]:typescript draft with revisions of "No bird but ..." dated December 28, 1986.
On leaf [5]:typescript draft of "No bird but ..." with revisions and reworking of stanza [1].
On leaf [6]:typescript draft with revisions of "No bird but ..." dated December 29, 1986; marginalia.
"No bird but lighter than one" published in: Final reckoning: poems 1982-1986/Irving Layton. Oakville, Ont.: Mosaic Press, 1987.
"Aesthetic cruelty," ibid.

FR 20/1
APPROACHING DOOMSDAY
1986.
[4]p., [4] leaves; 28 cm.
In part holograph.
Poem.
On p.[1,4]:2 holograph drafts with revisions.
On p.[2-3]:2 holograph drafts with revisions and reworking of stanza 3.
On leaves [1-2]:2 typescript drafts with revisions, dated December 27, 28, 1986.
On leaf [3]:typescript draft with holograph revisions.
On leaf [4]:typescript draft with revisions dated December 29, 1986; marginalia.
Published in: Final reckoning: poems 1982-1986/Irving Layton. Oakville, Ont.: Mosaic Press, 1987.

FR 21/1
CASA CACCIATORE
1986.
[2]p., [6] leaves; 28 cm.
In part holograph.
Poem.
On p.[1]:holograph draft with revisions and reworking of stanza 1.
On p.[2] and leaves [1-2]:3 holograph drafts with revisions and reworking of stanzas 1-3.
On leaf [3]:holograph draft with revisions.
On leaf [4]:2 holograph drafts with revisions.
On leaf [5]:2 holograph drafts with revisions dated December 19, 1986.
On leaf [6]:typescript draft; marginalia.
Published in: Final reckoning: poems 1982-1986/Irving Layton. Oakville, Ont.: Mosaic Press, 1987.

FR 22/1
MEMO TO A LITERARY PIMP
1986.
[3] leaves; 28 cm.
Typescript.
Poem.
On leaf [1]:holograph title.
On leaf [2]:typescript draft with holograph revisions dated August 18, 1986; marginalia.

...con't

FR 22/1...con't
On leaf [3]:typescript draft.
Published in: Final reckoning: poems 1982-1986/Irving Layton. Oakville, Ont.: Mosaic Press, 1987.

FR 23/1
THE PILES OF GREECE, THE PILES OF GREECE
[1986].
[2]p., [6] leaves; 28 cm.
Holograph.
Poem.
On leaf [1]:holograph title.
On p.[1]:draft with revisions and reworking of stanza 4; marginalia.
On p.[2]:2 drafts of stanzas 1 and 2 with revisions.
On leaf [2]:draft with revisions and reworking of stanza 3 titled "The Isles of Greece, the isles of Greece."
On leaf [3]:draft with revisions; stanzas 3 and 4 reversed.
On leaf [4]:draft with revisions and reworking of stanza 2.
On leaf [5]:draft with revisions and reworking of stanza 4.
On leaf [6]:draft with revisions titled "The new acropolis."
Published with further revisions in: Final reckoning: poems 1982-1986/Irving Layton. Oakville, Ont.: Mosaic Press, 1987.

FR 24/1
HERBERT VUNCE
[1986].
[2]p., [16] leaves; 28 cm.
In part holograph.
Poem.
On leaf [1]:typescript draft of stanza 1; holograph draft of stanzas 1-4.
On p.[1]:holograph draft with revisions titled "Norbert."
On p.[2]:holograph draft of personal letter.
On leaves [2-8]:7 typescript drafts with revisions; leaf [3] titled "Norbert"; leaf [7] titled "Mr. Norbert"; leaf 8 titled "Norman Vunce."
On verso of leaf [3]:3 typescript lines.
On leaf [9]:typescript draft of stanzas 1-3 and holograph draft of stanza 4 with revision titled "Vunce."
On leaf [10]:3 holograph drafts of stanza 4.
On leaves [11-12]:2 typescript drafts with revisions; leaf [1] titled "Norman Vunce"; marginalia on leaf [12].
On leaves [13-14]:2 typescript drafts titled "Norbert" with ms. revisions and

...con't

FR 24/1...con't
reworking of last 2 lines.
On leaf [15]:typescript draft with revisions; marginalia.
On leaf [16]:typescript draft with revisions.
Published in: Final reckoning: poems 1982-1986/Irving Layton. Oakville, Ont.: Mosaic Press, 1987.

FR 25/1
DIVERSE PLEASURES
[1986].
[5] leaves; 28 cm.
Holograph.
Poem.
On leaf [1]:draft of stanzas 1 and 4 crossed out; draft with revisions of stanzas 1-4.
On leaf [2]:draft with revisions of stanzas 1-4.
On leaf [3]:draft of stanzas 1-4 with revisions and reworking of stanza 3 titled "Purity."
On leaf [4]:draft with revisions of stanzas 1-4 titled "Going to church."
On leaf [5]:draft with revisions and reworking of stanza 5 titled "Suburban sabbath."
Published in: Final reckoning: poems 1982-1986/Irving Layton. Oakville, Ont.: Mosaic Press, 1987, (also in DD).

FR 26/1
TERRY FOX; SATURDAY NIGHT FARTICLE
[1986].
[2]p., [1] leaf; 1 leaf 9 cm. x 21 cm., 1 leaf 28 cm.
In part holograph.
2 poems.
On p.[1]:holograph draft of "Terry Fox."
On p.[2]:holograph draft with revisions of "Saturday night farticle."
On leaf [1]:typescript draft; marginalia.
"Terry Fox" published in: Final reckoning: poems 1982-1986/ Irving Layton. Oakville, Ont.: Mosaic Press, 1987.
"Saturday night farticle," ibid., (with further revisions).

FR 27/1
LEOPARDI IN MONTREAL
1984.
[16] leaves; 28 cm.
In part holograph signed.

...con't

FR 27/1...con't

Poem.
On leaf [1]:3 holograph drafts of "Adam Smith goes to heaven."
On leaf [2]:typescript draft of "Adam Smith goes to heaven."
On leaf [3]:typescript draft of "Adam Smith goes to heaven"; draft of "The rivals" titled "Strange pair."
On leaf [4]:typescript draft of "Adam Smith goes to heaven."
On leaf [5]:typescript draft with revisions of "Adam Smith goes to heaven."
On leaf [6]:4 holograph drafts of "Le menage" titled "Housecleaning"; marginalia.
On leaf [7]:1 typescript draft of "Le menage"; 4 holograph drafts of "The husking."
On leaf [8]:typescript draft of "Adam Smith goes to heaven"; holograph reworking of fragment beginning "And traded folly for sagacity...."
On verso of leaf [8]:3 holograph drafts of fragment beginning "Turning seventy I changed my hue..."; marginalia.
On leaf [9]:typescript draft of "The rivals."
On leaf [10]:typescript draft of "Adam Smith goes to heaven."
On leaf [11]:typescript draft of "Harlequinade."
On leaf [12]:typescript draft of "The husking"; 2 holograph drafts of "Machtpolitik."
On leaves [13-15]:3 typescript drafts of "The husking," "Le menage," "The rain and the wind," "Harlequinade," "Adam Smith goes to heaven," "Machtpolitik," "The rivals."
On leaf [16]:typescript draft of all of above mentioned poems with titles crossed out; title at head of page "Leopardi in Montreal."
Dated July, August, 1984.
Published with further revisions in: Final reckoning: poems 1982-1986/Irving Layton. Oakville, Ont.: Mosaic Press, 1987.

FR 28/1
TRENCH MOUTH; HARLEQUIN ROMANCE; INSECT REPELLENT; [THE CYST]
[1983].
[4] leaves; 29 cm.
In part holograph.
Four poems.
On leaf [1]:3 holograph drafts with revisions of "Trench mouth"; 2 drafts titled "Stalinist"; list of 4 poem titles by [Irving Layton].
On leaf [2]:holograph draft with revisions of "Trench mouth" titled "Hitlerist"; holograph draft of "Insect repellent"; holograph draft of "Harlequin romance"; notes on subject of "Wasps."
On leaf [3]:2 holograph drafts with revisions of "Trench mouth" titled "Hitlerist";

...con't

FR 28/1...con't

reworking of stanza 3.
On leaf [4]:holograph draft with revisions of "Trench mouth" titled "Stalinist"; draft of 2 stanzas of "[The cyst]" with reworking of stanza 1.
Drafts on verso of promotional material from "The Gucci bag."
Dated Piazza de Popula, August 20, 1983 and Umbrizi, August 26, 1983.
"Trench mouth" published with revisions in Final reckoning: poems 1982-1986/Irving Layton. Oakville, Ont.: Mosaic Press, 1987.
"[The cyst]" published with revisions in: The Gucci bag/Irving Layton. 2nd ed. Oakville, Ont.: Mosaic Press, 1984, (also in FR).
"Harlequin romance" not published to date.
"Insect repellent" not published to date.

FR 29/1
NIGHTMARE IN THE ANNEX
1986.
[4]p., [14] leaves; 28 cm.
In part holograph signed.
Poem.
On leaf [1]:holograph title.
On leaf [2]:holograph draft of 2 stanzas with revisions.
On p.[1]:holograph draft with revisions.
On p.[2]:holograph draft of stanzas 1 and 2 with revisions and reworking of stanza 2.
On leaves [3-4]:holograph draft with revisions; stanzas 3 and 4 reversed.
On p.[3-4]:holograph draft with revisions and reworking of stanza 4.
On leaf [5]:typescript draft with revisions and reworking of stanza 4.
On leaves [6-12]:7 typescript drafts with revisions.
On leaf [13]:typescript draft.
On leaf [14]:typescript (photocopy) draft with revisions dated May 28, [1986].
Ms. interpretation of poem at bottom of leaf [6] and on verso.
Leaves [5-7] dated May 11, 1986; leaf [8] dated May 12, 1986; leaves [9-10] dated May 14, 1986; leaf [11] dated May 15, 1986; leaf [12] dated May 18, 1986.
Published in: Final reckoning: poems 1982-1986/Irving Layton. Oakville, Ont.: Mosaic Press, 1987.

FR 30/1
WAGSCHAL EXHIBITION
1984.
[10] leaves; 3 leaves 29 cm., 7 leaves 28 cm. + 1 envelope.
Chiefly holograph.
Poem.
Two holograph drafts with revisions on verso of unaddressed envelope from Canadair, Montreal, Quebec.
On leaf [1]:holograph draft with reworking of stanza 1.
On leaves [2-4]:3 holograph drafts with revisions.
On leaf [5]:holograph draft with reworking of stanza 1.
On verso of leaf [5]:2 holograph drafts of stanza 4.
On leaves [6-8]:3 holograph drafts with revisions; draft on leaf [8] on verso of letter to Irving Layton from University of Toronto, President's Committee.
Leaves [9-10]:2 typescript drafts with revisions.
Leaves [1-3] on verso of promotional material from "The Gucci bag."
Dated Don Stewart Art Gallery, Montreal, November 15, 1984.
Published in Final reckoning: poems 1982-1986/Irving Layton. Oakville, Ont.: Mosaic Press, 1987.

FR 31/1
SATURDAY NIGHT FARTICLE
1986.
[9] leaves; 28 cm.
In part holograph.
Poem.
On leaf [1]:holograph draft with revisions and reworking of stanzas 1-2.
On leaf [2]:2 holograph drafts with revisions.
On leaf [3]:holograph draft of stanzas 1-2 with reworking of stanza 1.
On leaf [4]:holograph reworking of stanzas 3-4.
On leaf [5]:typescript draft of 4 stanzas with reworking of stanza 1.
On leaf [6]:typescript draft of 4 stanzas with revisions; holograph draft of stanzas 1-3 with revisions.
On leaf [7]:typescript draft of 4 stanzas with revisions and reworking of stanza 4.
On verso of leaf [7]:holograph reworking of stanza 4.
On leaves [8-9]:2 typescript drafts with revisions; leaf [8] dated August 8, 1986; marginalia.
Published in: Final reckoning: poems 1982-1986/Irving Layton. Oakville, Ont.: Mosaic Press, 1987.

FR 32/1
INTER-VIEW; NIGHTMARE IN THE ANNEX
1986.
[6]p., [4] leaves; 28 cm.
In part holograph signed.
2 poems.
On leaf [1]:holograph title "Interview."
On p.[1]:holograph draft with revisions of "Inter-View."
On p.[2,4,6]:3 typescript drafts of "Nightmare in the annex."
On leaves [2-3]:2 holograph (photocopy) drafts with revisions of "Inter-View," dated May 27, 1986.
On p.[3-5]:2 holograph drafts with revisions of "Inter-View."
On leaf [4]:typescript draft of "Inter-View," dated Montreal, May 27, 1986.
Page [5] titled "The Unicorn."
"Inter-View" published in: Final reckoning: poems 1982-1986/ Irving Layton. Oakville, Ont.: Mosaic Press, 1987.
"Nightmare in the annex," ibid.

FR 33/1
FINAL RECKONING: AFTER THEOGNIS; SOFT PORN; SEX APPEAL
1986.
[4]p., [5] leaves; 1 leaf 21 cm., 6 leaves 28 cm.
In part holograph.
3 poems.
On leaf [1]:holograph title "Final reckoning: after Theognis."
On p.[1]:holograph draft with revisions of "Final reckoning...," dated June 4, 1986.
On p.[2]:typescript draft of "Sex appeal."
On leaf [2]:typescript draft of "Soft porn" crossed out; holograph draft with revisions and reworking of "Final reckoning...."
On p.[3]:holograph draft with revisions of "Final reckoning...."
On p.[4]:typescript draft of "Soft porn."
On leaves [3-4]:2 typescript drafts with revisions of "Final reckoning ..." dated July 4, 13, 1986.
On leaf [5]:typescript (photocopy) of "Final reckoning...."
"Final reckoning: after Theognis" published in: Final reckoning: poems 1982-1986/Irving Layton. Oakville, Ont.: Mosaic Press, 1987.
"Soft porn," ibid.
"Sex appeal" published in: The Gucci bag/Irving Layton. Oakville, Ont.: Mosaic Press/Valley Edition, 1983, (also in GB2, MSGB).

FR 34/1
THEATRE OF DIONYSOS; BLACK TOURIST IN TINOS
1985.
[6]p., [9] leaves; 28 cm.
Holograph.
2 poems.
On leaf [1]:holograph title "Theatre of Dionysus."
On leaves [2-6] and p.[1,3]:7 drafts of 18-24 lines with revisions of "Theatre of Dionysos"; marginalia on leaf [2].
On p.[2]:draft of 4 stanzas with revisions of "Theatre of Dionysos."
On p.[4-5] and leaves [7-9]:5 drafts of 6 stanzas with revisions of "Theatre of Dionysos"; leaf [8] dated Athens, May 11, 1985.
On p.[6]:draft with revisions of "American tourist in Tinos" published as "Black tourist in Tinos."
Page [4] and leaf [7] titled "Ruined temple of Dionysus"; page [5] and leaf [9] titled "Ruined Dionysian temple"; leaf [8] titled "Ruins: the temple of Dionysus."
"Theatre of Dionysos" published with further revisions in: "Final reckoning: poems 1982-1986/Irving Layton. Oakville, Ont.: Mosaic Press, 1987.
"Black tourist in Tinos," ibid., (also in DD).

FR 35/1
FUNCTIONAL ILLITERATES
1986.
[6] leaves; 28 cm.
In part holograph.
Poem.
On leaf [1]:typescript draft of 3 stanzas titled "Canucky literati."
On leaf [2]:typescript draft with revisions and reworking of stanza 3, dated July 3, 1986.
On leaf [3]:typescript draft with revisions dated July 3, 1986.
On leaf [4]:typescript draft with ms. revisions dated July 8, 1986.
On leaf [5]:typescript draft with ms. revisions and reworking of stanzas 3-4, dated July 8, 1986; marginalia.
On leaf [6]:typescript draft with revisions dated July 25, [1986].
Published with revisions in: Final reckoning: poems 1982-1986/ Irving Layton. Oakville, Ont.: Mosaic Press, 1987.

FR 36/1
SIMPSON; INTER-VIEW; NIGHTMARE IN THE ANNEX; TWENTIETH CENTURY GOTHIC
1986.
[14]p., 7 leaves; 1 leaf 35 cm., 13 leaves 28 cm.
In part holograph.
4 poems.
On leaf [1]:holograph title "Simpson."
On p.[1]:holograph draft of 19 lines of "Simpson" with reworking of lines 1-9.
On p.[2]:holograph draft of "Inter-View" crossed out.
On p.[3-5]:2 holograph drafts of 22 lines of "Simpson" with revisions.
On p.[4,6,10]:3 typescript drafts of "Nightmare in the annex."
On p.[7,9,11]:3 holograph drafts of "Simpson" with revisions.
On p.[8,12]:2 typescript drafts of "Twentieth century gothic."
On leaf [2]:typescript draft of "Simpson" with revisions; marginalia.
On p.[13]:holograph draft of stanzas 3-4 with revisions.
On p.[14]:typescript draft of letter to the editor of Toronto Magazine, dated May 3, 1986.
On leaf [3]:typescript draft of "Authentic" with revisions; marginalia.
On leaf [4]:typescript draft of "Simpson" dated May 30; holograph title on verso.
On leaves [5-6]:typescript drafts of "Simpson"; leaf [6] dated October 28, 1986.
On leaf [7]:typescript draft of "Simpson" with revisions dated December 4, 1986.
Pages [1,11] and leaves [2-5] titled "Authentic"; page [9] titled "Authenticity."
"Simpson" published with further revisions in: Final reckoning: poems 1982-1986/Irving Layton. Oakville, Ont.: Mosaic Press, 1987.
"Nightmare in the annex," ibid.
"Twentieth century gothic," ibid.
"Inter-view," ibid.

FR 37/1
JUDGEMENT AT MURRAY'S
1985.
[10]p., [17] leaves; 28 cm.
In part holograph.
Poem.
On p.[1-4,6-9] and leaves [6-10,13]:13 holograph drafts with revisions; marginalia on verso of leaf 10.
On p.[5]:holograph draft of 9 lines with revisions.
On p.[10]:ms. draft with holograph revisions.
On leaves [1-5]:5 typescript drafts with revisions dated November 19, 1984.

...con't

FR 37/1...con't

On leaves [11-12,14]:3 typescript drafts with revisions dated January 22, 1985; holograph draft of 4 lines of stanza 2 on verso of leaf [12].
On leaf [15]:typescript draft with revisions dated January 26, 1985.
On leaves [16-17]:2 typescript drafts; leaf [16] dated January 26, 1985, leaf [17] dated February 4, 1985.
Published in: Final reckoning: poems 1982-1986/Irving Layton. Oakville, Ont.: Mosaic Press, 1987.

FR 38/1
FELLINI; BYRON IN VENICE
1984.
[4]p., [13] leaves; 28 cm.
In part holograph.
2 poems.
On p.[1,3] and leaves [1-7]:9 holograph drafts of "Fellini" with revisions; leaf [2] dated September 13, 1984; leaves [4-5,7] dated September 14, 1984.
On p.[2]:holograph draft of "Byron in Venice."
On p.[4]:2 holograph drafts of stanza 2 of "Fellini"; 2 holograph stanzas of "Byron in Venice."
On leaves [8-9]:2 photocopies of ms. drafts of "Fellini" with revisions, dated September 15, 1984.
On leaves [10-12]:3 typescript drafts of "Fellini" with revisions; leaves [10-12], dated September 15, 1984.
On leaf [13]:typescript draft of "Fellini" with revisions and reworking of last 2 lines, dated September 17, 1984.
"Fellini" published in: Final reckoning: poems 1982-1986/Irving Layton. Oakville, Ont.: Mosaic Press, 1987.
"Byron in Venice" not published to date.

FR 39/1
KITCH
[1986].
[8]p., [3] Leaves; 28 cm.
In part holograph.
Poem.
On p.[1]:1 ms. draft and 1 holograph draft; marginalia.
On p.[2]:ms. and holograph reworking of stanzas 1 and 3.
On p.[3-8] and leaf [1]:14 holograph drafts with revisions.

FR 39/1...con't

On leaf [2]:typescript with 2 drafts of stanza [1].
On leaf [3]:typescript draft.
Published in: Final reckoning: poems 1982-1986/Irving Layton. Oakville, Ont.: Mosaic Press, 1987.

FR 40/1
PRINCIPESSA ANNA; WEIRDO
[1986].
[6] leaves; 28 cm. + 1 file folder.
Chiefly holograph.
Two poems.
On leaf [1] and verso:holograph draft with revisions of "Principessa Anna."
On leaves [2-3]:holograph draft with revisions of "Principessa Anna"; marginalia.
On leaf [4]:holograph draft of "Principessa Anna."
On verso of leaf [4]:typescript draft of "Weirdo" crossed out.
On leaf [5]:typescript draft of "Principessa Anna" with portions crossed out.
On verso of leaf [5]:holograph draft with revisions of "Principessa Anna."
On leaf [6]:typescript draft with revisions of "Principessa Anna"; ms. note explaining numbering of drafts.
On leaf [7]:typescript (photocopy) with revisions titled "Principessa Anna."
Leaves [1,3,5-6] titled "Princess Anna."
On inside of file folder:3 holograph drafts of "Principessa Anna"; marginalia.
List of titles of poems by [Irving Layton]; holograph title "Principessa Anna" and marginalia on front cover of file folder.
"Principessa Anna" published in: Final reckoning: poems 1982-1986/Irving Layton. Oakville, Ont.: Mosaic Press, 1987.
"Weirdo" not published to date.

FR 41/1
BURNT OFFERING
1985.
[4]p., [6] leaves; 1 leaf 25 cm., 7 leaves 28 cm.
In part holograph.
Poem.
On p.[1]:holograph draft with reworking of stanza 3.
On p.[2-3] and leaves [1-2]:4 holograph drafts with revisions.
On p.[4]:holograph draft with revisions and reworking of stanza 4.
On leaf [3]:holograph draft.
On leaf [4]:holograph (photocopy) draft.
On leaves [5-6]:2 typescript drafts.

...con't

FR 41/1...con't

Leaves [2-6]:dated Montreal, March 30, 1985.
Published in: Final reckoning: poems 1982-1986/Irving Layton. Oakville, Ont.: Mosaic Press, 1987.

FR 42/1
TWO FOR THE ROAD FRANK
1985.
[2]p., [11] leaves; 1 leaf 21 cm., 1 leaf 14 cm., 10 leaves 28cm.
In part holograph.
Poem.
On leaf [1]:crossed out copy of letter from Lucinda Vardey to Peter Lindfoss; 2 holograph drafts of stanza 1.
On leaf [2]:ms. draft of stanza 1, dated February 5, 1985; marginalia; note concerning dinner engagement on verso.
On leaves [3-7]:5 typescript drafts of stanza [1] with revisions; leaf [5] dated February 5, 1985; leaf [6] dated February 4, [1985].
On p.[1]:holograph draft with revisions dated February 18, [1985].
On p.[2]:memo from Bill Abrams concerning material for "Viewpoints" quarterly.
On leaf [8]:typescript of stanza 1, 3 holograph drafts with revisions of stanzas [2-5].
On leaves [9-11]:3 typescript drafts with revisions, dated February 20, 1985.
On verso of leaf [11]:ms. interpretation of poem, dated February 21, 1985.
Published with revisions in: Final reckoning: poems 1982-1986/ Irving Layton. Oakville, Ont.: Mosaic Press, 1987.

FR 43/1
POPCORN
1984.
[7] leaves; 28 cm.
Holograph signed.
Poem.
On leaves [1,3,5]:3 drafts with revisions.
On leaf [2]:draft with revisions and reworking of stanza 1.
On leaf [4]:2 drafts with revisions.
On leaf [6]:2 drafts with revisions.
On leaf [7]:draft.
Holograph title on verso of leaves [6-7].
Dated San Jose, February 20, 1984.
Published in: Final reckoning: poems 1982-1986/Irving Layton. Oakville, Ont.: Mosaic Press, 1987.

FR 44/1
THE MASSACRE
1984.
[9] leaves; 28 cm. + 1 envelope.
Chiefly holograph.
Poem.
On verso of envelope:holograph draft of 6 lines; marginalia.
On leaves [1-8]:8 holograph drafts with revisions.
On verso of leaf [8]:partial draft of letter to [?] from [Irving Layton].
On leaf [9]:typescript draft of "The massacre."
Dated July 21, 1984.
Published in: Final reckoning: poems 1982-1986/Irving Layton. Oakville, Ont.: Mosaic Press, 1987.

FR 45/1
ETRUSCAN TOMBS; POTATOES
1984.
[6]p., [9] leaves; 6 leaves 28 cm., 6 leaves 30 cm.
Chiefly holograph.
Two poems.
On leaves [1-8] and p.[[1-3]:12 holograph drafts with revisions of "Etruscan tombs"; p.[3] titled "Norchia."
On p.[4]:holograph draft of "Potatoes."
Leaf [9]:photocopy of revised typescript draft of "Etruscan tombs."
"Etruscan tombs" dated Norchia, September 18, 1984.
"Etruscan tombs" published in Final reckoning: poems 1982-1986/ Irving Layton. Oakville, Ont.: Mosaic Press, 1987.
"Potatoes" not published to date.

FR 46/1
CRACKS IN THE ACROPOLIS
1984.
[6] leaves; 2 leaves 30 cm., 4 leaves 28 cm.
In part holograph.
Poem.
On leaf [1]:2 holograph drafts with revisions; one draft crossed out; sketches of human figures and note concerning sketches.
On leaf [2]:holograph draft with revisions titled "Des Moines tourist."
On leaf [3]:holograph draft with revisions.
On leaves [4-5]:2 typescript drafts with revisions.

...con't

FR 46/1...con't

On leaf [6]:photocopy of revised draft.
Dated September 19, 1984.
Published in Final reckoning: poems 1982-1986/Irving Layton. Oakville, Ont.: Mosaic Press, 1987.

FR 47/1
OPIUMS
1984.
[21] leaves; 28 cm.
In part holograph.
Poem.
On leaves [1-3] and verso:3 holograph drafts with revisions; marginalia on leaf 3.
On leaves [4-21]:10 typescript drafts with revisions.
Ms. note on theme of poem and marginalia on verso of leaf [17].
Dated July 9, 1984.
Published in: Final reckoning: poems 1982-1986/Irving Layton. Oakville, Ont.: Mosaic Press, 1987.

FR 48/1
DEVOTION; BYRON IN VENICE
[1986].
[2]p., 5 leaves ; 1 leaf 28 cm., 5 leaves 30 cm.
Holograph.
Poem.
On p.[1] and leaves [1-4]:5 drafts with revisions of "Devotion."
On p.[2]:draft with revisions of "Byron in Venice."
Leaf [5] photocopy of revised ms. draft.
"Devotion" published in Final reckoning: poems 1982-1986/ Irving Layton. Oakville, Ont.: Mosaic Press, 1987.
"Byron in Venice" not published to date.

GB - The Gucci Bag

GB 1/1
THE BREASTSTROKE
1981.
[1] leaf; 28 cm.
Typescript signed.
Poem.
Dated Cuba, December 30, 1981.
Black pen stroke through red ink signature.
Number "46" in upper left corner.
"The breaststroke" published as "[The breast stroke]."
Published in: The Gucci bag/Irving Layton. Oakville, Ont.: Mosaic Press/Valley Editions, 1983, (also in MSGB, GB2, WPJ, LPIL2, DD).

GB 2/1
THE DIVINE TOUCH
[1982].
[1] leaf; 28 cm.
Typescript signed.
Poem.
Published in: The Gucci bag/Irving Layton. Oakville, Ont.: Mosaic Press/Valley Editions, 1983, (also in WPJ, MSGB, GB2, DD).

GB 3/1
SAMANTHA CLARA LAYTON
1981.
[5]leaves; 28 cm.
In part holograph signed.
Poem.
One holograph, 5 typescript drafts with revisions.
On verso of leaf [1]:form letter from Canada Council regarding payment for Public Readings Program.
Leaf [1] dated Toronto, Ont., January 13, 1981.
Leaf [7] dated Toronto, [Ont.], January 20, 1981.
Published with further revisions in: The Gucci bag/Irving Layton. Oakville, Ont.: Mosaic Press/Valley Editions, 1983, (also in WPJ, MSGB, GB2).

GB 4/1
AN A PLUS; INSECT REPELLENT
[1982].
[3] leaves; 28 cm.

...con't

GB 4/1...con't
Chiefly holograph.
Two poems.
On leaf [1]:holograph draft with revisions of "An A plus."
On verso of leaf [1]:title "Poems for Jack the Ripper" and quotation from Psalms, Book 3:78.
On leaf [2]:holograph draft with revisions and reworking of last stanza of "An A plus."
On verso of leaf [2]:lines 1-4 of "Insect repellent."
On leaf [3]:typescript draft with revisions of "An A plus."
Holograph title "An A plus" on verso of leaf [3].
"An A plus" published with further revisions as "[The courage to be]."
"[The courage to be]" published in: The Gucci bag/Irving Layton. Oakville, Ont.: Mosaic Press/Valley Editions, 1983.
"Insect repellent" not published to date.

GB 5/1
BORIS PASTERNAK; FROM THE NETHER WORLD; BONDED; EPISTLE TO CATULLUS; IN REVENGE FOR OLGA AND BP
1981.
[8]p., [7] leaves; 28 cm.
In part holograph signed.
Five poems.
On leaves [1-7] and p.[1,3,5,7]:5 holograph, 6 typescript drafts with revisions of "Boris Pasternak."
On p.[2]:typescript draft of "In revenge for Olga and BP."
On p.[4]:typescript draft of "Epistle to Catullus."
On p.[6]:typescript draft of "From the nether world."
On p.[8]:typescript draft of "Bonded."
Yellow stains on p.[2].
"Boris Pasternak" dated Niagara-on-the-Lake, July 15, 1981.
Holograph title "Boris Pasternak" on verso of leaves [3,7].
"Boris Pasternak" published with further revisions in: The Gucci bag/Irving Layton. Oakville, Ont.: Mosaic Press/Valley Editions, 1983, (also in MSGB, GB2).
"From the nether world," ibid., (also in MSGB, GB2).
"Bonded," ibid., (also in MSGB, GB2, LPIL2, DD).
"Epistle to Catullus" published in: The Gucci bag/Irving Layton. 2nd ed. Oakville, Ont.: Mosaic Press/Valley Editions, 1984, (also in FR).
"In revenge for Olga and BP" not published to date.

GB 6/1
BLIND MAN'S B[L]UFF
[1982].
[5] leaves; 28 cm.
Typescript with holograph revisions.
Poem.
Five drafts.
Holograph title on verso of leaves [3-5].
Published in: The Gucci bag/Irving Layton. Oakville, Ont.: Mosaic Press/Valley Editions, 1983, (also in MSGB, GB2, LPIL2, DD).

GB 7/1
BONDED; [AH, NUTS]
[1982].
[1] leaf; 28 cm.
Holograph signed.
Two poems.
Three drafts of "Bonded"; 1 draft titled "The rivet"; draft of lines 1-12 of "[Ah, nuts]"; 8 line fragment beginning "Uptight as lawyers...."
Holograph title "Bonded" on verso.
"Bonded" published with revisions in: The Gucci bag/Irving Layton. Oakville, Ont.: Mosaic Press/Valley Editions, 1983, (also in MSGB, GB2, LPIL2, DD).
"[Ah, nuts]," ibid., (also in MSGB, GB2).

GB 8/1
THE CARVED NAKEDNESS; LA COMEDIA; AN OLD MAN'S WET DREAMS; FOR MY INCOMPARABLE GYPSY; THE WRAITH
[1982].
[6]p., [1] leaf; 28 cm.
In part holograph.
Five poems.
On leaf [1] and p.[1,3,5]:4 holograph drafts, 1 typescript draft of "The carved nakedness."
On p.[2]:typescript draft of "The wraith."
On p.[4]:typescript draft of "La comedia" with holograph signature.
On p.[6]:typescript draft of "An old man's wet dreams" with reference to "For my incomparable gypsy" in stanza 4; holograph title "The carved nakedness."
"The carved nakedness" published with further revisions in: The Gucci bag/Irving Layton. Oakville, Ont.: Mosaic Press/Valley Editions, 1983, (also in MSGB, GB2).
"La comedia," ibid., (also WPJ, MSGB, GB2).
"An old man's wet dreams," ibid., (with revisions).

...con't

GB 8/1...con't

"For my incomparable gypsy" published in For my brother Jesus/ Irving Layton. Toronto: McClelland and Stewart, 1976, (also in LPIL1, LPIL2, DD).
"The wraith" not published to date.

GB 9/1
THE CARILLON
[1982].
[6] leaves; 28 cm.
Chiefly holograph.
Poem.
On leaf [1]:2 holograph drafts of 3 stanzas with revisions.
On leaf [2]:holograph draft of 7 stanzas with revisions.
On leaf [3]:holograph draft of 7 stanzas with revisions; stanza 1 crossed out.
On leaf [4]:holograph draft of 8 stanzas with revisions.
On leaves [5-6]:2 typescript drafts of 8 stanzas with revisions.
Leaves [1-2] titled "The cracked bell."
Drafts 1-4 numbered.
Holograph title on verso of leaves [5-6].
Published with further revisions in: The Gucci bag/Irving Layton. Oakville, Ont.: Mosaic Press/Valley Editions, 1983, (also in MSGB, GB2).

GB 10/1
CENTRAL HEATING; [A CHARIOT FOR HARRIET]
[1982].
[4]p., 2 leaves; 28 cm.
In part holograph.
Two poems.
On p.[1,3]:2 holograph drafts with revisions of "Central heating."
On leaf [1]:typescript draft of "Central heating" with holograph reworking on last 4 lines.
On leaf [2]:typescript draft of "Central heating."
On p.[2,4]:typescript of 2 stanzas of "[A chariot for Harriet]" with holograph reworking of last stanza.
Holograph title "Central heating" on verso of leaf [2].
"Central heating" published in: The Gucci bag/Irving Layton. Oakville, Ont.: Mosaic Press/Valley Editions, 1983, (also in MSGB, GB2, DD).
"[A chariot for Harriet]" not published to date.

GB 11/1
THE DAZED FLY; BULL, MORE AND LESS
[1982].
[2] p., [5] leaves; 28 cm.
Chiefly holograph.
Two poems.
On leaves [1-3] and p.[1]:4 holograph drafts with revisions of "The dazed fly."
On leaf [4]:typescript draft of "The dazed fly."
On leaf [5]:typescript draft with revisions of "The dazed fly."
On verso of leaf [1]:title "Poems for Jack the Ripper" underlined; 2 quotations from Psalms, Book 2:53 and 2:59.
On p.[2]:typescript draft of "Bull, more and less."
Drafts [1-5] of "The dazed fly" numbered.
Holograph title "The dazed fly" on verso of leaf [5].
"The dazed fly" published with further revisions in: The Gucci bag/Irving Layton. Oakville, Ont.: Mosaic Press/Valley Editions, 1983, (also in MSGB, GB2).
"Bull, more and less" not published to date.

GB 12/1
DANCING MAN; AN A PLUS
[1982].
[2]p., [2] leaves; 3 leaves 28 cm. + 1 panel of brown envelope 26 cm.
In part holograph.
Two poems.
One holograph draft of "Dancing man" with reworking of stanzas 1,3-4 on back panel of brown envelope.
On leaf [1]:typescript draft of "Dancing man" titled "The [w]ind."
On verso of leaf [1]:typescript of 9 lines of essay used in foreword to "The Gucci bag."
On p.[1]:typescript draft of "Dancing man" with reworking of stanzas 3-4 titled "The [w]ind."
On p.[2]:typescript draft of "An A plus."
On leaf [2]:typescript draft of "Dancing man."
On verso of leaf [2]:typescript of lines 1-2 of "Dancing man."
"An A plus" dated Niagara-on-the-Lake, August 2, 1981.
"Dancing man" dated September 4, 1981.
Holograph title "Dancing man" on verso of leaf [3].
"An A plus" published with revisions as "[The courage to be]."
"Dancing man" published with further revisions in: The Gucci bag/Irving Layton. Oakville, Ont.: Mosaic Press/Valley Editions, 1983, (also in MSGB, GB2).
"[The courage to be]," ibid.

GB 13/1
DESCENT FROM EDEN; [THE WINGED HORSE]; THE CRACKED CRYSTAL BALL
[1982].
[2]p., [2] leaves; 28 cm.
Chiefly holograph.
Three poems.
On leaves [1-2]:2 holograph drafts with revisions of "Descent from Eden."
On verso of leaf [2]:typescript draft of lines 1-4 of "[The winged horse]."
On p.[1]:typescript draft with revisions of "Descent from Eden."
On p.[2]:typescript draft of "The cracked crystal ball"; holograph title "Descent from Eden."
"Descent from Eden" published with further revisions in: The Gucci bag/Irving Layton. Oakville, Ont.: Mosaic Press/Valley Editions, 1983, (also in MSGB, GB2).
"[The winged horse]," ibid., (also in MSGB, GB2).
"The cracked crystal ball" not published to date.

GB 14/1
DEAD SOULS; ODD OBSESSION; ADVICE TO OLD MAIDS; YIDS; STRIPPING TELEGRAM
1981.
[8]p., [1] leaf; 28 cm.
In part holograph.
Five poems.
On p.[1]:holograph draft of "Dead souls" with reworking of stanzas 1-2.
On p.[2]:typescript draft of "Yids."
On leaf [1]:2 holograph drafts with revisions of "Dead souls."
On verso of leaf [1]:holograph draft of line 1 of "Odd obsession."
On p.[3]:holograph draft with revisions of "Dead souls" titled "Doomed."
On p.[4,6]:2 typescript drafts of "Advice to old maids."
On p.[5]:holograph draft with revisions of "Dead souls" titled "The dead soul"; holograph draft of "Stripping telegram."
On p.[7]:typescript draft of "Dead souls."
On p.[8]:2 typescript drafts of fragment beginning "There are people who can't tell..."; holograph title "Dead souls."
"Stripping telegram" dated July 26, 1981.
"Dead souls" published in: The Gucci bag/Irving Layton. Oakville, Ont.: Mosaic Press/Valley Editions, 1983, (also in MSGB, GB2).
"Odd obsession," ibid., (also in MSGB, GB2, LPIL2, DD).
"Advice to old maids" not published to date.
"Yids" not published to date.
"Stripping telegram" not published to date.

GB 15/1
FOR THE WIFE OF JOHN MILTON
[1982].
[2]leaves; 28 cm.
In part holograph.
Poem.
On leaf [1]:2 holograph drafts with revisions.
On leaf [2]:3 typescript drafts.
Leaf [1] titled "Milton's wife."
Holograph title "For the wife of John Milton" on verso of leaf [2].
Published as "[For the wife of Mr. Milton]."
Published in: The Gucci bag/Irving Layton. Oakville, Ont.: Mosaic Press/Valley Editions, 1983, (also in MSGB, GB2).

GB 16/1
THE FURROW; THE CRACKED CRYSTAL BALL; YIDS; INSECT REPELLENT
1981.
[4]p., [1] leaf; 28 cm.
In part holograph.
Four poems.
On p.[1,3]:4 holograph drafts with revisions of "The furrow"; p.[3] titled "The gash."
On p.[2]:typescript draft with revisions of "The cracked crystal ball."
On p.[4]:typescript draft of "Yids."
On leaf [1]:3 typescript drafts with revisions of "The furrow"; 1 draft titled "The gash."
On verso of leaf [1]:typescript draft of "Insect repellent"; holograph title "The furrow."
"The furrow" dated August 2, 1981.
"The furrow" published in: The Gucci bag/Irving Layton. Oakville, Ont.: Mosaic Press/Valley Editions, 1983, (also in MSGB GB2).
"The cracked crystal ball" not published to date.
"Yids" not published to date.
"Insect repellent" not published to date.

GB 17/1
THE GARDEN
1981.
[2] leaves; 28 cm.
Holograph.

...con't

GB 17/1...con't

Poem.
On leaf [1]:draft of 9 stanzas with reworking of stanzas 4,6,9.
On leaf [2]:draft with reworking of stanza 10.
Holograph title on verso of leaf [2].
Dated July 18, 1981.
Published in: The Gucci bag/Irving Layton. Oakville, Ont.: Mosaic Press/Valley Editions, 1983, (also in WPJ, MSGB, GB2).

GB 18/1
MAKE ROOM WILLIAM BLAKE; LETTING GO; AN IDEAL HUSBAND
1981.
[4]p., [3] leaves; 28 cm.
Chiefly holograph.
Three poems.
On leaf [1]:3 holograph drafts of stanza 1, 2 drafts of stanza 2, 2 drafts of stanza 4 of "Make room William Blake."
On verso of leaf [1]:title "Poems for Jack the Ripper"; quotation from Psalms, Book 3:78.
On p.[1]:holograph draft with revisions of "Make room William Blake" titled "The water curse"; typescript draft of "Letting go" crossed out.
On p.[2,4]:2 typescript drafts of "An ideal husband."
On leaf [2]:holograph draft of "Make room William Blake" titled "Lest I become mad."
On p.[3]:1 typescript draft of "Make room William Blake" titled "Move over, William Blake."
On leaf [3]:typescript draft of "Make room William Blake"; signed holograph note concerning title of book.
"Make room William Blake" dated Niagara-on-the-Lake, August 2, 1981.
Holograph title "Make room William Blake" on verso of leaf [3].
"Make room William Blake" published with further revisions in: The Gucci bag/Irving Layton. Oakville, Ont.: Mosaic Press/ Valley Editions, 1983, (also in MSGB, GB2).
"Letting go" published in: The covenant/Irving Layton. Toronto: McClelland and Stewart, 1977, (also in GB, MSGB, GB2).
"An ideal husband" not published to date.

...con't

GB 19/1
NEIGHBOUR LOVE
[1982].
[4] leaves; 28 cm.
In part holograph.
Poem.
On leaves [1-2]:2 holograph drafts with revisions on verso of lined paper torn from notebook.
On leaf [3]:typescript draft with revisions.
On leaf [4]:typescript draft.
Holograph title "Love your neighbour" on verso of leaf [4].
Published with further revisions in: The Gucci bag/Irving Layton. Oakville, Ont.: Mosaic Press/Valley Editions, 1983, (also in MSGB, GB2).

GB 20/1
ODD OBSESSION
[1981].
[4] leaves; 28 cm.
In part holograph.
Poem.
On leaf [1]:holograph draft with revisions.
On verso of leaf [1]:holograph draft of line 1; list of miscellaneous household items.
On leaf [2]:holograph draft.
On leaf [3]:typescript draft.
On leaf [4]:typescript draft with revisions.
Holograph title on verso of leaf [4].
Published in: The Gucci bag/Irving Layton. Oakville, Ont.: Mosaic Press/Valley Editions, 1983, (also in MSGB, GB2, LPIL2, DD).

GB 21/1
TREES IN RAIN; THEY ALSO SERVE; IN REVENGE FOR OLGA AND BP; A CHARIOT FOR HARRIET
[1982].
[8]p., [4] leaves; 28 cm.
In part holograph.
Four poems.
On p.[1]:holograph draft, with revisions, of "Trees in rain"; typescript draft of 7 lines of "[A chariot for Harriet]."
On p.[2,6]:2 typescript drafts of "They also serve."
On leaf [1]:holograph draft with revisions of "Trees in rain."
On p.[3]:holograph draft of "Trees in rain"; typescript fragment "When it comes."

...con't

GB 21/1...con't

On p.[4]:typescript draft of "In revenge for Olga and BP."
On p.[5]:holograph draft with revisions of "Trees in rain."
On p.[7]:typescript draft of "Trees in rain" titled "Superman."
On p.[8]:typescript draft with revisions of "[A chariot for Harriet]."
On leaf [2]:typescript draft with revisions of "Trees in rain" titled "Nietzsche."
On verso of leaf [2]:line 1 of "Trees in rain"; holograph title "Nietzsche."
On leaves [3-4]:2 typescript drafts with revisions of "Trees in rain" titled "Nietzsche."
"Trees in rain" published with further revisions as "[Trees in late autumn]."
"[Trees in late autumn]" published in: The Gucci bag/Irving Layton. Oakville, Ont.: Mosaic Press/Valley Editions, 1983, (also in MSGB, GB2).
"They also serve," ibid., (also in MSGB, GB2).
"In revenge for Olga and BP" not published to date.
"[A chariot for Harriet]" not published to date.

GB 22/1
OF LEAVES AND LOVES
[1982].
[4] leaves; 28 cm.
In part holograph.
Poem.
On leaf [1]:2 holograph drafts with revisions.
On verso of leaf [1]:typescript draft of [table of] contents for "The Gucci bag."
On leaves [2-4]:3 typescript drafts.
Published in: The Gucci bag/Irving Layton. Oakville, Ont.: Mosaic Press/Valley Editions, 1983, (also in MSGB, GB2, LPIL2, DD).

GB 23/1
ORPHEUS IN OLD FOREST HILL; BLOSSOM; LOS AMERICANOS
[1982].
[6] leaves; 28 cm.
In part holograph.
Three poems.
On leaves [1-2]:2 holograph drafts with reworking of stanza [1] of "Orpheus in old Forest Hill" leaf [1] titled "Orpheus"; leaf [2] titled "Orpheus in Toronto."
On verso of leaf [2]:typescript draft of "Blossom."
On leaf [3]:holograph draft with revisions of "Orpheus in old Forest Hill"; marginalia.

...con't

GB 23/1...con't

On verso of leaf [3]:typescript draft of "Los Americanos"; marginalia.
On leaves [4-6]:3 typescript drafts of "Orpheus in old Forest Hill" with revisions. "Orpheus in old Forest Hill" published with further revisions in: The Gucci bag/Irving Layton. Oakville, Ont.: Mosaic Press/Valley Editions, 1983, (also in MSGB, GB2, LPIL2).
"Blossom," ibid., (also in WPJ, MSGB, GB2).
"Los Americanos," ibid., (also in MSGB, GB2).

GB 24/1
AN OLD MAN'S WET DREAMS; [PERFECTION]; THE CRACKED CRYSTAL BALL; BULL, MORE AND LESS; ADVICE FOR OLD MAIDS [1982].
[8]p., [5] leaves; 28 cm.
In part holograph.
Five poems.
On p.[1,3]:holograph draft with revisions of "An old man's wet dreams"; 6 lines on leaf [1] of "[Perfection]."
On p.[2]:typescript draft of "Bull, more and less."
On p.[4]:typescript draft of "The cracked crystal ball."
On p.[5] and leaf [1]:holograph draft of "An old man's wet dreams" titled "The harem"; typescript draft of line 1 of "The cracked crystal ball" on leaf [1].
On p.[6]:typescript draft of "Advice for old maids."
On verso of leaf [1]:typescript draft of line 1 of "The cracked crystal ball."
On p.[7]:holograph draft with revisions of "An old man's wet dreams" titled "The harem."
On p.[8]:typescript draft of "The cracked crystal ball."
On leaves [2-5]:4 typescript drafts with revisions of "An old man's wet dreams"; title on leaf [1] "The harem."
Holograph title "An old man's wet dreams" on verso of leaf [4].
"An old man's wet dreams" published in: The Gucci bag/Irving Layton. Oakville, Ont.: Mosaic Press/Valley Editions, 1983.
"[Perfection]," ibid., (also in MSGB, GB2).
"The cracked crystal ball" not published to date.
"Bull, more and less" not published to date.
"Advice for old maids" not published to date.

GB 25/1
PERFECTION; [THERE'S ALWAYS JOB]
[1982].
[2]p., [4] leaves ; 28 cm.

...con't

GB 25/1...con't
In part holograph.
Two poems.
On p.[1]:2 holograph drafts with revisions of "Perfection" titled "Light on leaves"; marginalia.
On p.[2]:typescript draft of "[There's always Job]."
On leaf [1]:holograph draft with revisions of "Perfection."
On leaves [2-3]:2 typescript drafts of "Perfection" titled "The perfect crime."
On leaf [4]:typescript draft with revisions of "Perfection."
Holograph title "Perfection" on verso of leaf [4].
"Perfection" published with further revisions in: The Gucci bag/ Irving Layton. Oakville, Ont.: Mosaic Press/Valley Editions, 1983, (also in MSGB, GB2).
"[There's always Job]," ibid., (also in MSGB, GB2).

GB 26/1
PORTRAIT OF A MODERN WOMAN
[1982].
[2] leaves; 28 cm.
In part holograph.
Poem.
On leaf [1]:holograph draft.
On verso of leaf [1]:typescript fragment beginning "A god made man from water and dust...."
On leaf [2]:typescript draft with revisions titled "Portrait of a young woman."
Holograph title on verso of leaf 2.
Published with further revisions in: The Gucci bag/Irving Layton. Oakville, Ont.: Mosaic Press/Valley Editions, 1983, (also in MSGB, GB2, DD).

GB 27/1
THE RECOVERY; AND IT CAME TO PASS
1981.
[6]p., [3] leaves; 28 cm.
In part holograph.
Two poems.
On p.[1]:holograph draft of lines 1-14 of "The recovery" with reworking of lines 1-10.
On p.[2,4,6]:3 typescript drafts of "And it came to pass."
On p.[3]:holograph draft with revisions of "The recovery."
On leaf [1]:holograph draft with revisions of "The recovery"; fragment beginning "We must leave each other she said...."

...con't

GB 27/1...con't

On p.[5]:holograph draft with revisions of "The recovery."
On leaves [2-3]:2 typescript drafts with revisions of "The recovery."
"The recovery" dated July 31, 1981.
Coffee [?] stains on leaf [1].
Holograph title on verso of leaf [3].
"The recovery" published with further revisions in: The Gucci bag/Irving Layton. Oakville, Ont.: Mosaic Press/Valley Editions, 1983, (also in MSGB, GB2).
"And it came to pass" not published to date.

GB 28/1
BALLAD; THE GARDEN; [THEY ALSO SERVE]; TERRY FOX; WHAT SHOULD BE DONE
1981.
[6]p., [7] leaves; 28 cm.
Chiefly holograph.
Five poems.
On leaf [1]:holograph draft with revisions of 6 stanzas of "Ballad"; typescript of lines 1-2 of "[They also serve]."
On leaf [2]:holograph draft with revisions of 7 stanzas of "Ballad."
On verso of leaf [2]:typescript draft of stanza 10 of "The garden."
On p.[1]:holograph draft with revisions of 7 stanzas of "Ballad" with reworking of stanza 4.
On p.[2]:typescript draft of "What should be done"; typescript note at bottom explaining title.
On leaf [3]:holograph draft of 7 stanzas of "Ballad."
On leaf [4]:holograph draft of 4 stanzas of "Ballad."
On p.[3]:holograph reworking of last stanza of "Ballad."
On p.[4]:typescript draft of stanzas 1-9 of "The garden."
On p.[5] and leaves [5-7]:4 typescript drafts with revisions of 8 stanzas of "Ballad."
On p.[6]:typescript draft of "Terry Fox."
Holograph title "A simple ballad" on verso of leaf [5].
"The garden" dated Niagara-on-the-Lake, July 18, 1981.
"Ballad" published with further revisions as "[The captive]."
"[The captive]" published in: The Gucci Bag/Irving Layton. Oakville, Ont.: Mosaic Press/Valley Editions, 1983, (also in MSGB, GB2).
"The garden," ibid., (also in WPJ, MSGB, GB2).
"[They also serve]," ibid., (also in MSGB, GB2).
"What should be done" not published to date.
"Terry Fox" published in: Final reckoning: poems 1982-1986/ Irving Layton. Oakville, Ont.: Mosaic Press, 1987.

GB 29/1
SELF OVERCOMING
1981.
[4] leaves; 1 leaf 8 cm. x 19 cm., 3 leaves 28 cm.
In part holograph.
Poem.
On leaf [1]:holograph draft on cover of note pad [?].
On leaves [2-4]:3 typescript drafts.
Holograph title and date on verso of leaves [3-4].
Dated August 1, 1981.
Published with revisions in: The Gucci bag/Irving Layton. Oakville: Mosaic Press/Valley Editions, 1983, (also MSGB, GB2).

GB 30/1
THE VACUUM; THE SMILE
1981.
[6]p., [2] leaves; 28 cm.
Chiefly holograph signed.
Two poems.
On p.[1,3,5]:3 holograph drafts with revisions of "The vacuum."
On p.[2,4,6]:3 holograph drafts of "The smile"; drafts on p.[2,6] crossed out.
On leaves [1-2]:2 typescript drafts of "The vacuum."
"The vacuum" dated Toronto, August 17, 1981.
"The smile" signed and dated Banff, August 15, 1981.
Marginalia and coffee [?] stain on p.[3].
Holograph title "The vacuum" on verso of leaf [2].
"The smile" published as "[Odd obsession]."
"The vacuum" published in: The Gucci bag/Irving Layton. Oakville, Ont.: Mosaic Press/Valley Editions, 1983, (also in MSGB, GB2).
"[Odd obsession]," ibid., (also in GB2, MSGB, LPIL2, DD).

GB 31/1
THE TALISMAN
[1982].
[6] leaves; 28 cm.
In part holograph.
Poem.
On leaves [1-2] and verso:2 holograph drafts on lined paper torn from notebook.
On leaf [3]:typescript draft with revisions.
On verso of leaf [3]:reworking of stanza 3.
On leaves [4-6]]:2 typescript drafts; marginalia on leaf [4].

...con't

GB 31/1...con't
On leaf [5]:typescript draft with revisions.
Drafts 1-2 numbered.
Holograph title on verso of leaves [4,6].
Last half of stanza 2 plus stanza 3 published as "The talisman."
Published in: The Gucci bag/Irving Layton. Oakville Ont.: Mosaic Press/Valley Editions, 1983, (also in MSGB, GB2).

GB 32/1
THERE'S ALWAYS JOB; BRING ON THE SKINHEADS; THE QUESTION
[1982].
[8]p., [2] leaves; 28 cm.
In part holograph.
Three poems.
On p.[1,3]:holograph draft with revisions of "There's always Job"; watermarks and yellow stain on both pages.
On p.[2]:untitled ms. poem.
On p.[4]:personal letter to Irving Layton.
On p.[5,7]:holograph draft with revisions of "There's always Job"; marginalia on p.[5].
On p.[6]:typescript draft of "Bring on the skinheads."
On p.[8]:typescript draft of "The question."
On leaves [1-2]:typescript draft of "There's always Job."
Holograph title "There's always Job" on verso of leaf [2].
"Bring on the skinheads" dated Niagara-on-the-Lake, July 15, 1981.
"There's always Job" published with further revisions in: The Gucci bag/Irving Layton. Oakville, Ont.: Mosaic Press/Valley Editions, 1983, (also in MSGB, GB2).
"Bring on the skinheads" not published to date.
"The question" not published to date.

GB 33/1
THE SWAMP
[1982].
[5] leaves; 28 cm.
Typescript.
Poem.
On leaf [1]:typescript draft of 8 stanzas.
On verso of leaf [1]:typescript of lines 1-3.
On leaves [2-5]:4 typescript drafts of 6 stanzas.

...con't

GB 33/1...con't

On verso of leaf [5]:typescript of line 1; holograph title.
Published with revisions in: The Gucci bag/Irving Layton. Oakville, Ont.: Mosaic Press/Valley Editions, 1983, (also in MSGB, GB2).

GB 33/2
[THE SWAMP]; ADVICE TO OLD MAIDS; BALLAD OF THE HOLSTEIN BULL; THE CRACKED CRYSTAL BALL; THE REVENGE I'D TAKE; YIDS
[1982].
[10]p., [1] leaf; 28 cm.
In part holograph.
Six poems.
On leaf [1]:holograph draft of "Yids"; typescript draft of lines 1-3 of "[The swamp]."
On p.[1]:holograph draft of "Yids."
On p.[2]:typescript draft of "Advice to old maids."
On p.[3,5,7]:3 holograph drafts with revisions of "Yids."
On p.[4]:holograph draft of "The revenge I'd take"; typescript draft of lines 1-7 of "[The swamp]."
On p.[6]:typescript draft of "Ballad of the Holstein bull."
On p.[8,10]:2 typescript drafts of "The cracked crystal ball."
On p.[9]:typescript draft of "Yids."
"[The swamp]" published in: The Gucci bag/Irving Layton. Oakville, Ont.: Mosaic Press/Valley Editions, 1983, (also in MSGB, GB2).
"Advice to old maids" not published to date.
"Ballad of the Holstein bull" not published to date.
"The cracked crystal ball" not published to date.
"The revenge I'd take" not published to date.
"Yids" not published to date.

GB 34/1
WHERE HAS THE GLORY FLED; AN A PLUS
[1982].
[4]p., [1] leaf; 28 cm.
In part holograph.
Two poems.
On p.[1]:holograph draft with revisions of "Where has the glory fled."
On p.[2,4]:2 typescript drafts of 8 stanzas of "An A plus."
On leaf [1]:typescript draft with revisions of "Where has the glory fled."
On p.[3]:typescript draft of "Where has the glory fled."
Holograph title "Where has the glory fled," on p.[4].

...con't

GB 34/1...con't

"An A plus" published as "[The courage to be]."
"Where has the glory fled" published with further revisions in: The Gucci bag/Irving Layton. Oakville, Ont.: Mosaic Press/Valley Editions, 1983, (also in MSGB, GB2).
"[The courage to be]," ibid., (with revisions).

GB 35/1
THE WINGED HORSE; [PERFECTION]; COMRADE UNDERSHAFTSKY; PRAYER FOR A LONG LIFE
[1982].
[4]p., [1] leaf; 28 cm.
In part holograph.
Four poems.
On p.[1]:holograph draft with revisions of "The winged horse."
On p.[2]:typescript draft with revisions of "Comrade Undershaftsky."
On leaf [1]:holograph draft with revisions of "The winged horse"; line 1 of "[Perfection]."
On verso of leaf [1]:typescript draft of stanza 1 of "[Perfection]."
On p.[3]:typescript draft of "The winged horse".
On p.[4]:typescript draft of "Prayer for a long life," holograph title "The winged horse."
"Prayer for a long life" dated Niagara-on-the-Lake, July 12, 1981.
"The winged horse" published in: The Gucci bag/Irving Layton. Oakville, Ont.: Mosaic Press/Valley Editions, 1983, (also in MSGB, GB2).
"[Perfection]," ibid., (also in MSGB, GB2).
"Comrade Undershaftsky" published in: The Gucci bag/Irving Layton. Toronto: McClelland and Stewart, 1983, (also in GB2).
"Prayer for a long life" not published to date.

GB 36/1
THE HAIRY MONSTER
[1982].
[2]p., [13] leaves; 28 cm.
In part holograph signed.
Poem.
On leaf [1]:1 typescript, 1 holograph draft with revisions.
On p.[1]:2 holograph drafts with revisions.
On p.[2]:holograph draft; list of titles of poems by [Irving Layton].
On leaves [2-8,10-13]:11 typescript drafts with revisions.

...con't

GB 36/1...con't

On leaf [9]:signed photocopy of typescript draft; list of titles of poems by [Irving Layton].
Drafts 1-2 numbered.
Published with further revisions in: The Gucci bag/Irving Layton. Oakville, Ont.: Mosaic Press/Valley Editions, 1983, (also in MSGB, GB2, DD).

GB 37/1
TRAGEDY
[1982].
[3] leaves; 1 leaf 18 cm., 2 leaves 28 cm.
In part holograph.
Poem.
On leaf [1]:holograph draft on 1/2 sheet of yellow lined paper.
On leaf [2]:typescript draft with holograph revisions; reworking of stanzas 1,5.
On leaf [3]:typescript draft.
Published with further revisions in: The Gucci bag/Irving Layton. Oakville, Ont.: Mosaic Press/Valley Editions, 1983, (also in MSGB, GB2).

GB 38/1
NOSTALGIA WHEN THE LEAVES BEGIN TO FALL; THE SWAMP
[1982].
[2]p., [2] leaves; 28 cm.
In part holograph.
Two poems.
On leaf [1]:holograph draft with revisions of "Nostalgia when the leaves begin to fall."
On verso of leaf [1]:typescript draft of 8 lines beginning "The long dark September nights have come."
On p.[1] and leaf [2]:2 typescript drafts of "Nostalgia when the leaves begin to fall."
On p.[2]:typescript draft of "The swamp."
Holograph title "Nostalgia" on p.[2] and verso of leaf [2].
"Nostalgia when the leaves begin to fall" published in: The Gucci bag/Irving Layotn. Oakville, Ont.: Mosaic Press/Valley Editions, 1983, (also in MSGB).
"The swamp," ibid., (also in MSGB, GB2).

GB 39/1
ZUCCHINI; EPISTLE TO CATULLUS; FROM THE NETHER WORLD
[1982].
[4]p., [1] leaf; 28 cm.
Typescript with holograph revisions.

...con't

GB 39/1...con't

Three poems.
On p.[1]:holograph draft with revisions of stanzas 1-5,7 of "Zucchini."
On p.[2]:typescript draft of "Epistle to Catullus."
On p.[3]:holograph draft of stanza 6 of "Zucchini"; fragment beginning "My words are an immense swamp...."
On p.[4]:typescript draft of "From the nether world."
On leaf [1]:typescript draft of "Zucchini."
Holograph title "Zucchini" on verso of leaf [1].
"Zucchini" published in: The Gucci bag/Irving Layton. Oakville, Ont.: Mosaic Press/Valley Editions, 1983, (also in MSGB, GB2).
"From the nether world," ibid., (also in MSGB, GB2).
"Epistle to Catullus" published in: The Gucci bag/Irving Layton. 2nd ed. Oakville, Ont.: Mosaic Press/Valley Editions, 1984, (also in FR).

GB2 - The Gucci Bag (2nd ed.)

GB2 1/1
EPISTLE TO CATULLUS
1983.
[6]p., [5] leaves; 28 cm.
In part holograph.
Poem.
On p.[1-6]:6 holograph drafts with revisions.
On leaf [1]:typescript draft with revisions.
On leaves [2-5]:4 typescript drafts.
Published in: The Gucci bag/Irving Layton. 2nd ed. Oakville, Ont.: Mosaic Press/Valley Editions, 1984, (also in FR).

GB2 2/1
BOSCHKA LAYTON 1921-1984
1984.
[6] leaves; 28 cm.
In part holograph signed.
Poem.
On leaves [1-2]:2 holograph drafts with revisions.
On leaves [3-5]:4 typescript drafts with revisions.
Leaves [4,6] photocopies of typescript drafts.
Dated Santa Rosa, February 17,19, 1984.
Published in: The Gucci bag/Irving Layton. 2nd ed. Oakville, Ont.: Mosaic Press/Valley Editions, 1984, (also in DD, FR).

GB2 3/1
CARMEN
[1983].
[11] leaves; 28 cm.
In part holograph.
Poem.
On leaves [1-3]:3 holograph drafts with revisions and reworking of stanza 1.
On leaves [4,7]:2 holograph drafts with revisions.
On leaves [5-6,8-9]:4 typescript drafts with revisions.
On leaf [10]:typescript draft with reworking of stanza 2.
Leaf [11] photocopy of typescript draft.
Holograph title on verso of leaves [7-9].
Typescript signature.
Marginalia on leaf [9].
Published in: The Gucci bag/Irving Layton. 2nd ed. Oakville, Ont.: Mosaic Press/Valley Editions, 1983, (also in MSGB, DD, FR).

GB2 3/2
CARMEN; AN OLD MAN'S WET DREAM
1983.
[2]p., [6] leaves; 28 cm.
In part holograph signed.
2 poems.
On leaf [1]:typescript (photocopy) draft of "Carmen" with reworking of stanza [2]; marginalia.
On leaf [2]:2 holograph drafts of stanza 2 of "Carmen" with revisions.
On p.[1]:2 holograph drafts of stanza 2 of "Carmen" with holograph and ms. revisions; marginalia.
On p.[2]:typescript draft with revisions of "An old man's wet dream."
On leaf [3]:typescript draft of "Carmen" with revisions and reworking of stanza 2.
On leaf [4]:typescript draft of "Carmen."
On leaves [5-6]:2 typescript drafts of "Carmen."
Leaves 4-6 dated Montreal, July 12, 1985.
"Carmen" published in: The Gucci bag/Irving Layton. 2nd ed.
Oakville, Ont.: Mosaic Press/Valley Editions, 1983, (also in MSGB, DD, FR).
"An old man's wet dream" published in: The Gucci bag/Irving Layton. Oakville, Ont.: Mosaic Press, 1983.

GB2 4/1
DIONYSIANS IN A BAD TIME; BOSCHKA LAYTON 1921-1984
1984.
[8]p., [14] leaves; 28 cm.
In part holograph.
Two poems.
On leaves [1-5] and p.[2-3,5,7]:8 holograph drafts with revisions of "Dionysians in a bad time."
On p.[4,6,8]:3 typescript drafts of "Boschka Layton 1921-1984."
On leaves [6-13]:8 typescript drafts with revisions of "Dionysians in a bad time"; title on p.[3,5] and leaf [6] "Dionysians in a dark age"; marginalia on leaf [12]."
On leaf [14]:typescript draft.
"Dionysians in a bad time" dated San Jose, March 3, 1984.
Holograph title "Dionysians in a bad time" on verso of leaves [6- 7,11-13].
"Dionysians in a bad time" published in: The Gucci bag/Irving Layton. 2nd ed. Oakville, Ont.: Mosaic Press/Valley Editions, 1984, (also in FR).
"Boschka Layton 1921-1984," ibid., (also in DD, FR).

GB2 5/1
LADY AURORA; BOSCHKA LAYTON 1921-1984
1984.
[6]p., [1] leaf; 28 cm.
In part holograph.
Two poems.
On p.[1,3,5]:3 holograph drafts of "Lady Aurora."
On p.[2,4,6]:3 typescript drafts of "Boschka Layton 1921-1984."
Leaf [1]:blank.
Drafts of "Lady Aurora" numbered.
"Lady Aurora" dated San Jose, February 22, 1984.
"Boschka Layton 1921-1984" dated Santa Rosa, February 17, 1984.
Holograph title "Lady Aurora" on p.[4-6] and leaf [1].
"Lady Aurora" published in: The Gucci bag/Irving Layton. 2nd ed. Oakville, Ont.: Mosaic Press/Valley Editions, 1984, (also in LPIL2, FR).
"Boschka Layton 1921-1984," ibid., (also in DD, FR).

GB2 5/2
LADY AURORA
1984.
[12] leaves; 28 cm.
In part holograph.
Poem.
On leaf [1]:holograph title, dated February 1984-December 30, 1986.
On leaf [2]:1 typescript draft with revisions; one holograph draft, dated San Jos, February 22, 1984 and December 4, 1986; marginalia.
On leaf [3]:typescript (photocopy) with revisions.
On verso of leaf [3]; ms. note: "worked on and finished July 12, 1985."
On leaf [4]:typescript draft with ms. revisions.
On leaf [5]:typescript draft with revision and reworking of stanza 1.
On leaf [6]:typescript draft.
On leaf [7]:typescript draft with revisions and reworking of stanzas 2-4.
On leaves [8-10]:3 holograph drafts with revisions.
On leaf [11]:typescript draft with revisions and reworking of stanzas 1,5-6.
On leaf [12]:typescript draft, dated Montreal, December 30, 1986; marginalia.
Leaves 3-7 dated San Jos, December 22, 1984.
Published with further revisions in: The Gucci bag/Irving Layton. 2nd ed. Oakville, Ont.: Mosaic Press, 1984, (also in FR).

GB2 6/1
THE CYST; TRENCH MOUTH
1983.
[7] leaves; 5 leaves, 29 cm., 2 leaves 34 cm. + 1 cardboard folder.
Holograph.
Poem.
On leaves [1-5]:5 drafts with revisions.
On leaf [6]:3 drafts with revisions.
On verso of leaf [6]:draft of "The cyst"; draft of "Trench mouth."
On leaf [7]:holograph draft; marginalia.
On verso of leaf [7]:holograph draft; "Ristorante la Fornarina Urbino" printed at bottom right corner.
On front of cardboard folder:1 holograph draft.
On back of cardboard folder:draft of lines 1-6.
Drafts accompanied by Raffaello reproduction with holograph note on verso re Raffaello's philosophy.
"The cyst" published in: The Gucci bag/Irving Layton. 2nd ed. Oakville, Ont. Mosaic Press/Valley Editions, 1984, (also in FR).
"Trench mouth," ibid., (also in FR).

GB2 7/1
FOR ETTORE WITH LOVE AND ADMIRATION
1983.
[11] leaves; 3 leaves 12 cm., 8 leaves 28 cm.
In part holograph.
Poem.
Leaves [1-3]:blank leaves with number "1" in upper right corner.
On leaf [4] and verso: ms. draft of themes in "For Ettore with love and admiration."
On leaf [5]:2 holograph drafts with revisions.
On leaf [6]:holograph draft of stanza 3; ms. note explaining blank leaves.
On leaves [7-11]:5 typescript drafts titled "To Ettore with love and admiration."
Leaves [5-6,11] on verso of promotional material for "The Gucci bag."
Dated September 5, 1983.
Published in: The Gucci bag/Irving Layton. 2nd ed. Oakville, Ont.: Mosaic Press/Valley Editions, 1984, (also in FR).

GB2 8/1
MONSTERS
1983.
[5] leaves; 28 cm.
Typescript.
Poem.
On leaf [1]:typescript draft with revisions and reworking of stanza [4]; marginalia.
On leaf [2]:typescript draft with revisions, dated July 2, [1986].
On leaf [3]:typescript draft with holograph and ms. revisions, dated July 7, 1986.
On leaf [4]:typescript draft with revisions, dated July 21, 1986.
On leaf [5]:typescript (photocopy) draft.
Published with further revisions in: The Gucci bag/Irving Layton. 2nd ed. Oakville, Ont.: Mosaic Press, 1984, (also in FR).

GB2 9/1
JUVENAL REDIVIVUS
1983.
[3] leaves; 28 cm.
In part holograph.
Poem.
On leaf [1]:typescript draft with holograph revisions and reworking of stanza 2.
On leaf [2]:holograph draft.
On leaf [3]:typescript draft.
Dated Rome, August 1983.
Published in: The Gucci bag/Irving Layton. 2nd ed. Oakville, Ont.: Mosaic Press, 1984, (also in FR).

GP - Seventy-five Greek Poems

GP 1/1
[ALAS], TOO NOISELESS
1974.
[1] leaf; 28 cm.
Typescript.
Poem.
Title on typescript "Too noiseless."
Published with revisions in: Seventy-five Greek poems/Irving Layton. Athens, Greece: Hermias, 1976.

GP 1/2
[ALAS], TOO NOISELESS
1974.
[11] leaves; 28 cm.
Typescript with holograph revisions.
Poem.
Eleven drafts.
Leaves [1-3,5-6] dated Piraeus, Greece, July 2, 1974.
Leaf [7] dated Piraeus, Greece, July 3, 1974.
Leaf [11] dated Molibos, July 12, 1974.
Leaves [1-5] titled "Too noiseless."
Stanza on leaf [10] crossed out.
Marginalia on verso of leaf [1].
Published in: Seventy-five Greek poems/Irving Layton. Athens, Greece: Hermias, 1976.

GP 2/1
THE BEARD; [ALAS, TOO NOISELESS]
1974.
[4]p., 3 leaves; 28 cm.
In part holograph.
Two poems.
On leaves [1-3] and p.[1,3-4]:2 holograph, 4 typescript drafts with revisions of "The beard."
On verso of leaf [1]:holograph reworking of last stanza of "The beard"; typescript fragment beginning "The tremulous moment he works and waits for...."
On p.[2]:typescript draft of "[Alas, too noiseless]."
"The beard" dated Molibos, July 16, 1974.
"[Alas, too noiseless]" dated Piraeus, July 2, 1974.

...con't

GP 2/1...con't

"The beard" published with further revisions in: Seventy-five Greek poems/Irving Layton. Athens, Greece: Hermias, 1974, (also in UE).
"[Alas, too noiseless]," ibid., (with revisions).

GP 3/1
A DREAM IN PANGRATI
1974.
[7] leaves; 28 cm.
In part holograph.
Poem.
Three holograph, 4 typescript numbered drafts with revisions.
Drafts on leaves [3-7] titled "The dream."
Dated Montreal, June 2, 1974.
Published with further revisions in: Seventy-five Greek poems/ Irving Layton. Athens, Greece: Hermias, 1974, (also in UE).

GP 4/1
BLACKOUT; ALAS, TOO NOISELESS
1974.
[2]p., [5] leaves; 28 cm.
In part holograph.
Two poems.
On leaf [1]:holograph draft of "Blackout" with reworking of stanzas 1-2.
On p.[1]:holograph draft with revisions of "Blackout."
On leaves [2-5]:3 typescript drafts with revisions of "Blackout."
On p.[2]:typescript draft with holograph revisions of "Alas, too noiseless."
"Blackout" dated Mithyma, Lesbos, July 21, 1974.
"Alas, too noiseless" dated Piraeus, Greece, July 2, 1974.
"Blackout" published in: Seventy-five Greek poems/Irving Layton. Athens, Greece: Hermias, 1974, (also in PIL, UE).
"Alas, too noiseless," ibid., (with revisions).

GP 5/1
BYRON EXHIBITION [AT THE BENAKI MUSEUM]
[1974].
[2]p.; 16 cm.
Holograph.
Poem.
On p. [1]:draft titled "Byron exhibition."
On p.[2]:list of titles of poems by [Irving Layton]; marginalia.
Published with revisions in: Seventy-five Greek poems/Irving Layton. Athens, Greece: Hermias, 1974, (also in UE).

GP 5/2
BYRON EXHIBITION AT THE BENAKI MUSEUM
1974.
[3] leaves; 28 cm.
Typescript.
Poem.
Four drafts with revisions.
Dated Athens, June 30, 1974. Published in: Seventy-five Greek poems/Irving Layton. Athens, Greece: Hermias, 1974, (also in UE).

GP 6/1
THE CASTLE; THE BEARD
1974.
[2]p., [10] leaves; 28 cm.
In part holograph.
Two poems.
On p.[1]:holograph draft of stanzas 1-3 of "The castle"; list of 9 titles of poems by [Irving Layton].
On p.[2]:typescript draft of "The beard."
On leaves [1-2]:holograph draft of "The castle" with revisions.
On leaves [3-10]:8 typescript drafts of "The castle" with revisions.
On verso of leaf [8]:typescript draft of stanzas [1-2] of "The castle."
Drafts 2-3 of "The castle" numbered.
"The beard" dated Myconos, June 28, 1974.
"The castle" dated Mithyma, Lesbos, July 18, 1974.
"The castle" published in: Seventy-five Greek poems/Irving Layton. Athens, Greece: Hermias, 1974, (also in UE, DD).
"The beard," ibid., (with revisions), (also in UE).

GP 7/1
THE FLYTRAP
[1973].
[4]p., [11] leaves; 2 leaves 30 cm., 11 leaves 28 cm.
Typescript with holograph revisions.
Poem.
On leaves [1-4,6-7,10-11] and p.[1,3]:10 drafts with revisions.
On leaf [5]:draft with reworking of stanzas 1,4.
On leaf [8]:draft of stanzas 1-2.
On recto and verso of leaf [9]: typescript fragments "It," "It is the death."
On p.[2]: 3 drafts of stanzas 1-2.
On p.[4]:draft with reworking of stanzas 1-2.

...con't

GP 7/1...con't

Leaf [2] titled "David and the fly."
Leaves [5-7,10-11] titled "Music for David's harp."
Published with further revisions as "[Flytrap]."
Published in: Seventy-five Greek poems/Irving Layton. Athens, Greece: Hermias, 1974, (also in UE, WPJ).

GP 7/2
FLYTRAP
[1973].
[9] leaves; 8 leaves 28 cm., 1 leaf 30 cm.
Typescript with holograph revisions.
Poem.
On leaves [1,2,5-9]:7 drafts with revisions.
On leaf [3]:draft of 14 lines in 2 stanzas.
On leaf [4]:draft of 10 lines. Leaves [1-4] titled "Music for David's harp."
Leaf [5] titled "Neocide."
Published with further revisions in: Seventy-five Greek poems/ Irving Layton. Athens, Greece: Hermias, 1974, (also in UE, WPJ).

GP 8/1
[KAZANTZAKIS]:GOD'S ATHLETE; F. NIETZSCHE; O JERUSALEM
1974.
[4] leaves; 16 cm.
Holograph.
Three poems.
On leaf [1]:draft of 11 lines with revisions of "[Kazantzakis]:God's athlete."
On leaves [2-3]:2 drafts with revisions of "[Kazantzakis]:God's athlete."
On verso of leaf [2]:draft of last 12 lines of "F. Nietzsche."
On leaf [4]:draft with revisions of "O Jerusalem."
On verso of leaf [4]:draft with revisions of lines 1-15 of "F. Nietzsche."
Dated Molibos, Lesbos, August 23, 1974.
"F. Nietzsche" published as "[The unwavering eye]."
"[Kazantzakis]:God's athlete" published with further revisions in: Seventy-five Greek poems/Irving Layton. Athens, Greece: Hermias, 1974, (also in FMBJ).
"[The unwavering eye]," ibid., (with further revisions), (also UE).
"O Jerusalem" published with further revisions in: For my brother Jesus/Irving Layton. Toronto: McClelland and Stewart, 1976, (also in UE, PIL, FMBJ, WPJ).

GP 8/2
[KAZANTZAKIS]: GOD'S ATHLETE
1974.
[11] leaves; 30 cm.
Holograph signed.
Poem.
Ten drafts with revisions.
Leaf [3] blank; marginalia on verso.
Drafts 1-2 numbered.
Dated Molibos, Lesbos, August 26, 1974.
Signature on leaves [7-11].
Published with further revisions in: Seventy-five Greek poems/ Irving Layton. Athens, Greece: Hermias, 1974, (also in FMBJ).

GP 9/1
HELIOS
1974.
[4]p.; 16 cm.
Holograph.
Poem.
On p.[1-2,4]:3 drafts with revisions; leaf 2 titled "Carpet merchant."
Marginalia on p.[3].
Dated Molibos, Hebros, July 23, 1974.
Published with further revisions in: Seventy-five Greek poems/ Irving Layton. Athens, Greece: Hermias, 1974, (also in UE).

GP 9/2
HELIOS
1974.
[7] leaves; 28 cm.
Typescript with holograph revisions.
Poem.
Seven drafts with revisions.
Leaf [2] titled "Carpet merchant."
Leaf [4] titled "For the ghost's of fish."
Leaves [5-6] titled "The carpet."
Published in: Seventy-five Greek poems/Irving Layton. Athens, Greece: Hermias, 1974, (also in UE).

GP 10/1
HELLENES; A POLITICAL DREAM
1974.
[2]p., [11] leaves; 28 cm.
In part holograph signed.
Two poems.
On leaf [1]:holograph draft with revisions of "Hellenes."
On p.[1] and leaves [2-11]:1 holograph, 10 typescript drafts with revisions of "Hellenes," p.[1] titled "Romeantics"; leaf [2] titled "Bitter lemons"; leaf [5] titled "Bitter fruit"; leaves [7-11] titled "Trojan women."
On p.[2]: typescript draft, signed, of "A political dream."
Drafts 1-4 numbered.
Marginalia on verso of leaf [1].
"Hellenes" dated July 23, 1974.
"Hellenes" published with further revisions in: Seventy-five Greek poems/Irving Layton. Athens, Greece: Hermias, 1974, (also in UE).
"A political dream" published in: Lovers and lesser men/Irving Layton. Toronto: McClelland and Stewart, 1973.

GP 11/1
ITHACA
1974.
[6]p.; 16 cm.
Holograph.
Poem.
Four drafts with revisions of stanzas 1-2,4.
Title on p.[3] "The tremulous moment."
Dated Molibos, Greece, June 13, 1974.
Marginalia on p.[2,6].
Published with further revisions in: Seventy-five Greek poems/ Irving Layton. Athens, Greece: Hermias, 1974, (also in UE, PIL, WPJ).

GP 11/2
ITHACA; ALAS, TOO NOISELESS
1974.
[11] leaves; 28 cm.
Typescript with holograph revisions signed.
Two poems.
On leaves [1-4]:4 drafts of stanzas [1-2,4].
On verso of leaf [1]:2 paragraphs of prose beginning "That awareness is the red

...con't

GP 11/2...con't

thread...."
On leaf [5]:draft of 4 stanzas with reworking of stanza 3.
On leaves [6-11]:6 drafts of 4 stanzas with revisions.
On verso of leaves [6-8]:6 lines of "Alas, too noiseless."
Title on leaves [2-4] "The tremulous moment."
Dated Molibos, Greece, July 14, 1974.
"Ithaca" published in "Seventy-five Greek poems/Irving Layton. Athens, Greece: Hermias, 1974, (also in UE, PIL, WPJ).
"Alas, too noiseless," ibid.

GP 12/1
FOR F.W.
[1973].
[4] leaves; 28 cm.
Typescript.
Poem.
Four drafts with revisions.
Published with further revisions as "[Reunion at the Hilton]."
Published in: Seventy-five Greek poems/Irving Layton. Athens, Greece: Hermias, 1974, (also in UE, DD).

GP 13/1
THE SHARK
1974.
[4]p., [1] leaf; 2 leaves 20 cm., 1 leaf 30 cm.
Chiefly holograph.
Poem.
On p.[1]:2 holograph drafts of "The shark" in margin of leaf torn from published poetry review [Ophalos].
On p.[2]:2 poems in Greek by [C. Cavafy?] on leaf from published poetry review [Ophalos].
On p.[3]:holograph draft in margin of table of contents page of published poetry review [Ophalos].
On p.[4]:front cover of published poetry review "Ophalos."
On leaf [1]:holograph draft of "The shark."
Dated Molibos, Lesbos, August 28, 1974.
Published in: Seventy-five Greek poems/Irving Layton. Athens, Greece: Hermias, 1975, (also in PIL, UE, WPJ).

GP 14/1
THE UNWAVERING EYE
[1974].
[2] leaves; 16 cm.
Holograph.
Poem.
Two drafts with revisions on lined paper torn from notebook.
On verso of leaf [2]:list of titles of poems in "The whole bloody bird" and "Nail polish."
Published with further revisions in: Seventy-five Greek poems/ Irving Layton. Athens, Greece: Hermias, 1974, (also in UE).

GP 14/2
THE UNWAVERING EYE
1974.
[13] leaves; 30 cm.
Holograph signed.
Poem.
On leaves [1-11]:11 drafts with revisions.
On leaves [12-13]:2 drafts with large portions crossed out.
Leaves [1-4,6-7,13] titled "F. Nietzsche."
Dated Molibos, Lesbos, August 24,25, 1974.
Published with further revisions in: Seventy-five Greek poems/ Irving Layton. Athens, Greece: Hermias, 1974.

IB - The Improved Binoculars

IB 1/1
BY ECSTASIES PERPLEXED
[1956].
[1] leaf; 20 cm.
Holograph signed.
Poem.
Published with revisions in: The improved binoculars/Irving Layton. Highlands, [N.C.]: Jonathan Williams, 1956, (also in CP65, CP71, DF, IB2, MOK, RC, SEL, LPIL1, LPIL2, DD).

IB 1/2
FOR AVIVA
1956.
[1] leaf; 20 cm.

...con't

IB 1/2...con't

Holograph signed.
Poem.
Dated April 4, 1956, Côte St. Luc, Quebec.
Published with revisions as "[By ecstasies perplexed]."
Published in: The improved binoculars/Irving Layton. Highlands, [N.C.]: Jonathan Williams, 1956, (also in CP65, CP71, DF, IB2, MOK, RC, SEL, LPIL1, LPIL2, DD).

IB 2/1
NAUSICAA
1956.
[1] leaf; 20 cm.
Holograph signed.
Poem.
Published in: The improved binoculars/Irving Layton. Highlands, N.C.: Jonathan Williams, 1956, (also in CP65, CP71, DF, GP, IB2, RC, SEL, LPIL1, LPIL2, WPJ, DD).

IB2 - The Improved Binoculars (2nd ed.)

IB2 1/1
ME, THE P.M., AND THE STARS
[1955].
[4]p.; 20 cm.
Holograph.
Poem.
Draft with revisions on lined yellow paper torn from daily journal dated May 5-8, 1953.
On p.[2]:list of English Literature assignments crossed out.
Published with further revisions in: The improved binoculars/ Irving Layton. 2nd ed. Highlands, N.C.: Jonathan Williams, 1956, (also in CGE, CP65, CP71, IB2, RC).

IMF - In the Midst of My Fever

IMF 1/1
PROTOTYPE
[1953].
[1] leaf; 20 cm.
Holograph.
Poem.
Draft on yellow lined paper torn from daily journal dated February 14, 1953.
Published with revisions as "For Priscilla."
Published in: In the midst of my fever/Irving Layton. [S.l.]: Divers Press, 1954.

LIM - A Laughter in the Mind

LIM 1/1
CAT DYING IN AUTUMN
[1957].
[1] leaf; 28 cm.
Typescript signed.
Poem.
Published with revisions in: A laughter in the mind/Irving Layton. Highlands,N.C.: Jonathan Williams, 1958, (also in CP65, CP71, DF, LIM2, RC, SEL, WPJ).

LIM 2/1
DENOUEMENT; EPITAPHS; TO R.E.
1942.
[2] leaves; 22 cm.
Typescript.
Three poems.
On leaf [1]:draft of "Denouement"; draft of "Epitaphs" (For a philosopher. For a wit).
On leaf [2]:draft of "To R.E."
"Denouement" published as pt.I of "Two songs for sweet voices."
Dated February 27, 1942.
Typescript signature.
"Two songs for sweet voices" published in: A laughter in the mind/Irving Layton. Highlands, N.C.: Jonathan Williams, 1958, (also in LPIL1, LPIL2).
"Epitaphs" published in: Here and now/Irving Layton. Montreal:First Statement, 1945, (also in BH).
"To R.E." published in McGill Daily, February 27th, 1942, (also in UP).

LIM 3/1
WHATEVER ELSE POETRY IS FREEDOM; PARTING; VICTORY; BAWDY BAWDY
1957.
[2]p., [5] leaves; 28 cm. + examination booklet jacket.
Holograph.
Four poems.
Recto of leaf [1] blank.
On verso of leaf [1] and on leaf [2]:draft with revisions of stanzas 1-6 of "Whatever else poetry is freedom."
On verso of leaf [3]:draft of poem titled "Bawdy bawdy."
On p.[1]:draft of 18 lines beginning "May you be proud and passionate...."
On p.[2] and top of leaves [4-5]:draft with revisions of "Parting."
On leaves [4-5]:draft with revisions of "Victory" with reworking of stanza 5.
"Parting" dated August 19, 1957, Lac Masson Que[bec].
"Whatever else poetry is freedom" published with further revisions in: A laughter in the mind/Irving Layton. Highlands, N.C.: Jonathan Williams, 1958, (also in CP65, CP71, DF, LIM2, PIL, RC, SEL, WPJ).
"Parting," ibid., (with revisions) (also in CP65, CP71, LIM2, RC, SEL).
"Victory," ibid., (with revisions) (also in CP71, LIM2, RC).
"Bawdy bawdy" not published to date.

LIM2 - A Laughter in the Mind (2nd ed.)

LIM2 1/1
LOVE IS AN IRREFUTABLE FIRE; FOR MAO-TSE-TUNG
[1958].
[12]p., [23] leaves; 28 cm. + 2 examination booklet jackets.
Holograph.
Two poems.
On p.[1-12] and leaves [1-23]:partial drafts of untitled poem with themes from "Love is an irrefutable fire" and "For Mao-tse- tung" interwoven throughout; p. [1,3-5] crossed out.
On leaves [21-23]:3 drafts of "Love is an irrefutable fire."
Drafts on lined pages torn from notebook, and two jackets from Sir George Williams College and Schools examination booklet.
Holograph titles on front jacket cover.
Marginalia on back jacket cover.
Cigarette burns on leaves [8-9].
"Love is an irrefutable fire" published with revisions in: A laughter in the mind/Irving Layton. 2nd ed. Montreal: Editions d'Orphée, 1959, (also in CP65, CP71, LIM).
"For Mao-tse-tung," ibid., (also in CP65, CP71, DF, PIL, RC, SEL, WPJ).

LIM2 2/1
MY FLESH COMFORTLESS
1958.
[17] leaves; 28 cm. + jacket of examination booklet.
Chiefly holograph.
Poem.
On leaf [1] and verso:notes on themes in poem.
On leaves [2-12]:7 holograph drafts with revisions; marginalia on leaves [4,8-9].
On leaves [13-14]:1 typescript draft with revisions.
On leaves [15-17]:holograph reworking of stanzas 1-4,9.
Leaves enclosed in jacket of Sir George Williams College and Schools examination booklet dated August 12, 1958.
Holograph title on cover.
Published with further revisions in: A laughter in the mind/ Irving Layton. 2nd ed. Montreal: Editions d'Orphe, 1959, (also in CP65, CP71, DF, RC, SEL, WPJ).

LIM2 3/1
YOUNG GIRLS DANCING AT CAMP LAJOIE
[1958].
[1] leaf; 28 cm.
Typescript with holograph revisions.
Poem.
Published with further revisions in: A red carpet for the sun/ Irving Layton. Toronto: McClelland and Stewart, 1959, (also in CP65, CP71).
Also published as "Young girls dancing" in: A laughter in the mind/Irving Layton. 2nd ed. Montreal: Editions d'Orphée, 1959.

LIM2 3/2
YOUNG GIRLS DANCING AT CAMP LAJOIE
[1958].
[1] leaf; 28 cm.
Typescript.
Poem.
Published with revisions in: A red carpet for the sun/Irving Layton. Toronto: McClelland and Stewart, 1959, (also in CP65, CP71).
Also published as "Young girls dancing" in: A laughter in the mind/Irving Layton. 2nd ed. Montreal: Editions d'Orphée, 1959.

LLM - Lovers and Lesser Men

LLM 1/1
SOME CANADIAN BIRDS IN OCTOBER
[1972].
[9] leaves; 28 cm.
Holograph signed.
Poem.
On leaf [1]:draft with revisions of stanzas 1-3 and reworking of lines 1-2.
On leaf [2]:2 drafts with revisions of stanzas 1-2.
On leaves [3-6,8-9]:5 drafts with revisions.
On leaf [7]:draft with revisions of stanzas 1-3.
Published with further revisions in: Lovers and lesser men/ Irving Layton. Toronto: McClelland and Stewart, 1973.

LLM 2/1
XMAS EVE 1971, ZIHUATANEJO
1971.
[1] leaf; 28 cm.
Holograph.
Poem.
Draft with revisions and reworking of last stanza.
Number "1" in upper right corner.
Published with further revisions in: Lovers and lesser men/ Irving Layton. Toronto: McClelland and Stewart, 1973, (also UE).

LLM 2/2
XMAS EVE 1971, ZIHUATANEJO
1971.
[1] leaf; 28 cm.
Holograph.
Poem.
Draft with revisions.
Number "2" in upper right corner.
Published with further revisions in: Lovers and lesser men/ Irving Layton. Toronto: McClelland and Stewart, 1973, (also UE).

LLM 2/3
XMAS EVE 1971, ZIHUATANEJO
1971.
[2]p.; 28 cm.
Holograph.
Poem.
On p.[1]:draft with revisions.
Number "3" in upper right corner.
On p.[2]:unidentified portion of personal letter.
Published with further revisions in: Lovers and lesser men/ Irving Layton. Toronto: McClelland and Stewart, 1973, (also UE).

LLM 2/4
CHRISTMAS EVE 1971, ZIHUATANEJO
1971.
[1] leaf; 28 cm.
Holograph.
Poem.
Draft with revisions.
Number "4" in upper right corner.
Published with further revisions as "[Xmas eve 1971, Zihuatanejo]."
Published in: Lovers and lesser men/Irving Layton. Toronto: McClelland and Stewart, 1973, (also in UE).

LLM 2/5
XMAS EVE 1971, ZIHUATANEJO
[1971].
[1] leaf; 28 cm.
Holograph.
Poem.
Draft with revisions.
Number "5" in upper right corner.
Published with further revisions in: Lovers and lesser men/ Irving Layton. Toronto: McClelland and Stewart, 1973, (also UE).

LP - The Long Pea-shooter

LP 1/1
CANADIAN SPRING
1954.
[1] leaf; 20 cm.
Holograph.
Poem.
Three stanzas of poem on lined yellow page torn from daily journal dated July 18, 1953.
Poem dated April 1, 1954.
Published with revisions in: The long pea-shooter/Irving Layton. Montreal: Laocoon Press, 1954, (also in UP).

LPIL2 - The Love Poems of Irving Layton

LPIL2 1/1
A MADRIGAL FOR ANNA; THE DEMON
[1983].
[8] p., 3 leaves; 28 cm.
Chiefly holograph.
Two poems.
On p.[1]:holograph draft of 7 lines of "A madrigal for Anna"; marginalia.
On p.[3]:2 holograph drafts of "A madrigal for Anna" titled "Song for Anna"; brown water [?] mark.
On p.[5]:holograph draft of "A madrigal for Anna"; brown water [?] mark.
On p.[2,4,6]:3 typescript drafts of "The demon."
On p.[7]:ms. draft of "A madrigal for Anna."
On p.[8]:partial draft of unidentified letter.
On leaves [1-3]:3 typescript drafts of "A madrigal for Anna"; marginalia on leaf [1].
Drafts 1-4 numbered.
"A madrigal for Anna" published in: The love poems of Irving Layton/Irving Layton. Oakville, Ont.: Mosaic Press, 1984, (also in FR).
"The demon" not published to date.

LR - The Laughing Rooster

LR 1/1
EL CAUDILLO
[1963].
[1] leaf; 28 cm.
Holograph.
Poem.
Published with revisions in: The laughing rooster/Irving Layton. Toronto: McClelland & Stewart, 1964, (also in CP65, CP71, DF, SEL).

LR 2/1
FOR MY GREEN OLD AGE
[1963].
[1] leaf; 30 cm.
Holograph.
Poem.
Draft with revisions on one half of cardboard file folder.
On verso: holograph list of personal names, and names of institutions.
Published with further revisions in: The laughing rooster/ Irving Layton. Toronto: McClelland and Stewart, 1964, (also in CP65, CP71, LR, LPIL1, LPIL2, DD).

LR 3/1
MONTGO
[1963].
[1] leaf; 25 cm.
Holograph.
Poem.
Draft with revisions.
Published with further revisions in: The laughing rooster/ Irving Layton. Toronto: McClelland and Stewart, 1964, (also in CP65, CP71).

LR 3/2
[AFTERMATH]
1963.
Holograph.
1 card; 16 cm.
Poem.
Draft with reworking of first stanza on verso of invitation to the "Cinquième salon du livre de Québec," October 1963; 2 lines on front of invitation.
Published with revisions in: The laughing rooster/Irving Layton. Toronto: McClelland and Stewart, 1964, (also in CP65, CP71).

MOK - Music on a Kazoo

MOK 1/1
MEETING
1956.
[1] leaf; 21 cm.
Holograph signed.
Poem.
Dated May 11, 1956.
Published in: Music on a kazoo/Irving Layton. Toronto: Contact,1956, (also in UP).

MOK 2/1
[THE NEWER CRITICS]
1956.
[1] leaf; 20 cm.
Holograph signed.
Poem.
Draft on blue airmail note paper. Dated June 4th, 1956.
Published in: Music on a kazoo/Irving Layton. Toronto: Contact Press, 1956, (also in UP).

MOK 3/1
WOMAN
[1955].
[1] leaf; 21 cm.
Holograph signed.
Poem.
Draft with revisions.
Published with further revisions in: Music on a kazoo/Irving Layton. [Toronto]: Contact Press, 1956, (also in CP65, CP71, DF, IB, IB2, RC, SEL, LPIL1, LPIL2, DD, WPJ).

MSGB - The Gucci Bag (McClelland and Stewart ed.)

MSGB 1/1
COMRADE UNDERSHAFTSKY; [THE SWAMP]; OF ONE FAIRY AND THREE GODDESSES
[1982].
[4]p., [2] leaves; 28 cm.
In part holograph.
Three poems.

...con't

MSGB 1/1...con't
On p.[1] and leaf [1]:2 holograph drafts with revisions of "Comrade Undershaftsky."
On p.[2]:typescript draft of "[The swamp]."
On p.[3]:typescript draft with revisions of "Comrade Undershaftsky."
On p.[4]:typescript draft of "Of one fairy and three goddesses."
On leaf [2]:typescript draft of "Comrade Undershaftsky."
Holograph title "Comrade Undershaftsky" on verso of leaf [4].
"Comrade Undershaftsky" published in: The Gucci bag/Irving Layton. Toronto: McClelland and Stewart, 1983, (also in GB2).
"[The swamp]" published in: The Gucci bag/Irving Layton. Oakville, Ont.: Mosaic Press/Valley Editions, 1983, (also in MSGB, GB2).
"Of one fairy and three goddesses," ibid., (also in MSGB, GB2 as "Of one fairy and two goddesses").

MSGB 2/1
WHITEHERN
[1983].
[4] leaves; 3 leaves 28 cm., 1 leaf 30 cm.
Chiefly holograph.
Poem.
On leaves [1-2]:2 holograph drafts with revisions. On verso of leaf [2]:outline of "Baker" family tree.
On leaves [3-4]:2 typescript drafts with revisions.
Leaf [3] titled "Canadian Forsyth Saga."
Brown stain on leaves [1-2].
Published in: The Gucci bag/Irving Layton. Toronto, Ont.: McClelland and Stewart, 1983, (also in GB2).

MSGB 3/1
ARISTOCRATS
[1982].
[6]p., [1] leaf; 3 leaves 28 cm., 1 leaf 25 cm.
Chiefly holograph.
Poem.
On p.[1-4]:4 holograph drafts with revisions.
On p.[5]:typescript draft with revisions.
On p.[6]:typescript of letter from Irving Layton to Hon.R.[Mc-?].
On leaf [1]:typescript draft on verso of printed promotional material for "The Gucci bag."
Published in: The Gucci bag/Irving Layton. Toronto: McClelland and Stewart, 1983, (also in GB2, DD).

MSGB 4/1
AUGUST STRINDBERG; LADY MACBETH; YEATS AT SIXTY FIVE; EMPTY WORDS; THE POET'S PLEA FOR JUSTICE
[1982].
[14]p., [4] leaves; 28 cm.
In part holograph.
Five poems.
On p.[1,5,7]:3 holograph drafts with revisions of "Lady MacBeth."
On p.[3]:holograph draft with revisions of "Lady MacBeth"; typescript draft of "Empty words."
On p.[2,10,12]:3 typescript drafts of "The poet's plea for justice."
On p.[4]:typescript draft beginning "Demented apes...."
On p.[6]:typescript draft beginning "Where is he...?" On p.[8]:typescript draft of "Yeat's at sixty five."
On p.[9,11,13] and leaves [1-4]:7 typescript drafts with revisions of "Lady MacBeth."
On p. [14]: typescript draft of "August Strindberg."
Leaf [4] on verso of promotional material from "The Gucci bag."
"August Strindberg" published in: The Gucci bag/Irving Layton. Toronto: McClelland and Stewart, 1983, (also in GB2).
"Lady MacBeth published in: The Gucci bag/Irving Layton. 2nd ed. Oakville,Ont.: Mosaic Press/Valley Editions, 1984, (also in DD, FR).
"Empty words," ibid.
"Yeat's at sixty five" published in: The Gucci bag/Irving Layton. Toronto: McClelland and Stewart, 1983, (also in GB2, LPIL2).
"The poet's plea for justice" not published to date.

MSGB 5/1
TIC TOC; HOLIDAY INN: TOKYO
[1983].
[2]p., [2] leaves; 2 leaves 28 cm., 1 leaf 29 cm.
In part holograph.
Two poems.
On leaf [1]:holograph draft, marginalia.
On p.[1]:typescript draft with revisions of "Holiday Inn Tokyo," "77A" in upper right corner.
On p.[2]:holograph draft with reworking of stanzas 3-4 of "Tic toc"; marginalia.
On leaf [2]:typescript draft of "Tic toc" on verso of promotional material from "The Gucci bag."
Rough pencil sketch on verso of leaf [1].
"Tic toc" published as "Tick tock."

...con't

MSGB 5/1...con't

"Tick tock" published in: The Gucci bag/Irving Layton. Toronto: McClelland and Stewart, 1983.
"Holiday Inn: Tokyo," ibid., (also in GB2).

NP - Nail Polish

NP 1/1
[AS SEEN THROUGH A GLASS DARKLY]
[1970].
[4]p., [2] leaves; 28 cm.
Chiefly holograph.
Poem.
On p.[1-4] and leaf [1]:5 holograph drafts with revisions.
On leaf [2]:typescript draft of stanzas 1-4.
Drafts on p.[1-4] and leaf [1] numbered 1-5.
Published with further revisions in: Nail polish/Irving Layton. Toronto: McClelland and Stewart, 1971, (also in UE).

NP 1/2
AS SEEN THROUGH A GLASS DARKLY
[1970].
[10] leaves; 28 cm.
Typescript with holograph revisions.
Poem.
On leaves [1-6]:3 drafts with revisions; marginalia on leaf [3].
On leaves [7-10]:7 drafts of stanza beginning "could it be their colour...."
Leaf [10]:reworking of stanza beginning "could it be their colour...."
Holograph title on verso of leaf [6].
Published with further revisions in: Nail polish/Irving Layton.
Toronto: McClelland and Stewart, 1971, (also in UE).

NP 2/1
DIONYSUS IN HAMPSTEAD
[1970].
[1] leaf; 28 cm.
Typescript with holograph revisions.
Poem.
Marginalia on verso.
Published with revisions in: Nail polish/Irving Layton. Toronto: McClelland and Stewart, 1971, (also in CP71, GP, UE).

NP 2/2
[DIONYSUS IN HAMPSTEAD]
[1970].
[1] leaf; 32 cm.
Holograph.
Poem.
On verso:last 4 lines of poem; observations on Vietnam and Cambodia.
Published with further revisions in: Nail polish/Irving Layton. Toronto: McClelland and Stewart, 1971, (also in CP71, GP, UE).

NP 2/3
[DIONYSUS IN HAMPSTEAD]; HUMAN AMONG HUMANS
[1970].
[2]p.; 28 cm.
Chiefly holograph.
Two poems.
On p.[1]:holograph draft with revisions of "[Dionysus in Hampstead].
On p.[2]:typescript draft of "Human among humans."
"Human among humans" published as "[Entry]."
"Dionysus in Hampstead" published with further revisions in: Nail polish/Irving Layton. Toronto: McClelland and Stewart, 1971. (also in CP71, GP, UE).
"[Entry]," ibid., (also in CP71, UE).

NP 2/4
[DIONYSUS IN HAMPSTEAD]
[1970].
[1] leaf; 28 cm.
Holograph.
Poem.
Draft with revisions.
Published with further revisions in: Nail polish/Irving Layton. Toronto: McClelland and Stewart, 1971, (also in CP71, GP, UE).

NP 2/5
[DIONYSUS IN HAMPSTEAD]; HUMAN AMONG HUMANS
[1970].
[2]p.; 28 cm.
Holograph.
Two poems.
On p.[1]:holograph draft with revisions of "[Dionysus in Hampstead]."
On p.[2]:typescript draft of "Human among humans."

...con't

NP 2/5...con't

"Human among humans" published as "[Entry]."
"Dionysus in Hampstead" published with further revisions in: Nail polish/Irving Layton. Toronto: McClelland and Stewart, 1971, (also in CP71, GP, UE).
"[Entry]," ibid.

NP 2/6
DIONYSUS IN HAMPSTEAD; HUMAN AMONG HUMANS
[1970].
[2]p.; 28 cm.
Typescript with holograph revisions.
Two poems.
On p.[1]:draft with revisions of "Dionysus in Hampstead."
On p.[2]:draft of "Human among humans"; holograph title "Dionysus in Hampstead."
"Human among humans" published as "[Entry]."
"Dionysus in Hampstead" published with further revisions in: Nail polish/Irving Layton. Toronto: McClelland and Stewart, 1971, (also in CP71, GP, UE).
"[Entry]," ibid.

NP 3/1
END OF THE WHITE MOUSE
[1970].
[3] leaves; 20 cm.
Holograph.
Poem.
Draft on unlined paper torn from notebook.
Marginalia on verso of leaf [1].
Published with revisions in: Nail polish/Irving Layton. Toronto: McClelland and Stewart, 1971, (also in CP71, UE, WPJ).

NP 3/2
[END OF THE WHITE MOUSE]
[1970].
[6] leaves; 28 cm.
Holograph.
Poem.
Three drafts with revisions on verso of loose leaf graph paper.
Marginalia on leaf [5].
Published with further revisions in: Nail polish/Irving Layton.
Toronto: McClelland and Stewart, 1971, (also in CP71, UE, WPJ).

NP 3/3
END OF THE WHITE MOUSE
[1970].
[14] leaves; 28 cm.
Typescript with holograph revisions signed.
Poem.
Seven drafts with revisions.
Published with further revisions in: Nail polish/Irving Layton. Toronto: McClelland and Stewart, 1971, (also in CP71, UE, WPJ).

NP 3/4
END OF THE WHITE MOUSE
[1970].
[5] leaves; 28 cm.
Typescript.
Poem.
On leaf [1]:draft with revisions of lines 1-33.
On leaf [2]:draft of lines 1-16.
On leaf [3]:draft of lines 1-25; holograph note concerning beginning of poem.
On leaf [4]:draft of lines 1-18.
On leaf [5]:draft with revisions of lines 1-32.
Published with further revisions in: Nail polish/Irving Layton. Toronto: McClelland and Stewart, 1971, (also in CP71, UE, WPJ).

NP 4/1
[FANATIC IN SAN FELIU]; LOBSTERS
[1970].
[4]p., [5] leaves; 28 cm.
In part holograph.
Two poems.
On p.[1-3] and leaf [1]:2 holograph drafts, one typescript draft with revisions of "[Fanatic in San Feliu]."
Fragment on p.[2] beginning "It is my virtue I repeat...."
On p.[4]:holograph draft of "Lobsters."
On leaves [2-5]:4 drafts of segment beginning "Wrong, wrong once more ..." (last stanza).
"Lobsters" published with revisions as "[As seen through the glass darkly]"
"[Fanatic in San Feliu]" published with further revisions in: Nail polish/Irving Layton. Toronto: McClelland and Stewart, 1971, (also in CP71, LPIL1, LPIL2).
"[As seen through a glass darkly]," ibid., (also in CP71, UE).

NP 4/2
FANATIC IN SAN FELIU; DARK LADY
[1970].
[2] leaves; 31 cm.
Typescript.
Two poems.
On leaf [1]:draft of stanzas 1-3 of "Fanatic in San Feliu."
On leaf [2]:draft of stanzas 4-5 of "Fanatic in San Feliu"; draft of "Dark lady."
Holograph title and note concerning publication on verso of leaf [2].
"Fanatic in San Feliu" published with revisions in: Nail polish/ Irving Layton. Toronto: McClelland and Stewart, 1971, (also in CP71, LPIL1, LPIL2).
"Dark lady," ibid.

NP 4/3
FANATIC IN SAN FELIU
[1970].
[6] leaves; 4 leaves 28 cm., 2 leaves 26 cm.
Typescript with holograph revisions.
Poem.
Three drafts.
Holograph note concerning publication on verso of leaf [6].
Title on leaf [3] "Fanatic."
Published with further revisions in: Nail polish/Irving Layton. Toronto: McClelland and Stewart, 1971, (also in CP71, LPIL1, LPIL2).

NP 5/1
FOR NATALYA CORREIA; GREY MORNING IN LISBON
[1970].
[2]p., [8] leaves; 8 leaves 27 cm., 1 leaf 25 cm.
In part holograph.
Two poems.
On p.[1]:2 holograph drafts with revisions of 10 lines of "For Natalya Correia"; line 1 of "Grey morning in Lisbon."
On p.[2]:holograph draft of stanzas 4-6 of "For Natalya Correia" with reworking of stanza 4; lines 1-4 of "Grey morning in Lisbon."
On leaf [1]:3 holograph drafts of varying lengths of stanzas 1-2 of "For Natalya Correia."
On leaves [2-8]:1 holograph and 6 typescript drafts with revisions of "For Natalya Correia."
Holograph title "For Marya Correia" on verso of leaves [7-8].

...con't

NP 5/1...con't

"For Natalya Correia" published in: Nail polish/Irving Layton. Toronto: McClelland and Stewart, 1971, (also in UE, WPJ).
"Grey morning in Lisbon," ibid.

NP 6/1
FROST AND FENCES
1969.
[21] leaves; 14 leaves 28 cm., 6 leaves 25 cm., 1 leaf 21 cm. x 15 cm.
Typescript with holograph revisions.
Poem.
Twenty-one drafts with revisions.
Leaves [1,5,7-8,11-12,16,18-21] titled "Requiescat"; leaves [12- 14] titled "In pacem."
Marginalia on leaf [17].
Holograph title "Frost and fences" on verso of leaf [21].
Dated: Inishmore, Aran Islands, [1969].
Published with further revisions in: Nail polish/Irving Layton. Toronto: McClelland and Stewart, 1971, (also in CP71).

NP 7/1
GOD IS LOVE; [PORTRAITS DRAWN FROM LIFE]
1970.
[14] leaves; 28 cm.
In part holograph.
Two poems.
Three holograph, 11 typescript drafts with revisions of "God is love."
At bottom of leaf [1] and on verso "Acknowledgements for reprints."
On verso of leaf [2]:typescript of lines 1-2 of "[Portraits drawn from life]."
Holograph title on verso of leaves [6,8,11-12,14].
Dated Lake Selby, August 21, 1970.
"God is love" published with further revisions in: Nail polish/ Irving Layton. Toronto: McClelland and Stewart, 1971, (also in CP71).
"[Portraits drawn from life]," ibid.

NP 8/1
GREY MORNING IN LISBON; [FROST AND FENCES]
[1970].
[2]p., [4] leaves; 27 cm.
Typescript with holograph revisions.
Two poems.

...con't

NP 8/1...con't

On p.[1] and leaves [1-4]:6 drafts with revisions of "Grey morning in Lisbon."
On p.[2]:draft of "[Frost and fences]."
Drafts of "Grey morning in Lisbon" numbered 1-6.
Holograph title "Grey morning in Lisbon" on verso of leaf [5].
"Grey morning in Lisbon" published with further revisions in: Nail polish/Irving Layton. Toronto: McClelland and Stewart, 1971, (also in CP71).
"[Frost and fences]," ibid., (with revisions), (also in CP71).

NP 9/1
HOMAGE TO ONASSIS
[1970].
[2]p., [8] leaves; 2 leaves 21 cm., 7 leaves 28 cm.
In part holograph.
Poem.
On p.[1]:holograph draft of 4 stanzas with reworking of stanza 1 titled "Epigram on Onassis."
On p.[2] and leaf [1]:2 holograph drafts with revisions; leaf [1] titled "That lovely pair."
On leaves [2-8]:7 typescript drafts with revisions.
On verso of leaf [8]:typescript draft of lines 1-2.
Holograph title on verso of leaves [7-8].
Marginalia on p.[1].
Drafts on p.[1-2] and leaf [1] numbered 1-3.
Published in: Nail polish/Irving Layton. Toronto: McClelland and Stewart, 1971.

NP 10/1
LAKE SELBY; TRUE LOVE
1970.
[2]p., [9] leaves; 28 cm.
Chiefly holograph.
Two poems.
On p.[1]:holograph draft of 23 lines of "Lake Selby"; fragment beginning "O this vain man's incurable...."
On p.[2]:typescript draft of "True love."
On leaf [1]:holograph draft of stanzas 1-2 of "Lake Selby."
On leaves [2-9]:2 holograph, 2 typescript drafts of "Lake Selby."
Holograph title "Lake Selby" on verso of leaves [8-9].
Note mentioning finished version on leaf [9].
Dated August 19, 1970.

...con't

NP 10/1...con't

"Lake Selby" published with further revisions in: Nail polish/ Irving Layton. Toronto: McClelland and Stewart, 1971, (also in CP71, UE).
"True love" not published to date.

NP 11/1
NAIL POLISH; HUNGRY CHRISTIANS; NO CURTAIN CALLS; END OF THE WHITE MOUSE; GOD IS LOVE
1970.
[10] p.,[2] leaves; 28 cm.
Chiefly holograph.
Five poems.
On leaf [1]:2 drafts of stanza 1, 4 drafts of stanza 3 of "Nail polish."
On p.[1]:draft of stanzas 1,3,5 of "Nail polish"; draft of "Hungry Christians" crossed out.
On p.[2]:2 fragments beginning "He speaks to me about my childhood ..." and "As you speak I know I am missing something...."
On p.[3]:2 drafts of stanzas 1,3-5, 2 drafts of stanza 2 of "Nail polish."
On p.[4]:4 typescript drafts of fragment "In homage to Daniel and Sinyavsky...."
On p.[5,7,9] and leaf [2]:3 holograph drafts, 1 typescript draft with revisions of "Nail polish."
On p.[6]:typescript draft with revisions of "No curtain calls."
On p.[8]:typescript draft with revisions of "End of the white mouse."
On p.[10]:typescript draft of "God is love" crossed out.
Drafts of "Nail polish" numbered 1-7.
Holograph title "Nail polish" on verso of leaf [2].
Dated Lake Selby, August 22, 1970.
"Nail polish" published with further revisions in: Nail polish/ Irving Layton. Toronto: McClelland & Stewart, 1971, (also in CP71).
"Hungry christians," ibid.
"No curtain calls," ibid., (also in CP71).
"End of the white mouse," ibid., (also in CP71, UE, WPJ).
"God is love," ibid., (also in CP71).

NP 12/1
NO CURTAIN CALLS
[1970].
[4] leaves; 28 cm.
In part holograph.
Poem.
One holograph draft; 3 typescript drafts with revisions.

...con't

NP 12/1...con't

Holograph title on verso of leaf [4].
Published with further revisions in: Nail polish/Irving Layton. Toronto: McClelland and Stewart, 1971, (also in CP71).

NP 13/1
PORTRAITS DRAWN FROM LIFE
[1970].
[2] leaves; 28 cm.
In part holograph.
Poem.
On leaf [1]:holograph draft of 7 stanzas titled "Portraits from life"; one stanza crossed out.
On leaf [2]:typescript draft with revisions.
Holograph title on verso of leaves [1-2].
Published in: Nail polish/Irving Layton. Toronto: McClelland and Stewart, 1971.

NP 14/1
[SHAKESPEARE]; SHORT SERMON ON GOD AND NATURE BY THE RABBI WHO SURVIVED AUSCHWITZ; [GOD IS LOVE]
[1970].
[6]p.; 28 cm.
Chiefly holograph.
Three poems.
On p.[1,3,5]:holograph draft of "[Shakespeare]" with revisions; marginalia on p.[1].
On p.[2,6]:2 typescript drafts of "Short sermon on God and nature...."
On p.[4]:typescript of lines 1-6 of "[God is love]."
Brown stains on p.[1-2].
"[Shakespeare]" published with further revisions in: Nail polish/Irving Layton. Toronto: McClelland and Stewart, 1971, (also in CP71, PIL, UE, WPJ).
"Short sermon on God and nature ..." ibid., (with revisions).
"[God is love]" ibid., (also in CP71).

NP 14/2
[SHAKESPEARE]; [POET'S LAMENT]; VERTICAL MAN; [GOD IS LOVE]
[1970].
[6]p.; 28 cm.
Chiefly holograph.
Four poems.
On p.[1,3,5]:draft of "[Shakespeare]" with revisions; marginalia.

...con't

NP 14/2...con't

On p.[2]:typescript draft of "[Poet's lament]" titled "Moon landing."
On p.[4]:typescript draft of lines 1-9 of "[God is love]."
On p.[6]:typescript draft of "Vertical man."
"Vertical man" published as "[The straight man]."
Drafts of "[Shakespeare]" numbered 2-1,2-2,2-3.
"[Shakespeare]" published with further revisions in: Nail polish/Irving Layton. Toronto: McClelland and Stewart, 1971, (also in CP71, PIL, UE, WPJ).
"[The straight man]," ibid., (with revisions), (also in CP71).
"[God is love]," ibid., (also in CP71).
"[Poet's lament]" not published to date.

NP 14/3
THE GREATNESS OF SHAKESPEARE; THE STRAIGHT MAN; [DIONYSIAN REVELLER]
[1970].
[6]p.; 28 cm.
Typescript with holograph revisions.
Three poems.
On p.[1,3,5]:draft of "The greatness of Shakespeare" with revisions.
On p.[2]:draft of "[Dionysian reveller]" On p.[4-6]:2 drafts of "The straight man."
Drafts of "The greatness of Shakespeare" numbered 3-1,3-2,3-3.
"The greatness of Shakespeare" published as "[Shakespeare]."
"[Shakespeare]" published with further revisions in: Nail polish/Irving Layton. Toronto: McClelland and Stewart, 1971, (also in CP71, PIL, UE, WPJ).
"The straight man," ibid., (with revisions), (also in CP71).
"[Dionysian reveller]," ibid., (also in CP71).

NP 14/4
SHAKESPEARE
[1970].
[3] leaves; 28 cm.
Typescript with holograph revisions.
Poem.
Marginalia on leaf [1].
Holograph title on verso of leaf [3].
Number "4" at top of leaf [1].
Published with further revisions in: Nail polish/Irving Layton. Toronto: McClelland and Stewart, 1971, (also in CP71, PIL, UE, WPJ).

NP 15/1
VERTICAL MAN
[1970].
[2]p.; 28 cm.
Holograph.
Poem.
On p.[1]:2 drafts with revisions of last stanza; reworking of lines 1-2.
On p.[2]:notice of annual meeting of "La ligue des droits de l'homme," dated June 3rd, 1969.
Bottom left corner torn from page.
Published with further revisions as "[The straight man]."
Published in: Nail polish/Irving Layton. Toronto: McClelland and Stewart, 1971, (also in CP71).

NP 15/2
[THE STRAIGHT MAN]
[1970].
[4]p.; 28 cm.
Holograph.
Poem.
On p.[1,3]:3 drafts with revisions.
On p.[2-4]:portion of personal letter to Layton.
Published with further revisions in: Nail polish/Irving Layton. Toronto: McClelland and Stewart, 1971, (also in CP71).

NP 15/3
VERTICAL MAN
[1970].
[1] leaf; 28 cm.
Typescript.
Poem.
Published with revisions as "[The straight man]."
Published in: Nail polish/Irving Layton. Toronto: McClelland and Stewart, 1971, (also in CP71).

NP 15/4 DAS NICHTS
[1970].
[1]p.; 28 cm.
Typescript.
Poem.
"Das nichts" published with revisions as "[The straight man]".
Published in: Nail polish/Irving Layton. Toronto: McClelland and Stewart, 1971, (also in CP71).

NP 16/1
KILMURVEY STRAND
[1970].
[3] leaves; 21 cm.
Holograph.
Poem.
On leaves [1-2]:draft with revisions on verso of pages torn from business ledger; number "16" in upper right corner of leaf [1].
On leaf [3]:reworking of stanzas 3-4.
Published with further revisions in: Nail polish/Irving Layton. Toronto: McClelland and Stewart, 1971, (also in CP71, UE).

NP 17/1
JULY 21, 1969; POET'S LAMENT
[1970].
[2]p., [2] leaves; 21 cm.
Holograph.
Two poems.
On leaf [1] and p.[1]:2 drafts with revisions of "Poet's lament."
On p.[2]:2 drafts of 10 and 16 lines each of "Poet's lament."
On leaf [2]:draft of "Poet's lament."
On verso of leaf [2]:2 drafts of "July 21, 1969."
"July 21, 1969" published in: Nail polish/Irving Layton. Toronto: McClelland and Stewart, 1971.
"Poet's lament" not published to date.

POM - Periods of the Moon

POM 1/1
FOR MUSIA'S GRANDCHILDREN; THE COLD GREEN ELEMENT
[1966].
[2]p.; 28 cm. folded to 21 cm.
In part holograph.
Two poems.
On p.[1]:draft of "For Musia's grandchildren."
On p.[2]:typescript of stanzas 1-5 of "The cold green element."
"For Musia's grandchildren" published with revisions in: Periods of the moon/Irving Layton. Toronto: McClelland and Stewart, 1967, (also in CP71, DF, SEL, LPIL1, WPJ, LPIL2, DD).
"The cold green element" published in: The cold green element/ Irving Layton. [Toronto]: Contact Press, 1955, (also in CP65, CP71, DF, IB, IB2, PIL, RC, SEL, WPJ).

POM 1/2
[FOR MUSIA'S GRANDCHILDREN]; THE COLD GREEN ELEMENT
[1966].
[2]p.; 28 cm. folded to 21 cm.
In part holograph.
Two poems. On p.[1]:holograph draft with revisions of stanza 3 of "[For Musia's grandchildren]."
On p.[2]:typescript of stanzas 6-8 of "The cold green element."
"[For Musia's grandchildren]" published in: Periods of the moon/ Irving Layton. Toronto: McClelland and Stewart, 1967, (also in CP71, DF, SEL, LPIL1, WPJ, LPIL2, DD).
"The cold green element" published in: The cold green element/ Irving Layton. [Toronto]: Contact Press, 1955, (also in CP65, CP71, DF IB IB2, PIL, RC, SEL, WPJ).

POM 1/3
FOR MUSIA'S GRANDCHILDREN; NO WILD DOG
[1966].
[3]p. on 1 leaf; 28 cm. folded to 21 cm.
In part holograph.
Two poems.
On p.[1]:holograph draft with revisions of first stanza of "For Musia's grandchildren"; at head of poem "The humans who look as if they were almost real."
On p.[2]:reworking of stanza 2 of "For Musia's grandchildren."
On p.[3]:typescript draft of "No wild dog."
"For Musia's grandchildren" published in: Periods of the moon/ Irving Layton. Toronto: McClelland and Stewart, 1967, (also in CP71, DF, SEL, LPIL1, WPJ, LPIL2, DD).
"No wild dog" published with revisions in: Balls for a one-armed juggler/Irving Layton. Toronto: McClelland and Stewart, 1963, (also in CP65, CP71, SEL).

POM 1/4
[FOR MUSIA'S GRANDCHILDREN]; NO WILD DOG
[1966].
[2]p.; 28 cm. folded to 21 cm.
In part holograph.
Two poems.
On p.[1]:holograph draft with revisions of stanzas 1-2 of "[For Musia's grandchildren]"; major portion of poem crossed out.
On p.[2]:typescript of "No wild dog."

...con't

POM 1/4...con't

"[For Musia's grandchildren]" published in: Periods of the moon/ Irving Layton. Toronto: McClelland and Stewart, 1967, (also in CP71, DF, SEL, LPIL1, WPJ, LPIL2, DD).

"No wild dog" published with revisions in: Balls for a one-armed juggler/Irving Layton. Toronto: McClelland and Stewart, 1963, (also in CP65, CP71, SEL).

POM 1/5

[FOR MUSIA'S GRANDCHILDREN]; CAIN

[1966].

[2]p.; 28 cm. folded to 21 cm.

In part holograph.

Two poems.

On p.[1]:holograph draft with revisions of stanzas 1-2 of "[For Musia's grandchildren]."

On p.[2]:typescript of stanza 1 of "Cain."

"[For Musia's grandchildren]" published in: Periods of the moon/ Irving Layton. Toronto: McClelland and Stewart, 1967, (also in CP71, DF, SEL, LPIL1, WPJ, LPIL2, DD).

"Cain" published in: A laughter in the mind/Irving Layton. Highlands, N.C.: Jonathan Williams, 1958, (also in CP65, CP71, DF, LIM2, PIL, SEL, WPJ).

POM 1/6

[FOR MUSIA'S GRANDCHILDREN]; SONG FOR NAOMI

[1966].

[3]p. on [1] leaf; 28 cm. folded to 21 cm.

In part holograph.

Two poems.

On p.[1]:holograph draft with revisions of stanza 3 of "[For Musia's grandchildren]."

On p.[2]:2 crossed out fragments from stanza 2 of "[For Musia's grandchildren]."

On p.[3]:typescript of stanzas 1-3 of "Song for Naomi."

"[For Musia's grandchildren]" published in: Periods of the moon/ Irving Layton. Toronto: McClelland and Stewart, 1967, (also in CP71, DF, SEL, LPIL1, WPJ, LPIL2, DD).

"Song for Naomi" published in: The improved binoculars/Irving Layton. Highlands, [N.C.]: Jonathan Williams, 1956, (also in BC, CP65, CP71, DF, IB2, PIL, SEL, WPJ).

POM 1/7
[FOR MUSIA'S GRANDCHILDREN]; SONG FOR NAOMI
[1966].
[2]p.; 28 cm. folded to 21 cm.
In part holograph.
Two poems.
On p.[1]:two fragments from stanza 3 of "[For Musia's grandchildren]"; one fragment crossed out.
On p.[2]:typescript of last stanza of "Song for Naomi."
"[For Musia's grandchildren]" published in: Periods of the moon/ Irving Layton. Toronto: McClelland and Stewart, 1967, (also in CP71, DF, SEL, LPIL1, WPJ, LPIL2, DD).
"Song for Naomi" published in: The improved binoculars/Irving Layton. Highlands, [N.C.]: Jonathan Williams, 1956, (also in BC, CP65, CP71, DF, IB2, PIL, SEL, WPJ).

POM 1/8
FOR MUSIA'S GRANDCHILDREN
[1966].
[7] leaves; 28 cm.
Typescript with holograph revisions.
Poem.
Seven drafts.
Published with further revisions in: Periods of the moon/Irving Layton. Toronto: McClelland and Stewart, 1967, (also in CP71, DF, SEL, LPIL1, WPJ, LPIL2, DD).

POM 2/1
FREEDOM; MISUNDERSTANDING
[1966].
[3]p. on [1] leaf; 28 cm. x 21cm. folded to 14 cm. x 21 cm.
Chiefly holograph.
Two poems.
On p.[1]:holograph draft with revisions of "Freedom."
On p.[2]:holograph draft with revisions of "Freedom"; major portion crossed out.
On p.[3]:typescript draft of "Misunderstanding."
"Freedom" published with further revisions in: Periods of the moon/Irving Layton. Toronto: McClelland and Stewart, 1967. (also in CP71).
"Misunderstanding" published in: The long pea-shooter/Irving Layton Montreal: Laocoon Press, 1954, (also in CP65, CP71, PIL, RC, SEL, LPIL1, WPJ, LPIL2, DD).

POM 3/1
INSOMNIA; ON THE ASSASSINATION OF PRESIDENT KENNEDY
1966.
[7] leaves; 6 leaves 25 cm., 1 leaf 28 cm.
Chiefly holograph.
Two poems.
One typescript; 6 holograph drafts with revisions of "Insomnia."
On verso of leaf [1]:offprint of "On the assassination of President Kennedy," Queen's Quarterly, Winter, 1964, vol.LXX, no.4.
"Insomnia" dated March 5, 1966.
"Insomnia" published in: Periods of the moon/Irving Layton. Toronto: McClelland and Stewart, 1967, (also in CP71, DF, LPIL1, LPIL2, DD).
"On the assassination of President Kennedy" published in: The laughing rooster/Irving Layton. Toronto: McClelland and Stewart, 1964, (also in CP65, CP71).

POM 4/1
ONCE A SINGLE HAIR
1966.
[2]p., [7] leaves; 28 cm.
Chiefly holograph.
Poem.
On p.[1-2] and leaves [1-6]:8 holograph drafts.
On leaf [7]:typescript draft of 19 lines beginning"Once ignited and kept aglow...."
Drafts 1-3 numbered.
Marginalia on verso of leaf [6].
Dated March 6, 1966 "Once a single hair" published with revisions as "Mahogany red."
Published in: Periods of the moon/Irving Layton. Toronto: McClelland and Stewart, 1967, (also in CP71, DF, PIL, SEL, LPIL1, LPIL2).

POM 5/1
WATER SKIER
[1966].
[1] leaf; 28 cm.
Typescript.
Poem.
Thirty-two lines on theme of "[Poros]."
On verso:landscape and miscellaneous sketches in black ink.
Published with revisions as "[Poros]."
Published in: Periods of the moon/Irving Layton. Toronto: McClelland and Stewart, 1967, (also in GP).

POM 6/1
REPLY TO A RHYMING NOTARY
1966.
[7] leaves; 2 leaves 25 cm., 5 leaves 28 cm.
In part holograph.
Poem.
On leaf [1] and verso:holograph draft of stanzas 2-3 with revisions.
On leaves [2-6]:4 typescript drafts with revisions; 1 carbon copy; leaf [3] titled "For Gerald Cooper."
On leaf [7]:typescript draft titled "Reply to a versifying notary"; 6 questions on theme and style of poem.
At bottom of leaf [6]:holograph note dated March 1, 1966; marginalia.
Published with further revisions in: Periods of the moon/Irving Layton. Toronto: McClelland and Stewart, 1967.

POM 7/1
WESTMINSTER ABBEY
[1966].
[3] leaves; 28 cm.
Typescript with holograph revisions.
Poem.
Sketch of clasped hands on verso of leaf [2].
Published with further revisions in: Periods of the moon/Irving Layton. Toronto, Ont.: McClelland and Stewart, 1967, (also in CP71, DF, SEL).

POM 8/1
COLLABORATION; NO EXIT
[1967].
[1] bag; 13 cm. x 29 cm.
Holograph.
Two poems.
Holograph draft of "Collaboration" on back of airline motion-sickness bag.
On front of bag:draft of four line poem titled "No exit."
"Collaboration" published in: Periods of the moon/Irving Layton. Toronto: McClelland and Stewart, 1971, (also in CP71).
"No exit" not published to date.

POM 9/1
AT THE BELSEN MEMORIAL; QUAY SCENE
[1966].
[2]p.; 28 cm.
Holograph.
Two poems.
On p.[1]:draft with revisions of "At the Belsen Memorial" on lined loose leaf paper.
On p.[2]:draft with revisions of "Quay scene."
"At the Belsen Memorial" published with further revisions in: Periods of the moon/Irving Layton. Toronto: McClelland and Stewart, 1967.
"Quay scene," ibid.

PV - The Pole-vaulter

PV 1/1
FOR NADEZHDA MANDELSTAM
1973.
[7] leaves; 28 cm.
In part holograph.
Poem.
On leaf [1]:holograph draft of stanzas [3-6].
On leaves [2-7]:1 holograph and 4 typescript drafts with revisions.
Drafts 1-6 numbered.
Dated January 15, 1973.
Published with revisions in: The pole-vaulter/Irving Layton. Toronto: McClelland and Stewart, 1974.

PV 1/2
FOR NADEZHDA MANDELSTAM
[1973].
[1] leaf; 28 cm.
Typescript.
Poem.
Draft with revisions.
Typescript signature.
Holograph title on verso.
Published in: The pole-vaulter/Irving Layton. Toronto: McClelland and Stewart, 1974.

PV 2/1
ADAM AND EVE
[1973].
[2] leaves; 30 cm.
Typescript.
Poem.
On leaf [1]:draft of lines 1-15.
On leaf [2]:draft of lines 1-14.
Holograph title on verso of leaf [2].
Published with revisions in: The pole-vaulter/Irving Layton. Toronto: McClelland and Stewart, 1974.

PV 3/1
AMERICAN YOUNG WOMAN IN PATMOS
[1973].
[2] leaves; 28 cm.
Typescript.
Poem.
Two drafts with revisions.
Published with further revisions in: The pole-vaulter/Irving Layton. Toronto: McClelland and Stewart, 1974, (also in GP).

PV 4/1
THE ANIMAL ACROSS THE STREET
[1973].
[5] leaves; 28 cm.
Typescript.
Poem.
Five drafts with revisions.
Typescript signature on leaves [1,4-5].
Published with further revisions in: The pole-vaulter/Irving Layton. Toronto: McClelland and Stewart, 1974.

PV 5/1
ASIAN SUITE
[1973].
[2]p., [2] leaves; 28 cm.
Chiefly holograph.
Poem.
On leaf [1]:typescript draft with holograph revisions and reworking of stanza 5.
On leaf [2] and p.[1]:2 holograph drafts.

...con't

PV 5/1...con't

On p.[2]:typescript draft with holograph revisions.
Published with further revisions in: The pole-vaulter/Irving Layton. Toronto: McClelland and Stewart, 1974.

PV 6/1
AUSTRALIAN BUSH
1974.
[6] leaves; 25 cm.
In part holograph signed.
Poem.
On leaves [1-6]:1 holograph, 3 typescript drafts with revisions.
Dated Woodford, New South Wales, February 10, 1974.
Published with further revisions in: The pole-vaulter/Irving Layton. Toronto: McClelland and Stewart, 1974, (also in UE).

PV 7/1
THE BASIN
[1973].
[5] leaves; 28 cm.
Typescript with holograph revisions.
Poem.
On leaves [1-5]:5 drafts of 33 lines.
On verso of leaf [2]:draft of lines 1-8.
Drafts 1-4 numbered.
Holograph title on verso of leaves [3-4].
Published with revisions in: The pole-vaulter/Irving Layton. Toronto: McClelland and Stewart, 1974, (also in GP).

PV 7/2
THE BASIN
[1973].
[1] leaf; 28 cm.
Typescript.
Poem.
Published with revisions in: The pole-vaulter/Irving Layton. Toronto: McClelland and Stewart, 1974, (also in GP).

PV 8/1
BEDBUGS AND OTHER VERMIN
1973.
[6] leaves; 1 leaf 28 cm., 5 leaves 30 cm.
In part holograph.
Poem.
On leaves [1-6]:2 holograph, 4 typescript drafts with revisions; marginalia on leaf [4].
At bottom of leaves [1-2] and on verso:typescript fragment beginning "He thought for a diversion or relief...."
On verso of leaves [3,6]:typescript draft of stanzas [3-6].
Leaves [3-5] titled "Red bed bugs and other vermin."
Dated Molibos, September 6, 1973.
Published with revisions as "[Bedbugs]."
Published in: The pole-vaulter/Irving Layton. Toronto: McClelland and Stewart, 1974.

PV 9/1
POET ON COS
[1973].
[2] leaves; 28 cm.
Typescript with holograph revisions.
Poem.
Two drafts with revisions.
Published with further revisions in: The pole-vaulter/Irving Layton. Toronto: McClelland and Stewart, 1974, (also in GP).

PV 10/1
DEPARTED
[1973].
[2] leaves; 1 leaf 28 cm., 1 leaf 30 cm.
Typescript with holograph corrections.
Poem.
Two drafts.
On verso of leaf [1]:first three words of line 1.
Published in: The pole-vaulter/Irving Layton. Toronto: McClelland and Stewart, 1974, (also in UE).

PV 11/1
DISPLACED PERSON
[1973].
[13] leaves; 28 cm.
Typescript with holograph revisions.
Poem.
On leaf [1]:draft of 7 stanzas.
On verso of leaf [1]:holograph draft of stanza 8.
On leaves [2-3]:2 drafts of 8 stanzas.
Leaf [4] blank.
On leaves [5-10]:6 drafts of 7 stanzas.
On leaves [11-12]:2 drafts of 5 stanzas.
On leaf [13]:draft of 6 stanzas with reworking of stanza 1.
On verso of leaf [13]:draft of stanza [1].
Published with further revisions in: The pole-vaulter/Irving Layton. Toronto: McClelland and Stewart, 1974, (also in FMBJ).

PV 12/1
BODHIDHARMA
1973.
[4] leaves; 2 leaves 9 cm. x 18 cm., 1 leaf 17 cm., 1 leaf 21 cm.
Holograph.
Poem.
Four drafts with revisions.
Leaves [1-2] on verso of passenger ticket booklet from Thai International [Airlines].
Leaf [2] dated Airport, Quala Lumpur, December 8, 1973.
Leaf [3] dated Singapore, December 8, 1973.
Leaf [4] dated Bali, December 10, 1973.
Published in: The pole-vaulter/Irving Layton. Toronto. McClelland and Stewart, 1974, (also in UE).

PV 13/1
BUDAPEST; [LURES]
1973.
[2]p., [15] leaves; 30 cm.
Typescript with holograph revisions.
Poem.
On leaf [1]:draft of lines 1-39 of "Budapest."
On leaves [2-13]:6 drafts of "Budapest."
On leaves [14-15] and p.[1]:3 fragments of "Budapest" beginning "This poet's colours...."

...con't

PV 13/1...con't

On p.[2]:draft of "[Lures]."
Typescript signature on leaf [11].
Dated Budapest, July 15, 1973.
Holograph title "Budapest" on verso of leaves [1,3,7,9,13-15].
"Budapest" published with further revisions in: The pole-vaulter/Irving Layton. Toronto: McClelland and Stewart, 1974.
"[Lures]," ibid.

PV 14/1
THE COASTAL MIND
1974.
[3] leaves; 26 cm.
Holograph.
Poem.
Three drafts with revisions; dated March 3, 1974.
Published with further revisions in: The pole-vaulter/Irving Layton. Toronto: McClelland and Stewart, 1974, (also in UE).

PV 14/2
[THE COASTAL MIND]
1974.
[8]p. on 2 leaves; 28 cm. folded to 25 cm.
Holograph.
Poem.
On p.[1-2]:draft with revisions and reworking of last 21 lines.
On p.[3-4]:draft.
On p.[5-8]:2 drafts with revisions.
Dated March 2, 1974.
Published with further revisions in: The pole-vaulter/Irving Layton. Toronto: McClelland and Stewart, 1974, (also in UE).

PV 14/3
THE COASTAL MIND
1974.
[6] leaves; 4 leaves 26 cm., 2 leaves 33 cm.
In part holograph.
Poem.
On leaves [1,3]:2 holograph drafts with revisions; numbered 7-8.
Leaf [2] blank.
On leaves [4-5]:2 typescript drafts.

...con't

PV 14/3...con't

On leaf [6]:typescript draft with revisions; note to publisher at bottom of page; list of four titles of poems by [Irving Layton] in upper right corner.
Published with further revisions in: The pole-vaulter/ Irving Layton. Toronto: McClelland and Stewart, 1974, (also in UE).

PV 14/4
THE COASTAL MIND
1974.
[1] leaf; 33 cm.
Typescript.
Poem.
Yellow stained leaf, folded in four.
Typescript signature.
Marginalia on verso.
Published in: The pole-vaulter/Irving Layton. Toronto: McClelland and Stewart, 1974, (also in UE).

PV 15/1
THE FINAL SOLUTION
[1973].
[2] leaves; 30 cm.
Typescript with holograph revisions.
Poem.
Typescript signature on leaf [2].
Holograph title on verso of leaves [1-2].
Published with further revisions in: The pole-vaulter/Irving Layton. Toronto: McClelland and Stewart, 1974, (also in UE).

PV 16/1
FOR ANDREI AMALRIK
[1973].
[8] leaves; 6 leaves 28 cm., 2 leaves 30 cm.
In part holograph.
Poem.
On leaf [1]:typescript draft of 35 lines.
On leaf [2]:holograph draft of stanzas 1-2 and 3 lines of stanza 3.
On leaves [3-4]:2 holograph drafts with revisions.
On leaf [5]:typescript draft.
On leaf [6]:typescript draft with revisions.
Leaf [7] blank.

...con't

PV 16/1...con't
On leaf [8]:typescript draft with revisions.
Drafts 1-6 numbered.
Holograph title on verso of leaf [1].
Published with further revisions in: The pole-vaulter/Irving Layton. Toronto: McClelland and Stewart, 1974, (also in UE).

PV 17/1
FOR ANNE FRANK
[1973].
1 bag; 31 cm.
Holograph.
Poem.
Draft of "For Anne Frank" pt.II written on back of paper bag.
Ms. address [?] covering part of text.
Published with revisions in: The pole-vaulter/Irving Layton. Toronto: McClelland and Stewart, 1974.

PV 17/2
FOR ANNE FRANK
1973.
[3] leaves; 30 cm.
Typescript with holograph revisions.
Poem.
Three drafts with typescript signature.
Dated Vienna, July 11, 1973.
Published with further revisions in: The pole-vaulter/Irving Layton. Toronto: McClelland and Stewart, 1974.

PV 18/1
FOR A YOUNG POET WHO HANGED HIMSELF
[1973].
[2]p., [1] leaf; 28 cm.
Chiefly holograph.
Poem.
On p.[1]:holograph draft with revisions and reworking of stanzas 2-4.
On p.[2]:typescript draft with reworking of stanzas 3-4.
On leaf [1]:holograph draft.
Published in: The pole-vaulter/Irving Layton. Toronto: McClelland and Stewart, 1974.

PV 18/2
TO A YOUNG POET WHO HANGED HIMSELF
[1973].
[4] leaves; 1 leaf 28 cm., 3 leaves 30 cm.
Typescript.
Poem.
Four drafts with revisions.
On verso of leaf [3]:draft of line 1.
On verso of leaf [4]:draft of lines 1-2 crossed out.
Leaves [1,3-4] titled "For John Berryman."
"To a young poet who hanged himself" published with further revisions as "[For a young poet who hanged himself]."
Published in: The pole-vaulter/Irving Layton. Toronto: McClelland and Stewart, 1974.

PV 19/1
FOR THE FRAULEIN FROM HAMBURG; [PROTEUS AND NYMPH]
[1973].
[6] leaves; 30 cm.
Typescript with holograph revisions.
Two poems.
On leaf [1]:draft of 6 stanzas of "For the fraulein from Hamburg" with reworking of stanza 4.
On verso of leaf [1]:draft of lines 1-4 of "[Proteus and nymph]."
On leaf [2]:draft of 5 stanzas of "For the fraulein from Hamburg" with reworking of stanza 4.
On leaves [3-5]:3 drafts of 6 stanzas of "For the fraulein from Hamburg" with revisions; leaf [3] titled "For the woman from Hamburg."
On leaf [6]:draft of 6 stanzas of "For the fraulein from Hamburg"with reworking of stanza 6.
"For the fraulein from Hamburg" published with further revisions in: The pole-vaulter/Irving Layton. Toronto: McClelland and Stewart, 1974, (also in UE).
"[Proteus and nymph]," ibid., (also in GP, UE, LPIL1, LPIL2, WPJ, DD).

PV 19/2
FOR THE FRAULEIN FROM HAMBURG
[1973].
[3] leaves; 30 cm.
Typescript with holograph revisions.
Poem.
On leaf [1]:draft of 7 stanzas with reworking of stanzas 1-4.

...con't

PV 19/2...con't

On leaf [2]:draft of 5 stanzas with stanza 3 crossed out and reworking of stanza 4.
On leaf [3]:draft of 4 stanzas with revisions.
Published in: The pole-vaulter/Irving Layton. Toronto: McClelland and Stewart, 1974, (also in UE).

PV 20/1
GANNYMEDE; [THE FINAL SOLUTION]
[1973].
[1] leaf; 30 cm.
Typescript with holograph revisions.
Two poems.
Draft of "Gannymede"; fragment "Its all" at bottom of page.
On verso:draft of lines 1-3 of "[The final solution]"; holograph title.
"Gannymede" published in: The pole-vaulter/Irving Layton. Toronto: McClelland and Stewart, 1974, (also in GP, UE).
"[The final solution]," ibid., (also in UE).

PV 21/1
GREEK EPIGRAM; A TAILOR'S VIEW OF HISTORY
[1973].
[2]p., [1] leaf; 30 cm.
Typescript.
Two poems.
On p.[1] and leaf [1]:3 drafts of "Greek epigram."
On p.[2]:draft of "A tailor's view of history."
Holograph title "Greek Epigram" on p.[1] and verso of p.[2].
"Greek epigram" published in: The pole-vaulter/Irving Layton. Toronto: McClelland and Stewart, 1974, (also in GP).
"A tailor's view of history," ibid., (with revisions).

PV 22/1
GREEK FLY
[1973].
[2] leaves; 28 cm.
Typescript with holograph revisions.
Poem.
Dated Molibos, Lesbos, August 6, 1[9]73.
Published with further revisions in: The pole-vaulter/Irving Layton. Toronto: McClelland and Stewart, 1974, (also in GP, UE).

PV 23/1
HIT PARADE
[1973].
[1] leaf; 30 cm.
Typescript with holograph revisions.
Poem.
Holograph title on verso.
Published in: The pole-vaulter/Irving Layton. Toronto: McClelland and Stewart, 1974.

PV 24/1
HONEYMOON; [MARY]; CHILEAN CHILL
[1973].
[2]p.; 28 cm.
In part holograph.
Three poems.
On p.[1]:typescript draft of 7 lines of "Honeymoon"; holograph draft of stanzas 1-3 of "Chilean chill."
On p.[2]:holograph draft of stanzas 1-3 of "Chilean chill; typescript of stanzas 1-3 of "[Mary]."
"Chilean chill" published as "[Poetry and the class war]."
"Honeymoon" published in: The pole-vaulter/Irving Layton. Toronto: McClelland and Stewart, 1974.
["Mary]," ibid., (with revisions).
"[Poetry and the class war]," ibid., (with revisions).

PV 25/1
THE IDEAL AMONG VACATIONERS
[1973].
[2]p.; 25 cm.
Holograph.
Poem.
Draft with revisions.
Two fragments beginning "If you want to find innocence and grace..." at bottom of p.[1] and on p.[2].
Published with further revisions as "[The ideal among vacationists]."
Published in: The pole-vaulter/Irving Layton. Toronto: McClelland and Stewart, 1974, (also in GP, UE).

PV 25/2
THE IDEAL AMONG VACATIONERS
1973.
[5] leaves; 3 leaves 28 cm., 2 leaves 30 cm.
In part holograph.
Poem.
Two holograph, 3 typescript drafts with revisions.
"Plato in Molibos 1973" at bottom of leaf [3].
Dated Molibos, September 11, 1973.
Published with further revisions as "[The ideal among vacationists]."
Published in: The pole-vaulter/Irving Layton. Toronto: McClelland and Stewart, 1974, (also in GP, UE).

PV 26/1
JIJIMUGE
[1973].
[2] leaves; 29 cm.
Typescript.
Poem.
Two drafts.
Published in: The pole-vaulter/Irving Layton. Toronto: McClelland and Stewart, 1974.

PV 27/1
LILLIAN ROXON
[1973].
[7] leaves; 4 leaves 28 cm., 3 leaves 30 cm.
In part holograph.
Poem.
On leaf [1]:2 holograph drafts of stanzas 1-2.
On leaves [2-7]:2 holograph, 4 typescript drafts with revisions.
On verso of leaf [7]:typescript of line 1 Drafts 1-2 numbered.
Published with further revisions in: The pole-vaulter/Irving Layton. Toronto: McClelland and Stewart, 1974, (also in PIL, UE).

PV 28/1
LULLABY
[1973].
[3] leaves; 30 cm.
Typescript.
Poem.
Three drafts.

...con't

PV 28/1...con't

Leaf [2] titled "Blue Danube."
Holograph title on verso of leaf [2].
Published with revisions in: The pole-vaulter/Irving Layton. Toronto: McClelland and Stewart, 1974.

PV 29/1
MADONNA AND DIONYSOS
[1973].
[6] leaves; 30 cm.
Typescript with holograph revisions.
Poem.
Six drafts.
On verso of leaves [3-4,6]:3 partial drafts.
Published in: The pole-vaulter/Irving Layton. Toronto: McClelland and Stewart, 1974, (also in GP).

PV 30/1
MARRIAGE
[1973].
[1] leaf; 30 cm.
Typescript with holograph revisions.
Poem.
Published in: The pole-vaulter/Irving Layton. Toronto: McClelland and Stewart, 1974, (also in UE).

PV 31/1
MARY
[1973].
[3] leaves; 28 cm.
Typescript with holograph revisions.
Poem.
On leaf [1]:draft with reworking of stanza 3.
On leaves [2-3]:two drafts with revisions.
Published with further revisions in: The pole-vaulter/Irving Layton. Toronto: McClelland and Stewart, 1974.

PV 32/1
A MIDSUMMER'S DREAM IN THE VIENNA STADPARK; [THE FINAL SOLUTION]
1973.
[4] leaves; 28cm.

...con't

PV 32/1...con't

Typescript with holograph revisions.
Two poems.
On leaves [1-4]:4 drafts of "A midsummer's dream in the Vienna Stadpark" with reworking of stanzas 4-5.
Leaves [1-3] titled "A midsummer's dream in the Vienna Woods."
On verso of leaf [1]:lines 1-6 of "[The final solution]."
"A midsummer's dream in the Vienna Stadpark" dated July 13, 1973.
Holograph title "A midsummer's dream in the Vienna Stadpark" on verso of leaves [1,3-4].
"A midsummer's dream in the Vienna Stadpark" published in: The pole-vaulter/Irving Layton. Toronto: McClelland and Stewart, 1974, (also in UE, WPJ).
"[The final solution]," ibid., (also in UE).

PV 33/1
MY FAIR LADY FROM BREMEN
[1973].
[3] leaves; 30 cm.
Typescript.
Poem.
Three drafts.
Published with revisions in: The pole-vaulter/Irving Layton. Toronto: McClelland and Stewart, 1974.

PV 34/1
MITHYMNA CEMETERY
1973.
[2]p.; 19 cm.
In part holograph.
Poem.
Draft with revisions on "Acknowledgements" page torn from unidentified monograph.
Dated Molibos, September 5, 1973.
Published with further revisions in: The pole-vaulter/Irving Layton. Toronto: McClelland and Stewart, 1974, (also in GP, UE).

PV 34/2
MITHYMNA CEMETERY
1973.
[3] leaves; 1 leaf 28 cm., 2 leaves 30 cm.

...con't

PV 34/2...con't
Typescript with holograph revisions.
Poem.
On leaves [1-2]:2 drafts with reworking of stanza 3; lines 1-3 repeated at bottom of leaf [1].
At bottom of leaf [1]:lines 1-3 .
On leaf [3]:draft with revisions.
Dated Mithymna, Lesbos, September 5, 1973.
Published with further revisions in: The pole-vaulter/Irving Layton. Toronto: McClelland and Stewart, 1974, (also in GP, UE).

PV 35/1
POET'S BUST; [REVOLUTION]
[1973].
[4]p., [4] leaves; 4 leaves 28 cm., 2 leaves 30 cm.
Chiefly holograph.
Two poems.
On leaves [1-4] and p.[1-3]:7 holograph, 4 typescript drafts with revisions of "Poet's bust."
At bottom of p.[2]:4 drafts with revisions of "[Revolution]."
On p.[4]:typescript draft of 2 paragraphs of an essay on subject of female book reviewers, dated Molibos, Lesbos, Sept. 8, 1973.
"Poet's bust" published with further revisions in: The pole- vaulter/Irving Layton. Toronto: McClelland and Stewart, 1974, (also in UE).
"[Revolution]," ibid., (with revisions).

PV 36/1
POETRY AND THE CLASS WAR
[1973].
[2]p., [3] leaves; 28 cm.
In part holograph.
Poem.
On p.[1]:2 holograph drafts with revisions of stanzas 1-3 titled "Culture and the class war."
On p.[2]:holograph draft with revisions titled "The class war."
On leaves [1-2]:2 typescript drafts with revisions of stanzas 1-5 titled "The class war."
On leaf [3]:holograph draft with revisions.
Published in: The pole-vaulter/Irving Layton. Toronto: McClelland and Stewart, 1976.

...con't

PV 37/1
PROTEUS AND NYMPH
[1973].
[5] leaves; 1 leaf 28 cm., 4 leaves 30 cm.
In part holograph.
Poem.
On leaves [1-3]:1 holograph, 2 typescript drafts with revisions.
On verso of leaf [1]:personal letter to [Irving Layton ?].
On verso of leaf [3]:typescript of lines 1-5 crossed out.
On leaf [4]:typescript draft with revisions and reworking of stanza 2.
On verso of leaf [4]:2 holograph drafts of stanza 2 with revisions.
On leaf [5]:typescript draft with revisions.
Leaves [2-5] titled "Satyr and nymph."
Published in: The pole-vaulter/Irving Layton. Toronto: McClelland and Stewart, 1974, (also in GP, UE, LPIL1, LPIL2, WPJ, DD).

PV 38/1
POSTCARD; ADAM AND EVE
[1973].
[5] leaves; 30 cm.
Typescript with holograph revisions.
Two poems.
On leaf [1]:drafts of stanza 1-3 of "Postcard" with reworking of stanza 3; draft of "Adam and Eve."
On leaves [2-5]:4 drafts with revisions of "Postcard."
On verso of leaves [2-3]:fragment beginning "In Venice when...."
Drafts 1-4 numbered.
Holograph title "Postcard" on verso of leaf [4].
"Postcard" published with further revisions in: The pole-vaulter/Irving Layton. Toronto: McClelland & Stewart, 1974, (also in UE).
"Adam and Eve," ibid.

PV 39/1
THE POLE-VAULTER
[1973].
[7] leaves; 1 leaf 28 cm., 6 leaves 30 cm.
Typescript with holograph revisions.
Poem.
Seven drafts.
Leaves [1-2,4] titled "Sorrows of a Canadian priapus"; marginalia on leaf [4].
Holograph title "Sorrows of a Canadian priapus" on verso of leaves [1-2].

...con't

PV 39/1...con't

Holograph title "The pole vaulter" on verso of leaves [2-4].
Fragment "the animals" on verso of leaf [1].
Published with further revisions as "[Pole-vaulter]".
Published in: The pole-vaulter/Irving Layton. Toronto: McClelland and Stewart, 1974, (also in PIL, UE).

PV 40/1
REQUIEM FOR A.M. KLEIN; [FOR A YOUNG POET WHO HANGED HIMSELF]
[1973].
[8]leaves; 28 cm.
Chiefly holograph.
Two poems.
On leaf [1]:holograph draft of 5 stanzas with revisions; stanzas 1-3 used in "[For a young poet who hanged himself]."
On leaf [2]:holograph draft of stanzas 1-3,8 of "Requiem for A.M. Klein" with revisions and reworking of stanza 5.
On leaf [3]:holograph draft of stanzas 1-5 of "Requiem for A.M. Klein" with revisions and reworking of stanza 5.
On leaves [4-6]:2 holograph drafts, 1 typescript draft of stanzas 1-7 of "Requiem for A.M. Klein" with revisions.
On leaves [7-8]:2 typescript drafts of "Requiem for A.M. Klein" with revisions.
Holograph title on verso of leaf [8].
"Requiem for A.M. Klein" published in: The pole-vaulter/Irving Layton. Toronto: McClelland and Stewart, 1974, (also in UE).
"[For a young poet who hanged himself]," ibid.

PV 41/1
SEPTEMBER WOMAN
[1973].
[3] leaves; 2 leaves 30 cm., 1 leaf 28 cm.
Typescript.
Poem.
On leaf [1]:draft of 7 stanzas with revisions and reworking of stanza 5; leaf repaired with scotch tape.
On leaf [2]:draft of 8 stanzas.
On leaf [3]:draft with revisions.
Published with further revisions in: The pole-vaulter/Irving Layton. Toronto: McClelland and Stewart, 1974, (also in DD).

PV 42/1
THE SHADOW
1973.
[6] leaves; 4 leaves 28 cm., 2 leaves 30 cm.
Typescript.
Poem.
Three drafts with revisions.
On verso of leaf [6]:5 lines beginning "The warm summery evening..." crossed out.
Holograph title on verso of leaves [2,4].
Dated Vienna, July 10, 1973.
Published with further revisions in: The pole-vaulter/Irving Layton. Toronto: McClelland and Stewart, 1974, (also in UE).

PV 43/1
TO THE WOMAN WITH THE SPEAKING EYES
[1973].
[2] leaves; 30 cm.
Typescript with holograph revisions.
Poem.
Two drafts.
Published with further revisions in: The pole-vaulter/Irving Layton. Toronto: McClelland and Stewart, 1974, (also in UE, DD).

PV 44/1
WHAT I TOLD THE GHOST OF HAROLD LASKI
[1973].
[3] leaves; 30 cm.
Typescript with holograph revisions.
Poem.
On leaf [1]:draft with revisions of stanzas 1-4 and lines 1-6 of stanza 5.
On leaves [2-3]:2 drafts of stanzas 5-7.
Published with further revisions in: The pole-vaulter/Irving Layton. Toronto: McClelland and Stewart, 1974, (also in UE).

PV 45/1
FOR THE YOUNG COUPLE AT LUM FONG HOTEL; REVOLUTION
1973.
[8] p., [8] leaves; 28 cm.
Chiefly holograph.
Two poems.
On p.[1,3-8] and leaves [1-8]:8 holograph, 9 typescript drafts with revisions and

...con't

PV 39/1...con't

reworking of "For the young couple at Lum Fong Hotel"; marginalia on verso of leaf [1].
On p.[2]:typescript draft of "Revolution."
Drafts of "For the young couple at Lum Fong Hotel" numbered 1-15.
"For the young couple at Lum Fong Hotel" dated Penang, December 6, 1973.
"For the young couple at Lum Fong Hotel" published with further revisions as "[Young couple at Lum Fong Hotel]."
"[Young couple at Lum Fong Hotel]" published in: The pole- vaulter/Irving Layton. Toronto: McClelland & Stewart, 1974, (also in UE, DD).
"Revolution," ibid.

PV 46/1
GROUND FOR DIVORCE
[1973].
[2] leaves; 30 cm.
Typescript.
Poem.
Two drafts with revisions.
On verso of leaf [2]:typescript draft of lines 1-2.
Published with further revisions as "[The solitary]."
Published in: The pole-vaulter/Irving Layton. Toronto: McClelland and Stewart, 1974.

PV 47/1
THE THREE SISTERS; [FOR NADEZHDA MANDELSTAM]
1974.
[12] leaves; 1 leaf 19 cm., 11 leaves 26 cm.
In part holograph.
Two poems.
On leaves [1-5]:2 holograph, 3 typescript drafts with revisions of "The three sisters."
On verso of leaf [2]:typescript draft of lines 1-4 of "[For Nadezhda Mandelstam]."
On leaf [6]:typescript draft with revisions and reworking of stanza 1 of "The three sisters."
On leaf [7]:2 typescript drafts with reworking of stanzas 1,3 of "The three sisters."
On leaf [8]:typescript draft with revisions of "The three sisters."
On leaf [9]:typescript draft of "The three sisters."
On leaf [10]:3 typescript drafts of stanza 1 of "The three sisters."
On leaves [11-12]:2 typescript drafts with revisions of "The three sisters."
Dated Katoomba, New South Wales, February 10, 1974.

...con't

PV 47/1...con't

"The three sisters" published with further revisions in: The pole-vaulter/Irving Layton. Toronto: McClelland and Stewart, 1974.
"[For Nadezhda Mandelstam]," ibid.

PV 48/1
TERRORISTS
[1973].
[1] leaf; 30 cm.
Typescript.
Poem.
Published with revisions in: The pole-vaulter/Irving Layton. Toronto: McClelland and Stewart, 1974, (also in UE).

PV 49/1
A TAILOR'S VIEW OF HISTORY
[1973].
[4]p., [3] leaves; 30 cm.
Typescript.
Poem.
On p.[1]:draft with reworking of stanzas 1-2.
On p.[2-4] and leaf [1]:4 drafts.
On leaf [2]:draft with reworking of stanzas 5-6.
On leaf [3]:draft with revisions.
Holograph title on verso of leaves [2-3].
Published with further revisions in: The pole-vaulter/Irving Layton. Toronto: McClelland and Stewart, 1974.

PV 50/1
RELIGIOUS POET; [THE IDEAL AMONG VACATIONISTS]
[1973].
[2] leaves; 30 cm.
Chiefly holograph.
Two poems.
On leaf [1]:2 holograph drafts with revisions of "Religious poet."
On verso of leaf [1]:typescript draft of lines 1-4 of "[The ideal among vacationists]."
On leaf [2]:typescript draft with revisions of "Religious poet."
"Religious poet" published with further revisions as "[Religious poet 1973 AD]."
"[Religious poet 1973 AD]" published in: The pole-vaulter/ Irving Layton. Toronto: McClelland and Stewart, 1974.
"[The ideal among vacationists]," ibid., (also in GP, UE).

PV 51/1
THE BLACK QUEEN; [LINES FOR MY GRANDCHILDREN]; ALCAEUS REFLECTS ON A CHANCE ENCOUNTER
[1973].
[4]p., [8] leaves; 28 cm.
Typescript with holograph revisions.
Three poems.
On p.[1,3] and leaves [1-8]:10 drafts with revisions of "The black queen."
On p.[2]:lines 1-15 of "[Lines for my grandchildren]."
On p.[4]:lines 1-13 of "Alcaeus reflects on a chance encounter."
"The black queen" published with further revisions in: The pole-vaulter/Irving Layton. Toronto: McClelland and Stewart, 1974. (also in UE).
[Lines for my grandchildren]," ibid.
"Alcaeus reflects on a chance encounter" not published to date.

SF - The Swinging Flesh

SF 1/1
THE CAGED BIRD
[1960].
[6]p.; 28 cm.
Chiefly holograph.
Poem.
On p.[1-2]:holograph draft with revisions titled "The Wolfgang Russ."
On p.[3,5,]:typescript draft with revisions.
On p.[4,6]:holograph draft with revisions titled "Gulls and the caged bird."
Published in: The swinging flesh/Irving Layton. Toronto: McClelland and Stewart, 1961, (also in CP65, CP71, DF).

SF 2/1
THE BLACK MOTHS
[1960].
[3]p. on 1 leaf; 28 cm.
Holograph.
Poem.
On p.[1]:draft with revisions of stanzas 1-6.
On p.[2]:2 drafts of stanza beginning "I with my third love shall now ascend...."
On p.[3]:3 drafts of stanza 4; one draft of stanza 5.
Published with further revisions as "[I know the dark and hovering moth]."
Published in: The swinging flesh/Irving Layton. Toronto: McClelland and Stewart, 1961, (also in CP65, CP71, DF, SEL).

SF 2/2
[I KNOW THE DARK AND HOVERING MOTH]
[1960].
[3]p. on 1 leaf; 28 cm.
Holograph.
Poem.
On p.[1-2]:2 drafts of stanzas 1-4.
On p.[3]:4 stanzas of 4 lines with revisions on theme of black moths.
Published with further revisions in: The swinging flesh/Irving Layton. Toronto: McClelland and Stewart, 1961, (also in CP65, CP71, DF, SEL, LPIL1, LPIL2).

SF 3/1
KEINE LAZAROVITCH 1870-1959
[1960].
[14] leaves; 28 cm.
Holograph.
Poem.
On leaf [1]:8 lines beginning "My mother had black eyebrows."
On leaves [2-11,13-14]:12 drafts with revisions; marginalia on leaf [3].
On leaf [12]:2 drafts of stanza 2.
Leaf [7] titled "Klara Lazarovitch 1870-1959."
Accompanied by 24 cm. x 10 cm. envelope with "Drafts of Keine Lazarovitch 1870-1959" on front panel.
Published with further revisions in: The swinging flesh/Irving Layton. Toronto: McClelland and Stewart, 1961, (also in CP65, CP71, DF, PIL, SEL, WPJ).

SP - The Shattered Plinths

SP 1/1
FANTASIA IN BLACK; THE WAY KEATS WOULD NOT HAVE TOLD IT; AFTER AUSCHWITZ
[1967].
[12]p., [8] leaves; 28 cm.
In part holograph.
Three poems.
On p.[1,3,5,7,9,11] and leaves [1-8]:five holograph and 9 typescript drafts with revisions of "Fantasia in black"; drafts numbered 1-13.
On p.[2,4,8]:3 typescript drafts with revisions of "The way Keats would not have told it."
On p.[6]:typescript draft of lines 1-4 of "The way Keats would not have told it."
On p.[10]:typescript fragment beginning "An elderly poetic statesman...."

...con't

SP 1/1...con't

On p.[12]:typescript draft with revisions of "After Auschwitz."
Holograph title "Fantasia in black" on verso of leaf [8].
"The way Keats would not have told it" published with further revisions as "[The way Keats never would have told it]."
"Fantasia in black" published in: The shattered plinths/Irving Layton. Toronto: McClelland and Stewart, 1968, (also in CP71).
"[The way Keats never would have told it]," ibid."
"After Auschwitz" published with revisions in: The whole bloody bird/Irving Layton. Toronto: McClelland and Stewart, 1969, (also in CP71, UE, WPJ).

SP 2/1
FOR A GIRL WITH WIDE APART EYES
[1967].
[1] leaf; 28 cm.
Typescript with holograph revision.
Poem.
Published as "For the girl with wide apart eyes."
Published with revisions in: The shattered plinths/Irving Layton. Toronto: McClelland and Stewart, 1968, (also in LPIL1, LPIL2).

SP 2/2
FOR A GIRL WITH WIDE APART EYES
[1967].
[1] leaf; 28 cm.
Typescript.
Poem.
Published as "For the girl with wide apart eyes."
Published with revisions in: The shattered plinths/Irving Layton. Toronto: McClelland and Stewart, 1968, (also in LPIL1, LPIL2).

SP 2/3
FOR A GIRL WITH WIDE APART EYES
[1967].
[1] leaf; 28 cm.
Typescript.
Poem.
Published as "For the girl with wide apart eyes."
Published with revisions in: The shattered plinths/Irving Layton. Toronto: McClelland and Stewart, 1968, (also in LPIL1, LPIL2).

SP 3/1
ART; AN ODD LOVE POEM; ON THIS FAR SHORE
[1967].
[7]p. on 3 leaves; 28 cm.
Chiefly holograph.
Three poems.
On p.[1,4,6]:2 holograph drafts, 1 typescript draft of "Art."
On p.[2,7]:1 holograph draft and 1 typescript draft of "An odd love poem"; leaf [7] titled "A twist of lemon."
On p.[3]:typescript draft of "On this far shore."
Also on p.[4]:typescript draft of lines 1-7 of "An odd love poem."
On p.[5]:typescript draft of lines 1-10 of "An odd love poem."
Holograph title "The graveyard" on verso of leaf [7].
"Art" published with revisions as "[The graveyard]."
"An odd love poem" published with revisions as "[Love poem with an odd twist]."
"[The graveyard]" published in: The shattered plinths/Irving Layton. Toronto: McClelland and Stewart, 1968, (also in CP71, DF, SEL, WPJ).
"[Love poem with an odd twist]," ibid., (also in CP71, SEL, LPIL1, LPIL2).
"On this far shore," ibid., (with revisions), (also in CP71).

SP 4/1
IROQUOIS IN NICE
[1967].
[7] leaves; 28 cm.
In part holograph.
Poem.
On leaves [1-5]:2 holograph, 1 typescript draft with revisions; marginalia on leaf [3].
On leaves [6-7]:2 typescript drafts of 17 lines beginning "It was his irony that mainly puzzled me...."
Holograph title "Iroquois in Nice" on verso of leaf [7].
Title on leaf [4] "Stranger in paradise."
Published with further revisions in: The shattered plinths/ Irving Layton. Toronto: McClelland and Stewart, 1968, (also WPJ).

SP 5/1
[LIKE A MOTHER DEMENTED]; POET AT SINAI
[1967].
[2]p.; 28 cm.
Chiefly holograph.
Two poems.

...con't

SP 5/1...con't

On p.[1]:typescript draft of "Poet at Sinai."
On p.[2]:holograph draft of "[Like a mother demented]."
"[Like a mother demented]" published with revisions in: The shattered plinths/Irving Layton. Toronto: McClelland and Stewart, 1968, (also in CP71, DF, SEL, WPJ).
"Poet at Sinai," ibid., (with revisions), (also in CP71).

SP 5/2
LIKE A MOTHER DEMENTED; [MODERN GREEK POET]
[1967].
[2]p.; 28 cm.
Chiefly holograph.
Two poems.
On p.[1]:holograph draft of stanzas 1-4,6 of "Like a mother demented."
On p.[2]:typescript draft of stanzas 1-2 of "[Modern Greek poet]"; holograph draft of stanza 7 of "Like a mother demented."
"Like a mother demented" published with revisions in: The shattered plinths/Irving Layton. Toronto: McClelland and Stewart, 1968, (also in CP71, DF, SEL, WPJ).
"[Modern Greek poet]" ibid., (also in CP71, GP, SP).

SP 5/3
LIKE A MOTHER DEMENTED; AS YOU WISH SIR
[1967].
[2]p.; 28 cm.
Chiefly holograph.
Two poems.
On p.[1]:holograph draft of stanzas 1-4,6-7 of "Like a mother demented."
On p.[2]:typescript draft of "As you wish sir."
"Like a mother demented" published with revisions in: The shattered plinths/Irving Layton. Toronto: McClelland and Stewart, 1968, (also in CP71, DF, SEL, WPJ).
"As you wish sir" not published to date.

SP 5/4
LIKE A MOTHER DEMENTED
[1967].
[2] leaves; 28 cm.
In part holograph.
Poem.
On leaf [1]:typescript draft of stanzas 1-4,6-7 with reworking of stanza 7.
On leaf [2]:2 holograph drafts of stanza 5.

...con't

SP 5/4...con't

On verso of leaf [1]:typescript draft of lines 1-3.
Published with revisions in: The shattered plinths/Irving Layton. Toronto: McClelland and Stewart, 1968, (also in CP71, DF, SEL, WPJ).

SP 6/1
[MARCHE MUNICIPAL[E]; [VILLAGE FUNERAL]; [FOR THE CAUSE]; MID EAST CRISIS
[1967].
[6]p. on 3 leaves; 1 leaf 28 cm., 1 leaf 21 cm., 1 leaf 28 cm. folded to 21 cm.
Chiefly holograph.
Four poems.
On p.[1-2,4-6]:2 holograph drafts of poem with themes from "March municipale" and "[Village funeral]."
On p.[3]: typescript draft of "Mid East crisis."
Also on p.[6]: typescript draft of "[For the cause]."
Holograph title "March municipale" on p.[6].
"March municipale" published with revisions in: The shattered plinths/Irving Layton. Toronto: McClelland and Stewart, 1968, (also in CP71, DF, SEL).
"[Village funeral]," ibid., (also in CP71).
"[For the cause]," ibid., (also in CP71).
"Mid East crisis" not published to date.

SP 6/2
MARCHE MUNICIPALE
[1967].
[1] leaf; 28 cm.
Typescript with holograph revisions.
Poem.
Published with further revisions in: The shattered plinths/ Irving Layton. Toronto: McClelland and Stewart, 1968, (also in CP71, DF, SEL).

SP 6/3
MARCHE MUNICIPALE
[1967].
[1] leaf; 28 cm.
Typescript with holograph revisions.
Poem.
Published with further revisions in: The shattered plinths/ Irving Layton. Toronto: McClelland and Stewart, 1968, (also in CP71, DF, SEL).

SP 7/1
MEDITERRANEAN CEMETERY; TALK AT TWILIGHT; PRELUDE
[1967].
[6]p., [2] leaves; 28 cm.
Chiefly holograph.
Three poems.
On p.[1,3,5]:3 holograph drafts with revisions of "Mediterranean cemetery."
On leaves [1-2]:2 typescript drafts of "Mediterranean cemetery."
On p.[2,4]:2 typescript drafts of "Talk at twilight"; drafts on p.[2] crossed out.
On p.[6]:typescript draft of "Prelude."
Holograph title on verso of leaf [2].
Drafts on p.[1,3,5,] numbered 1-3.
"Mediterranean cemetery" published with further revisions in: The shattered plinths/Irving Layton. Toronto: McClelland and Stewart, 1968, (also in CP71).
"Talk at twilight," ibid., (also CP71, DF, SP, LPIL1, LPIL2, DD).
"Prelude," ibid., (also in CP71, DF, SP, LPIL1, LPIL2).

SP 8/1
OIL SLICK ON THE RIVIERA
[1967].
[4] leaves, [8] p.; 28 cm.
Chiefly holograph.
Poem.
On leaf [1]:holograph draft with revisions; fragment at top of page beginning "And no matter what horrible things are being done...."
On p.[1]:holograph reworking of stanzas 1-2.
On p.[3]:holograph draft with reworking of stanzas 1-2.
On p.[5]:holograph draft with last stanza at head of page.
On p.[7] and leaves [2-3]:3 holograph drafts with revisions.
On leaf [4]:typescript draft of stanzas 1-2,4 and 2 lines of stanza 3.
On p.[2,4,6,8]:typescript draft of foreword to "The shattered plinths"; dated Nice, France, 1968.
Drafts numbered.
Holograph title on verso of leaf 4.
Published with further revisions in: The shattered plinths/ Irving Layton. Toronto: McClelland and Stewart, 1968.

SP 9/1
ON THIS FAR SHORE; [MID-EAST CRISIS]
[1967].
[3]p. on [1] leaf; 28 cm.
In part holograph.
Two poems.
On p.[1]:typescript draft of "On this far shore" with one extra stanza beginning "And what if it isn't a holy scroll...."
On p.[2-3]:5 drafts of "[Mid-east crisis]."
"On this far shore" published with revisions in: The shattered plinths/Irving Layton. Toronto: McClelland and Stewart, 1968, (also in CP71).
"[Mid-east crisis]" not published to date.

SP 10/1
PRELUDE; OIL SLICK ON THE RIVIERA
[1967].
[2]p., [1] leaf; 28 cm.
Chiefly holograph.
Two poems.
On p.[1] and leaf [1]:4 drafts of "Prelude" with revisions.
On p.[2]:typescript of "Oil slick on the Riviera."
P.[1] titled "Beach episode"; leaf [1] titled "Praeludium."
Drafts 1-2 numbered.
Holograph title "Prelude" on verso of leaf [1].
"Prelude" published with further revisions in: The shattered plinths/Irving Layton. Toronto: McClelland and Stewart, 1968, (also in CP71, DF, LPIL1, LPIL2).
"Oil slick on the Riviera," ibid., (also in CP71, SEL).

SP 11/1
QUEER HATE POEM
[1967].
[1] leaf; 28 cm. folded to 21 cm.
Holograph.
Poem.
Draft with revisions.
Published with further revisions in: The shattered plinths/ Irving Layton. Toronto: McClelland and Stewart, 1968, (also in CP71).

SP 12/1
THE RED MOUJHIK
1967.
[5] leaves; 28 cm.
Typescript with holograph revisions.
Poem.
On leaf [1]:draft with revisions and reworking of stanzas 6,8.
On verso of leaf [1]:reworking of stanza 8; typescript of line 1.
On leaf [2]:draft of stanzas 1-6,8 with revisions.
Leaf [3]:carbon copy of leaf [2].
On leaves [4-5]:2 drafts with revisions.
Dated June 6, 1967.
Published with further revisions in: The shattered plinths/ Irving Layton. Toronto: McClelland and Stewart, 1968.

SP 13/1
THE SWEET LIGHT STRIKES MY EYES; HOMAGE TO ROUMANIA; TO A GENERATION OF POETS; IMPARTIALITY; THE FINAL IRONY
[1967].
[12]p., [3] leaves; 28 cm.
Chiefly holograph.
Five poems.
On p.[1,3,5,7,9,11] and leaves [1-3]:8 drafts with revisions of "The sweet light strikes my eyes."
On p.[2]:typescript draft of "To a generation of poets."
On p.[4]:typescript of draft "Homage to Roumania."
On p.[6,12]:2 typescript drafts of "The final irony."
On p.[8,10]:2 typescript drafts of "Impartiality."
Page [4] repaired with scotch tape, section missing from bottom centre.
"Impartiality" published as "[Poetess]."
"The sweet light strikes my eyes" published with further revisions in: The shattered plinths/Irving Layton. Toronto: McClelland and Stewart, 1968, (also in CP71, DF, SEL).
"Homage to Roumania," ibid., (with revisions).
"To a generation of poets," ibid.
"[Poetess]," ibid., (with revisions), (also in UP).
"The final irony" not published to date.

SP 14/1
[TAMED BIRDS]; AUTOPSY ON ABERFAN
[1967].
[3]p. on [1] leaf; 28 cm. folded to 21 cm.
Chiefly holograph.
Two poems.
On p.[1]:3 holograph drafts of stanza 1 of "[Tamed birds]"; 2 drafts crossed out.
On p.[2]:typescript draft of 2 lines with title "Poetry"; and 1 line of "Autopsy on Aberfan."
On p.[3]:typescript of "Autopsy on Aberfan"; and holograph fragment beginning "It's like laughing at a funeral...."
"[Tamed birds]" published with revisions in: The shattered plinths/Irving Layton. Toronto: McClelland and Stewart, 1968, (also in CP71).
"Autopsy on Aberfan," ibid., (also in CP71).

SP 14/2
[TAMED BIRDS]; COUNSEL FOR MY STUNG LOVE
[1967].
[3]p. on [1] leaf; 28 cm. folded to 21 cm.
Chiefly holograph.
Two poems.
On p.[1]:holograph draft of "[Tamed birds]" with revisions and reworking of stanza 3; stanzas 1-2 and 2 lines at bottom of page crossed out.
On p.[2]:holograph draft of "[Tamed birds]" with revisions and reworking of stanza 3.
On p.[3]:typescript of "Counsel for my stung love" with revisions.
"[Tamed birds]" published with further revisions in: The shattered plinths/Irving Layton. Toronto: McClelland and Stewart, 1968, (also in CP71).
"Counsel for my stung love," ibid., (also in CP71).

SP 15/1
TO WRITE AN OLD FASHIONED POEM
[1967].
[2]p., [6] leaves; 28 cm.
In part holograph.
Poem.
One holograph and 3 typescript drafts with revisions.
Drafts 1-3 numbered.
Published with further revisions in: The shattered plinths/ Irving Layton. Toronto: McClelland and Stewart, 1968, (also in CP71).

SP 16/1
YET WHAT IF THE SURVIVORS; ONE LAST TRY AT A FINAL SOLUTION; CLEAVAGES
[1967].
[8]p., [7] leaves; 28 cm.
In part holograph.
Three poems.
On p.[1]:holograph draft of 24 lines with themes and images of "Yet what if the survivors."
On p.[2,4]:2 typescript drafts with revisions of "Cleavages."
On p.[3,5,7] and leaves [1-3]:5 holograph drafts of 8 stanzas with revisions of "Yet what if the survivors."
On leaves [4,7]:3 holograph drafts with revisions of "Yet what if the survivors."
On p.[6,8]:2 typescript drafts of "One last try at a final solution."
Holograph title "What if the survivors" on verso of leaf [7].
"Yet what if the survivors" published with further revisions in: The shattered plinths/Irving Layton. Toronto: McClelland and Stewart, 1968, (also in CP71, DF, SEL).
"One last try at a final solution," ibid., (also in CP71).
"Cleavages" published with further revisions in: The whole bloody bird/Irving Layton. Toronto: McClelland and Stewart, 1968, (also in CP71).

SP 17/1
HE SAW THEM AT FIRST; LET GENTILITY CRY OUT; [PEACEMONGER]; TO THE RUSSIANS AT THE U.N.; [A SORT OF AFTER DINNER SPEECH]; AFTER THE BATTLE OF SINAI
1967.
[12]p.; 28 cm.
Chiefly holograph.
Six poems.
On p.[1-2,7,9,11]:2 holograph drafts, 1 typescript draft with revisions of "He saw them at first."
On p.[2]:typescript fragment of "[Peacemonger]" beginning with "After our lovemaking...."
On p.[3]:holograph draft of stanzas 4-6 of "He saw them at first."
On p.[4,6]:2 typescript drafts of "To the Russians at the U.N."
On p.[5]:2 holograph drafts of stanzas 1-3 of "He saw them at first."
On p.[8]:holograph draft of stanzas 4-5 of "He saw them at first"; typescript draft of "After the battle of Sinai."
On p.[10]:typescript draft of "Let gentility cry out."
On p.[12]:typescript of lines 1-12 of "[A sort of after dinner speech]."

...con't

SP 17/1...con't

Holograph title "He saw them at first" in margin of p.[1].
"To the Russians at the U.N." dated July 1967.
"He saw them at first" published with revisions in: The shattered plinths/Irving Layton. Toronto: McClelland and Stewart, 1983. (also CP71).
"[Peacemonger]," ibid., (also in CP71, DF, GP, LPIL1, LPIL2).
"To the Russians at the U.N.," ibid., (also in CP71).
"[A sort of after dinner speech]," ibid., (also in CP71).
"After the battle of Sinai," ibid., (also in CP71) "Let gentility cry out," ibid., (also in CP71).

TD - The Tightrope Dancer

TD 1/1
THE ACCIDENT; [CHECKMATE]
[1977].
[2] leaves; 1 leaf 21 cm., 1 leaf 28 cm.
In part holograph.
Two poems.
On leaf [1]:holograph draft of 6 lines of "The accident" titled "Modern loves"; holograph draft of "[Checkmate]" crossed out.
On leaf [2]:typescript draft of "The accident."
"The accident" published with revisions in: The tightrope dancer/Irving Layton. Toronto: McClelland and Stewart, 1978.
"[Checkmate]," ibid., (with revisions).

TD 2/1
AFTER A SLEEPLESS NIGHT; THE ORACLE; LIFEBUOY; THE RED CHAMBERPOT; [THE SQUINT]
[1977].
[8]p. on [3] leaves; 28 cm. folded to 22 cm.
Chiefly holograph.
Five poems. On p.[1]:holograph draft of "[The squint]."
On p.[2]:holograph draft with revisions of "After a sleepless night."
On p.[3]:typescript draft of "The red chamberpot."
On p.[4]:holograph draft with revisions of "After a sleepless night" titled "Images to live by."
On p.[5]:2 holograph drafts with revisions of "The oracle."
On p.[6]:typescript draft of "Lifebuoy"; holograph draft with revisions of "After a sleepless night."

...con't

TD 2/1...con't

On p.[7-8]:2 holograph drafts with revisions of "[The squint]."
"Lifebuoy" published with revisions as "[At the chill centre]."
"After a sleepless night" published with further revisions in: The tightrope dancer/Irving Layton. Toronto: McClelland and Stewart, 1978.
"The oracle," ibid., (with revisions).
"[At the chill centre]," ibid.
"The red chamberpot" published with revisions in: For my neighbours in hell/Irving Layton. Oakville, Ont.: Mosaic Press/Valley Editions, 1980.
"[The squint]" not published to date.

TD 3/1
ARAB HARIKIRI
[1977].
[2] leaves; 1 leaf 21 cm., 1 leaf 28 cm.
In part holograph.
Poem.
Two holograph, 3 typescript drafts with revisions.
Published with further revisions in: The tightrope dancer/ Irving Layton. Toronto: McClelland and Stewart, 1978.

TD 4/1
BRAVO, DEATH, I LOVE YOU; GOD AND JOHN DEWEY; THE GREEK LIGHT; THE GOAT; THE ORACLE; THE LIFEBUOY; MEDUSAS
[1977].
[12]p.; 28 cm.
Typescript with holograph revisions.
Seven poems.
On p.[1,3,5,7,9,11]:5 drafts with revisions of "Bravo, death, I love you"; p.[5] titled "Death of a tyrant."
On p.[2]:draft of "God and John Dewey."
On p.[4]:draft of "The Greek light."
On p.[6]:draft of "The goat."
On p.[8]:draft of "The oracle."
On p.[10]:draft of "The lifebuoy."
On p.[12]:draft of "Medusas."
"The Greek light" dated Ios, June 28, 1977.
"The lifebuoy" published with revisions as "[At the chill centre]."
"Bravo, death, I love you" published with further revisions in: The tightrope dancer/Irving Layton. Toronto: McClelland and Stewart, 1978.
"The Greek light," ibid., (with revisions).

...con't

TD 4/1...con't

"The goat," ibid., (with revisions).
"The oracle," ibid., (with revisions).
"[At the chill centre]," ibid (with revisions).
"Medusas," ibid., (with revisions).
"God and John Dewey" published on cover jacket and on title page of: For my neighbours in hell/Irving Layton. Oakville, Ont.: Mosaic Press/Valley Editions, [1980].

TD 5/1
FLIES; MEMO TO SIR MORTIMER
[1977].
[4]p., [1] leaf; 1 leaf 21 cm., 2 leaves 28 cm.
In part holograph.
Two poems.
On leaf [1]:holograph draft of part I of "Flies."
On p.[1]:typescript draft of parts I and II of "Flies."
On p.[2]:3 typescript drafts of "Memo to Sir Mortimer."
On p.[3]:typescript draft of part III, and lines 1-2 of part I of "Flies."
On p.[4]:typescript draft of parts I and II, and lines 1-5 of part III of "Flies."
"Flies" published with further revisions in: The tightrope dancer/Irving Layton. Toronto: McClelland & Stewart, 1978, (also in WPJ).
"Memo to Sir Mortimer," ibid.

TD 6/1
FLOWERS HE'LL NEVER SMELL
1977.
2p., 5 leaves; 3 leaves 21 cm., 3 leaves 28 cm.
In part holograph.
Poem.
On p.[1-2] and leaves [1-2]:4 holograph drafts with revisions.
On leaves [3-5]:3 typescript drafts with revisions.
Leaves [3-4] titled "Flowers he won't pick."
Published with further revisions in: The tightrope dancer/ Irving Layton. Toronto: McClelland and Stewart, 1978.

TD 7/1
THE GOAT; STARTREK; AFTER A SLEEPLESS NIGHT; [THE SQUINT]
1977.
[4]p., [3] leaves; 28 cm.
In part holograph.

...con't

TD 7/1...con't

Four poems.
On p.[1]:holograph draft with revisions of stanzas 1-2 of "The goat"; typescript draft of "[The squint]".
On p.[2]:2 typescript drafts of "Startrek."
On leaf [1]:holograph reworking of stanza 3 of "Startrek."
On p.[3] and leaves [2-3]:3 typescript drafts of "The goat."
On p.[4]:typescript draft of "After a sleepless night."
On verso of leaf [3]:typescript of line 1 of "The goat."
"Startrek" published as "Star trek."
Dated Siprios [?], June 22, 1977.
"The goat" published with further revisions in: The tightrope dancer/Irving Layton. Toronto: McClelland and Stewart, 1978.
"Star trek," ibid.
"After a sleepless night," ibid.
"[The squint]" not published to date

TD 8/1
GOODNIGHT SWEET LADY
[1977].
[3] leaves; 28 cm..
Typescript.
Poem.
Three drafts.
Leaf [2] titled "Lady, where's my hat."
Published with revisions in: The tightrope dancer/Irving Layton. Toronto: McClelland and Stewart, 1978, (also in LPIL1).

TD 8/2
WHERE'S MY DAMNED HAT; PARDON ME LADY
[1977].
[2]p., [4] leaves; 2 leaves 21 cm., 3 leaves 28 cm.
In part holograph.
Two poems.
On leaves [1-2]:2 holograph drafts with revisions of "Where's my damned hat."
On p.[1]:typescript draft of "Where's my damned hat"; typescript draft of "Pardon me lady."
On p.[2]:typescript draft of "Pardon me lady."
On leaf [3]:typescript draft of "Where's my damned hat" with reworking of stanzas 1-2.
On leaf [4]:typescript draft of "Where's my damned hat."

...con't

TD 8/2...con't

Leaves [2,4] and p.[1] titled "Lady where's my hat."
"Where's my damned hat" published with revisions as "[Goodnight sweet lady]."
"[Goodnight sweet lady]" published in: The tightrope dancer/ Irving Layton. Toronto: McClelland and Stewart, 1978, (also in LPIL1).
"Pardon me lady" published with revisions in: For my neighbours in hell/Irving Layton. Oakville, Ont.: Mosaic Press/Valley Editions, [1980].

TD 9/1
GREEK DANCERS
1977.
[4]p., [5] leaves; 3 leaves 21 cm., 4 leaves 29 cm.
In part holograph.
Poem.
On p.[1,2,4] and leaf [1]:4 holograph drafts with revisions.
On p.[3]:holograph draft of stanzas 1-3.
On leaves [2-5]:4 typescript drafts with revisions.
Drafts 1-5 numbered.
Dated Molibos, July 18, 1977.
Published with further revisions in: The tightrope dancer/ Irving Layton. Toronto: McClelland and Stewart, 1978.

TD 10/1
INTIMATIONS
1977.
[2]p., [2] leaves; 2 leaves 21 cm., 1 leaf 28 cm.
Chiefly holograph.
Poem.
On p.[1-2] and leaf [1]:3 holograph drafts of 4 stanzas with revisions.
On leaf [2]:typescript draft of 4 stanzas with revisions.
Dated July 8, 1977.
Published with further revisions in: The tightrope dancer/ Irving Layton. Toronto: McClelland and Stewart, 1978.

TD 11/1
WHEN DEATH COMES FOR YOU; KEEP DYING
[1977].
[2]p; 28 cm.
In part holograph.
Two poems.
On p.[1]:2 holograph drafts of "When death comes for you"; 2 typescript drafts of

...con't

TD 11/1...con't

"Keep dying."
On p.[2]:3 typescript drafts of "When death comes for you."
"When death comes for you" published with revisions in: The tightrope dancer/Irving Layton. Toronto: McClelland and Stewart, 1978, (also in DD).
"Keep dying" not published to date.

TD 12/1
THE TIGHTROPE DANCER
[1977].
[6] leaves; 3 leaves 21 cm., 3 leaves 29 cm.
In part holograph.
Poem.
On leaf [1]:2 holograph drafts of 2 stanzas each with revisions.
On leaves [2-3]:2 holograph drafts of 2 stanzas with revisions.
On leaves [4,6]:2 typescript drafts of 2 stanzas.
On leaf [5]:typescript draft of 2 stanzas with reworking of stanza 2.
Leaves [2,3-4] titled "The madman"; leaves [5-6] titled "The tightrope walker."
Stanza 2 published with further revisions as "The tightrope dancer." Published in: The tightrope dancer/Irving Layton. Toronto: McClelland and Stewart, 1978, (also in DD).

TD 13/1
MEMO TO SIR MORTIMER
[1977].
[1] leaf; 28 cm.
Typescript.
Poem.
Two typescript drafts; draft on verso crossed out.
Published in: The tightrope dancer/Irving Layton. Toronto: McClelland and Stewart, 1978.

TD 14/1
ODD COUPLE; MERCENARIES
[1977].
[4] leaves; 2 leaves 21 cm., 2 leaves 30 cm.
In part holograph.
Two poems.
On leaves [1-2]:2 holograph drafts of "Odd couple"; leaf [2] titled "Progress of an affair."
On leaf [3]:2 typescript drafts of "Mercenaries"; typescript draft of "Odd couple"

...con't

TD 14/1...con't

titled "Progress of an affair."
On leaf [4]:typescript draft of "Odd couple" with reworking of last stanza.
"Mercenaries" published with revisions as 1 titled stanza of "[The cracked mirror]."
"Odd couple" published with revisions in: The tightrope dancer/ Irving Layton. Toronto: McClelland and Stewart, 1978.
"[The cracked mirror]" published in: For my neighbours in hell/ Irving Layton. Oakville, Ont.: Mosaic Press/Valley Editions, [1980].

TD 15/1
MISHNAH AND THE ETERNAL SHMUCK; AN AGING GREEK POET; DON'T BLAME THE APPLE; PRIVATE ENTERPRISE; [PLATO WAS AN ASSHOLE]
1977.
[4]p., [2] leaves; 3 leaves 21 cm., 1 leaf 29 cm.
Chiefly holograph.
Five poems.
On p.[1]:2 holograph drafts of "Private enterprise"; fragment beginning "In the 20th century..."; 1 draft of "Private enterprise" crossed out.
On p.[2]:2 holograph drafts of "Aging Greek poet"; 2 holograph drafts of "Don't blame the apple"; titled "Original sin"; fragment beginning "Cynicism is the ideology..." crossed out; 1 draft of "Aging Greek poet" and 1 draft of "Don't blame the apple" crossed out.
On leaf [1]:holograph draft of "Mishnah and the eternal shmuck."
On leaf [2]:holograph draft of "Mishnah and the eternal shmuck"; fragment beginning "Like love, power..."; marginalia.
On p.[3]:typescript draft of lines 1-4 of "[Plato was an asshole]"; typescript draft of "Don't blame the apple"; typescript draft of "Private enterprise."
On p.[4]:typescript draft of line [1] of "[Plato was an asshole]"; typescript draft of "Mishnah and the eternal shmuck"; typescript draft of "Aging Greek poet."
"Mishnah and the eternal shmuck" dated Molibos, July 19, 1977.
"An aging Greek poet" published as "[Beatitude]."
"Mishnah and the eternal shmuck" published in: The tightrope dancer/Irving Layton. Toronto: McClelland and Stewart, 1978.
"[Beatitude]," ibid.
"Don't blame the apple," ibid.
"[Plato was an asshole]" published in: For my neighbours in hell/Irving Layton. Oakville, Ont.: Mosaic Press/Valley Editions, [1980].
"Private enterprise" not published to date.

TD 16/1
THE MONSTER
[1977].
[4] leaves; 2 leaves 21 cm., 2 leaves 30 cm.
In part holograph.
Poem.
On leaves [1-2]:2 holograph drafts with revisions.
On leaf [3]:typescript draft with revisions.
On leaf [4]:typescript draft.
Published with further revisions in: The tightrope dancer/ Irving Layton. Toronto: McClelland and Stewart, 1978.

TD 17/1
THE LATEST WRINKLE
[1977].
[4] leaves; [1] leaf 21 cm., 3 leaves 30 cm.
In part holograph.
Poem.
On leaf [1]:holograph draft with revisions.
On leaves [2-3]:3 typescript drafts titled "The new wrinkle."
On leaf [4]:typescript draft of lines 1-6.
On verso of leaf [4]:typescript draft of line 1.
Published with further revisions in: The tightrope dancer/ Irving Layton. Toronto: McClelland and Stewart, 1978.

TD 18/1
THE PAPAL ELECTION
[1977].
[4]p.; 2 leaves of 21 cm. folded to 16 cm.
Holograph.
Poem.
On p.[1-2]:3 holograph drafts with revisions.
On p.[3-4]:2 holograph drafts with revisions.
P.[2-3] titled "Who's got the longest."
Holograph title on p.[4].
Published with further revisions in: The tightrope dancer/ Irving Layton. Toronto: McClelland and Stewart, 1978.

TD 18/2
THE PAPAL ELECTION
[1977].
[7] leaves; 28 cm.
Typescript.
Poem.
On leaves [1,6]:2 typescript drafts with revisions.
On leaves [2-5,7]:5 typescript drafts.
Leaves [2,4] titled "A present for the pope."
Coffee [?] stains on leaf [1].
Published with further revisions in: The tightrope dancer/ Irving Layton. Toronto: McClelland and Stewart, 1978.

TD 19/1
THE PROFESSIONAL; SIR MORTIMER
1977.
[2]p., [1] leaf; 1 leaf 21 cm., 1 leaf 28 cm.
In part holograph.
Two poems.
On leaf [1]:holograph draft with revisions of "The professional."
On p.[1]:typescript draft of "The professional"; typescript draft of "Sir Mortimer."
On p.[2]:typescript draft of "Sir Mortimer" crossed out.
"The professional" dated Molibos, July 14, 1977.
"The professional" published with further revisions in: The tightrope dancer/Irving Layton. Toronto: McClelland and Stewart, 1978.
"Sir Mortimer," ibid.

TD 20/1
THE PRUSSIAN SCHOOLMASTER; [GAY SUNSHINE ANTHOLOGY]
[1977].
[5] leaves; 1 leaf 21 cm., 4 leaves 28 cm.
In part holograph.
Two poems.
On leaves [1-2]:2 holograph drafts of "The Prussian schoolmaster" with revisions.
On verso of leaf [2]:typescript draft of lines 1-6 of "[Gay sunshine anthology]."
On leaves [3-5]:3 typescript drafts of "The Prussian schoolmaster" with revisions.
On leaf [3]:lines 1-4 of "[Gay sunshine anthology]."
On verso of leaf [5]:typescript draft of lines 1-6 of "The Prussian schoolmaster."
"The Prussian schoolmaster" published with further revisions as "[Dialectical leap]."
"[Dialectical leap]" published in: The tightrope dancer/Irving Layton. Toronto:

...con't

TD 20/1...con't

McClelland and Stewart, 1978.
"[Gay sunshine anthology]" published in: Europe and other bad news/Irving Layton. Toronto: McClelland and Stewart, 1981.

TD 21/1
SMOKE; MOLIBOS
1977.
[4]p., [1] leaf; 2 leaves 21 cm., 1 leaf 30 cm.
In part holograph.
Two poems.
On p.[1-2]:2 holograph drafts with revisions of "Smoke."
On leaf [1]:holograph draft of "Smoke" with revisions and reworking of stanza 2.
On p.[3]:typescript draft with revisions of "Smoke"; 2 lines at bottom of page crossed out.
On p.[4]:typescript draft of "Molibos" crossed out.
"Molibos" dated Molibos, July 23, 1977.
"Smoke" published with further revisions in: The tightrope dancer/Irving Layton. Toronto: McClelland and Stewart, 1978, (also in LPIL1, LPIL2, DD).
"Molibos" published in: Droppings from heaven/Irving Layton. Toronto: McClelland and Stewart, 1979.

TD 22/1
SIR MORTIMER
[1977].
[3] leaves; 2 leaves 21 cm., 1 leaf 28 cm.
Chiefly holograph.
Poem.
On leaves [1-2]:2 holograph drafts with revisions.
On leaf [3]:2 typescript drafts with revisions.
Published with further revisions in: The tightrope dancer/ Irving Layton. Toronto: McClelland and Stewart, 1978.

TD 23/1
SCHADENFREUDE
[1977].
[4] leaves; 2 leaves 21 cm., 2 leaves 30 cm.
In part holograph.
Poem.
On leaves [1-2]:2 holograph drafts with revisions.
On leaf [3]:typescript draft with revisions.

...con't

TD 23/1...con't

On leaf [4]:typescript draft.
Published with further revisions in: The tightrope dancer/ Irving Layton. Toronto: McClelland and Stewart, 1978.

TD 24/1
SIR; [YOU ALLOWED THE GENERALISSIMO]
[1977].
[2]p., [10] leaves; 1 leaf 21 cm., 10 leaves 28 cm.
In part holograph.
Two poems.
On p.[1]:holograph draft with revisions, of 17 lines of "Sir."
On p.[2]:holograph draft of 14 lines of "Sir"; typescript draft of ["You allowed the generalissimo"].
On leaf [1] and verso of leaf [1]:holograph draft of 20 lines of "Sir."
On leaf [2]:typescript draft of "Sir" with revisions and reworking of last stanza.
On leaves [3,7-9]:4 typescript drafts of "Sir."
On leaves [4-6,10]:4 typescript drafts with revisions of "Sir."
"Sir" published with further revisions in: The tightrope dancer/ Irving Layton. Toronto: McClelland and Stewart, 1978.
"[You allowed the generalissimo]," ibid.

TD 25/1
WATCH OUT FOR HIS LEFT; [COMRADE]; [WHEN DEATH SAYS COME]
1977.
[4]p., [6] leaves; 2 leaves 21 cm., 5 leaves 28 cm.
In part holograph.
Three poems.
On p.[1-2]:holograph draft of 8 stanzas of "Watch out for his left"; stanzas 4-6 used in "[When death says come]."
On leaf [1]:holograph draft of 6 stanzas of "Watch out for his left."
On p.[3]:holograph draft of 10 stanzas of "Watch out for his left," stanzas 6-8 used in "[When death says come]"; holograph draft of 6 stanzas of "Watch out for his left."
On p.[4]:typescript draft of "[Comrade]."
On leaf [2]:typescript draft of 6 stanzas of "Watch out for his left."
On leaves [3-6]:3 typescript drafts with revisions, of 6 stanzas of "Watch out for his left."
On verso of leaf [4]:typescript draft of stanzas 1-2 of "Watch out for his left."
"Watch out for his left" dated Molibos, June 7, 1977.
"Watch out for his left" published with further revisions in: The tightrope

...con't

TD 25/1...con't

dancer/Irving Layton. Toronto: McClelland and Stewart, 1978.
"[Comrade]," ibid.
"[When death says come]" published in: For my neighbours in hell/Irving Layton. Oakville, Ont.: Mosaic Press/Valley Editions, [1980].

TD 26/1
COMRADE
1977.
[4] leaves; 1 leaf 21 cm., 3 leaves 28 cm.
In part holograph.
Poem.
On leaf [1]:holograph draft with revisions.
On leaf [2]:typescript draft with repetition of lines 1-2; typescript fragment "Aobe [sic] the rocking green bottle"; title "Arise ye prisoners."
On verso of leaf [2]:holograph list of words with Greek translation; typescript fragment "Above the rocking green bottle."
On leaves [3-4]:2 typescript drafts with titles "The surprise" and "Surprise everyone."
Dated June 7, 1977.
Published in: The tightrope dancer/Irving Layton. Toronto: McClelland and Stewart, 1978.

TD 27/1
THE PRIZE
[1977].
[4] leaves; 29 cm.
Typescript.
Poem.
Four drafts.
Number "73" in lower left corner of leaf [3].
Published in: The tightrope dancer/Irving Layton. Toronto: McClelland and Stewart, 1978.

TD 28/1
CHECKMATE; [THE ACCIDENT]; [HOMAGE TO SIR MORTIMER]
1977.
[2]p., [3] leaves; 3 leaves 21 cm., 1 leaf 28 cm.
Chiefly holograph.
Three poems.

...con't

TD 28/1...con't

On p.[1]:holograph draft of "Checkmate"; theme and images used in "[Homage to Sir Mortimer]."
On p.[2]:holograph draft of poem beginning "Bad movies are cultural barometers...."
On leaves [1-2]:2 holograph drafts with revisions of "Checkmate."
On leaf [3]:typescript draft of "Checkmate"; typescript draft of "[The accident]."
"Checkmate" dated Molibos, Greece, July 14, 1977.
"Checkmate" published with further revisions in: The tightrope dancer/Irving Layton. Toronto: McClelland and Stewart, 1978.
"[The accident]," ibid., (with revisions).
"[Homage to Sir Mortimer]" published in: For my neighbours in hell/Irving Layton. Oakville, Ont.: Mosaic Press/Valley Editions, [1980].

TD 29/1
YOU ALLOWED THE GENERALISSIMO; [WATCH OUT FOR HIS LEFT]
[1977].
[2]p., [2] leaves; 28 cm.
In part holograph.
Two poems.
On leaf [1]:holograph draft with revisions of "You allowed the generalissimo."
On p.[1]:typescript draft of "You allowed the generalissimo."
On p.[2]:typescript draft of [Watch out for his left]."
On leaf [2]:typescript draft of "You allowed the generalissimo"; typescript draft of fragment "Hatched into the May sunshine they totter."
On verso of leaf [2]:typescript draft of 4 lines beginning "Hatched into the May sunshine...."
"You allowed the generalissimo" published in: The tightrope dancer/Irving Layton. Toronto: McClelland and Stewart, 1978.
"[Watch out for his left]," ibid., (with revisions).

TD 30/1
YOU COME TO ME; TELL IT TO MAGGIE; PARADOX
[1977].
[4]p., [2] leaves; 3 leaves 21 cm., 1 leaf 28 cm.
Chiefly holograph.
Three poems.
On leaf [1]:holograph draft with reworking of stanza 2 of "You come to me."
On leaf [2] and p.[1]:2 holograph drafts with revisions of "You come to me."
On p.[2]:holograph draft of "Paradox."
On p.[3]:typescript draft of "You come to me"; typescript draft of "Tell it to

...con't

TD 30/1...con't
Maggie," crossed out.
On p.[4]:typescript draft of "Paradox"; 2 typescript drafts of "Tell it to Maggie."
"Tell it to Maggie" published as "[Tell it to Peggy]."
"You come to me" published with revisions in: The tightrope dancer/Irving Layton. Toronto: McClelland and Stewart, 1978.
"[Tell it to Peggy]," ibid.
"Paradox" published in: For my neighbours in Hell/Irving Layton. Oakville, Ont.: Mosaic Press/Valley Editions, [1980]

UN - Unpublished

UN 1/1
FRIED FISH
1966.
3 leaves; 2 leaves 25 cm., 1 leaf 28 cm.
Chiefly holograph.
Poem.
One typescript, 2 holograph drafts with revisions.
Leaf [2] titled "Worn down."
Published with further revisions as "[Fried fish my love]."
Dated March 6, 1966.
Published in: Intercourse 2:16-17 Spring 66.
No monograph publication to date.

UN 2/1
SELF THERAPY
1987.
[1]p., [4] leaves; 28 cm.
In part holograph.
Poem.
On p.[1]:holograph draft with revisions; marginalia.
On p.[2]:photocopy from ABC Radio National Guide, December 1986.
On leaf [1]:typescript draft with revisions.
On leaf [2]:typescript draft with revisions dated September 14, 1985.
On leaf [3]:typescript draft with revisions dated January 1, 1987; marginalia.
On leaf [4]:typescript draft.
Not published to date.

UN 3/1
QUIDNUNC
[1978?].
[2] leaves; 30 cm.
Chiefly holograph.
Poem.
On leaf [1]:2 holograph drafts with revisions.
On leaf [2]:typescript draft of "Quidnunc"; typescript draft of 2 lines from foreword to "The tightrope dancer" beginning "When I was just starting on my fantastic career...."
"Quidnunc" not published to date.

UN 4/1
ADVICE TO A FRIEND ON HIS 60TH BIRTHDAY
[197-?].
[3] leaves; 2 leaves 21 cm., 1 leaf 28 cm.
Chiefly holograph.
Poem.
On leaf [1] and verso:3 holograph drafts.
On leaf [2]:holograph draft.
On leaf [3]:2 typescript drafts.
Not published to date.

UN 5/1
THE BIGGEST SHOW IN TOWN
1981.
[9] leaves; 28 cm.
In part holograph.
Poem.
On leaves [1-3]:3 holograph drafts with revisions; drafts on leaves [2-3] titled "Entertainment."
On leaves [4-9]:6 typescript drafts.
Dated Niagara-on-the-Lake, July 26, 1981.
Not published to date.

UN 6/1
TO IRVING SANS LOVE
[1969?]
[7] leaves; 28 cm. In part holograph signed.
Poem.
On leaf [1]:holograph draft with revisions of stanzas 1-4,6; ms. draft of 9 lines titled "to irving sans love."

...con't

UN 6/1...con't

On leaves [2-3]:2 holograph drafts with revisions of stanzas 1- 4,6.
On verso of leaf [2]:holograph draft of stanza 5 crossed out.
On leaves [4-7]:4 typescript drafts with revisions; leaves
[2,4,6-7] titled "To Irving sans love (revised version)."
On verso of leaf [4]:typescript of line 1.
Published in: University of Guelph Ontarian. January 23, 1969.
No monograph publication to date.

UN 7/1
FILL IN THE BLANK; MONSTERS; KAKANIA
[198-?].
[10]p., [21] leaves; 5 leaves 28 cm., 21 leaves 25 cm.
In part holograph.
Three poems.
On p.[1,3,5,7,9]:5 holograph drafts with revisions of "Fill in the blank."
On p.[2,4,6,8,10]:5 typescript drafts of "Kakania."
On leaves [1-18,20-21]:20 typescript drafts with revisions of "Fill in the blank"; leaves [1-3,6-9,12-14,16-17] titled "Lawyers."
On leaf [19]:typescript draft with revisions of "Monsters."
Leaves [1-21] on verso of printed promotional material for "The Gucci bag."
"Fill in the blank" not published to date.
"Monsters" published in: The Gucci bag/Irving Layton. 2nd ed. Oakville, Ont.: Mosaic Press/Valley Editions, 1984, (also in FR).
"Kakania" not published to date.

UN 8/1
POTATOES
1984.
[2]p., [1] leaf; 30 cm.
In part holograph.
Poem.
On p.[1]:1 ms. draft with theme and images of "Potatoes"; 1 holograph draft of "Potatoes."
On p.[2]:2 ms. drafts with theme and images of "Potatoes"; marginalia explaining authorship of drafts.
On p.[3]:holograph draft.
Dated Fiono, September 20, 1984.
Not published to date.

UN 9/1
CLAWS
[198-?].
[8] leaves; 28 cm.
In part holograph.
Poem.
On leaf [1]:holograph draft with revisions.
On verso of leaf [1]:ms. draft of poem signed M. Blue, October, 1979.
On leaves [2-5]:4 typescript drafts.
On leaf [6]:typescript draft with reworking of stanza 3.
On leaves [7-8]:3 typescript drafts with revisions.
Holograph title on verso of leaf [8].
Not published to date.

UN 10/1
A CHARIOT FOR HARRIET
[1982?].
[5] leaves; 28 cm.
Chiefly holograph.
Poem.
On leaves [1-3]:3 holograph drafts with revisions.
On leaves [4-5]:typescript draft.
On verso of leaf [5]:fragment "Can make his heart prance."
Not published to date.

UN 11/1
WEIRDO
1984.
[6] leaves; 28 cm.
In part holograph.
Poem.
On leaves [1-3]:3 holograph drafts with revisions; cigarette burn on leaf [1]; marginalia on leaf [3].
On leaf [4]:typescript draft; ms. interpretation of poem; marginalia.
On leaves [5-6]:2 typescript drafts with revisions.
Drafts numbered.
Dated Montreal, July 9, 1984.
Not published to date.

UN 12/1
CONTEXT; WHERE HAS THE GLORY FLED; MAKE ROOM WILLIAM BLAKE
[198-?].
[4]p.; 28 cm.
In part holograph.
Three poems.
On p.[1]:holograph draft of "Context."
On p.[2]:typescript draft of "Where has the glory fled."
On p.[3]:typescript draft of "Context" with revisions and reworking of stanza 6.
On p.[4]:typescript draft of "Make room William Blake"; holograph title "Context."
"Context," not published to date.
"Where has the glory fled" published in: The Gucci bag/Irving Layton. Oakville, Ont.: Mosaic Press/Valley Editions, 1983, (also in GB, MSGB, GB2).
"Make room William Blake," ibid., (also in GB, MSGB, GB2).

UN 13/1
UNDESERVED
[197-?].
[4] leaves; 2 leaves 21 cm., 2 leaves 28 cm.
In part holograph.
Poem.
On recto and verso of leaf [1]:holograph draft with revisions.
On leaf [2]:holograph draft with revisions.
On leaf [3]:typescript draft with holograph revisions and reworking of stanza 5; coffee [?] stain on verso.
On leaf [4]:typescript draft with holograph revisions.
Not published to date.

UN 14/1
DEAD MOTHWINGS
[198-?].
[2] leaves; 28 cm.
Typescript with holograph revisions.
Poem.
On leaf [1]:1 typescript draft, 1 holograph draft.
On verso of leaf [1]:typescript draft of lines 1-4.
On leaf [2]:typescript draft.
Not published to date.

UN 15/1
CANUCKY SHMUCKISM
[19-?].
[1] leaf; 28 cm.
Typescript.
Poem.
Not published to date.

UN 16/1
THE WRAITH; TERRY FOX
[197-?].
[5] leaves.
In part holograph.
Two poems.
On leaf [1]:typescript draft of "The wraith" with holograph revisions and reworking of stanza 4.
On verso of leaf [1]:typescript draft of line 1 of "The wraith."
On leaf [2]:holograph draft with revisions of "The wraith" titled "Poet and women."
On verso of leaf [2]]:holograph draft of "Terry Fox."
On leaf [3]:holograph draft with revisions of "The wraith."
On leaves [4-5]:two typescript drafts of "The wraith."
Holograph title "The wraith" on verso of leaves [4-5].
"The wraith" not published to date.
"Terry Fox" published with revisions in: Final reckoning: poems 1982-1986/Irving Layton. Oakville, Ont.: Mosaic Press, 1987.

UN 17/1
CLIO'S FAVOURITES
[197-?].
[2] leaves; 28 cm.
In part holograph.
Poem.
On leaves [1-2]:1 holograph, 1 typescript draft with revisions.
Number "5" in upper left corner of leaf [1].
Not published to date.

UN 18/1
FANTASIES OF A STONE; [POROS]
[197-?]
[1] leaf; 28 cm.
Typescript with holograph revisions.
Two poems.

...con't

UN 18/1...con't

On recto:draft of "Fantasies of a stone."
On verso:fragment of "[Poros]" beginning "Pulling the skier over waves and fish...."
"Fantasies of a stone" not published to date.
"[Poros]" published in: Periods of the moon/Irving Layton. Toronto: McClelland and Stewart, 1967.

UN 19/1
BYRON IN VENICE
1984.
[21] leaves; 1 leaf 28 cm.; 20 leaves 30 cm.
In part holograph signed.
Poem.
On leaf [1]:holograph draft with revisions and reworking of stanza 3.
On verso of leaf [1]:holograph draft partially crossed out with reworking of stanzas 1-2.
On leaf [2]:ms. draft with revisions, signed by Irving Layton.
On leaves [3-7]:5 holograph drafts with revisions.
Leaf 8 photocopy of holograph draft.
On leaf [9]:typescript draft.
On leaf [10]:typescript draft with revisions and reworking of stanzas 2-4.
On leaf [11]:holograph draft with reworking of stanza 4.
On leaf [12]:holograph draft partially crossed out with reworking of stanza 4.
On leaves [13-17]:5 typescript drafts with revisions.
On leaf [18]:holograph draft of stanza 4.
Leaves [19-20]:photocopies of 2 typescript drafts with revisions.
On leaf [21]:typescript draft with revisions.
Dated Fiano, Romano, September 17, 1984.
Not published to date.

UN 20/1
HALF OF FOREVER; PLATO WAS AN ASSHOLE
[197-?].
[2]p., [3] leaves; 2 leaves 21 cm., 2 leaves 29 cm.
In part holograph.
Two poems.
On leaves [1-2]:2 holograph drafts with revisions of "Half of forever."
On p.[1]:typescript draft of "Half of forever."
On p.[2]:typescript draft of "Plato was an asshole."
On leaf [3]:typescript draft with revisions of "Half of forever."

...con't

UN 20/1...con't

"Half of forever" not published to date.
"Plato was an asshole" published in: For my neighbours in hell/ Irving Layton. Oakville, Ont.: Mosaic Press/Valley Editions, [1980].

UN 21/1
JAMSMEAR; DAPHNIS AND CHLOE
[197-?].
[2]p., [1] leaf; 28 cm.
In part holograph.
Two poems.
On leaf [1]:holograph draft with revisions of "Jamsmear"; typescript of lines 1-8 of "Daphnis and Chloe."
On p.[1]:typescript draft of "Jamsmear."
On p.[2]:typescript draft of "Daphnis and Chloe."
"Jamsmear" not published to date.
"Daphnis and Chloe" published in: For my brother Jesus/Irving Layton. Toronto: McClelland and Stewart, 1976.

UN 22/1
THE INITIATES; BOSCHKA LAYTON 1921-1984
1984.
[4]p., [12] leaves; 28 cm.
In part holograph signed.
Two poems.
On leaves [1-7] and p.[1,3]:9 holograph drafts with revisions of "The initiates"; p.[1] titled "The Berkeley Frisson."
On p.[2,4]:2 typescript drafts of "Boschka Layton 1921-1984."
On leaves [8-11]:4 typescript drafts with revisions of "The initiates"; marginalia on leaf [11].
On leaf [12]:typescript draft of "The initiates"; holograph titles of 2 poems by [Irving Layton] on verso.
"The initiates" dated Berkeley, February 21, 1984.
"Boschka Layton 1921-1984" dated Santa Rosa, February 17, 1984.
Holograph title "The initiates" on verso of leaves [4-7,9-11].
"The initiates" not published to date.
"Boschka Layton 1921-1984" published in: The Gucci bag/Irving Layton. 2nd ed. Oakville, Ont.: Mosaic Press/Valley Editions, 1984, (also in GB2, DD, FR).

UN 22/2
THE INITIATES
[1984].
[8] leaves; 28 cm.
Typescript with holograph revisions.
Poem.
Eight drafts of "The initiates."
Dated Berkeley, California, February 21, 1984.
Not published to date.

UN 23/1
THE SHINING
1981.
[3] leaves; 28 cm.
Typescript.
Poem.
Three drafts.
Dated Banff, August 15, 1981.
Not published to date.

UN 24/1
SPAGHETTI WESTERN
[197-?].
[4] leaves; 1 leaf 21 cm., 3 leaves 29 cm.
In part holograph.
Poem.
On leaf [1]:holograph draft with revisions.
On leaves [2-4]:3 typescript drafts with revisions.
Marginalia on recto and verso of leaf [4].
Not published to date.

UN 25/1
THE SPURT
[197-?].
[2] leaves; 30 cm.
Typescript with holograph revisions.
Poem.
Two drafts.
Not published to date.

UN 26/1
THE TRAGEDY OF OLD AGE
[197-?].
[8] leaves; 28 cm.
Chiefly holograph.
Poem.
On leaves [1-6]:6 holograph drafts with revisions; marginalia on leaf [4].
On leaf [7]:typescript draft with revisions.
On leaf [8]:typescript draft.
Holograph title on verso of leaves [6,8].
Not published to date.

WBB - The Whole Bloody Bird

WBB 1/1
ELEPHANT
[1968].
[1] leaf; 30 cm.
Holograph.
Poem.
Draft with revisions.
Published with further revisions in: The whole bloody bird/ Irving Layton. Toronto: McClelland and Stewart, 1969, (also in CP71, UE).

WBB 2/1
DEADALIVE
1967.
[4] leaves; 28 cm.
Chiefly holograph.
Poem.
Three holograph drafts with revisions; 1 typescript draft.
Drafts on leaves [1-3] numbered.
Dated February 3, 1967.
Deadalive" published in Canadian Jewish Chronicle Review, February 10, 1967, p.8.
Stanza 2 published as "[Modern miracle]." Published in: The whole bloody bird/Irving Layton. Toronto: McClelland and Stewart, 1969, (also in CP71).

WBB 3/1
[NEPALESE WOMAN AND CHILD]
[1968].
[1] leaf; 34 cm. folded to 22 cm.
Holograph.
Poem.
Published with revisions in: The whole bloody bird/Irving Layton. Toronto: McClelland and Stewart, 1969, (also in CP71, UE).

WBB 4/1
THE SHRINKING GENERAL
[1968].
[1] leaf; 30 cm.
Holograph.
Poem.
Draft with revisions of 4 stanzas on back leaf of file folder.
"The shattered plinths" at head of poem.
Marginalia at bottom of leaf and on verso.
Published with further revisions in: The whole bloody bird/ Irving Layton. Toronto: McClelland and Stewart, 1969.

WBB 4/2
WHO'S SEEN DE GAULLE?
[1968].
[3] leaves; 1 leaf 27 cm., 2 leaves 28 cm.
Typescript.
Poem.
On leaf [1]:draft of stanzas 1-6 with revisions.
On leaf [2]:draft with revisions and reworking of stanza 7.
On leaf [3]:draft with revisions.
Leaf [2] titled "A modern fable."
"Who's seen De Gaulle" published with further revisions as "[The shrinking general]."
Published in: The whole bloody bird/Irving Layton. Toronto: McClelland and Stewart, 1969.

E - Essays

E/1
CANADIAN POEMS 1850-1952
[1953].
[2] leaves.
Typescript.
Partial draft of introduction beginning "Canada may be said to have been waiting in snowed-in silence..." published in: Canadian poems 1850-1952/ed. by Louis Dudek and Irving Layton. Toronto: Contact Press, 1953.

E/2
[THE COLLECTED POEMS OF IRVING LAYTON]
1971.
[7] leaves; 28 cm.
Typescript.
Dated Toronto, Ontario May 20, 1971.
Draft of foreword to "The collected poems."
Published in: The collected poems of Irving Layton. Toronto: McClelland and Stewart, 1971.

E/3
[LOVE WHERE THE NIGHTS ARE LONG]
[1962].
[5] leaves.
Typescript with holograph revisions.
Foreword to: Love where the nights are long/Irving Layton. Toronto: McClelland and Stewart, 1962.

E/4
[POEMS TO COLOR]
[1970].
[3] leaves; 28 cm.
Typescript with holograph corrections.
Draft of introduction to: Poems to color/ed. by Rick Fritz and Ross Ringler.[S.l.:s.n.], 1970.

E/5
[THE POLE VAULTER]
[1974].
[3] leaves; 28 cm.
Typescript with holograph revisions.
Draft of foreword to: The pole-vaulter/Irving Layton. Toronto: McClelland and Stewart, 1974.

E/6
REFLECTIONS ON THE VICTORY OF THE LABOUR PARTY; [LETTER]
1950.
[3] leaves; 35 cm.
Typescript with holograph revisions signed.
On leaves [1-2]:essay on victory of the Labour Party.
On leaf [3]:unsigned typescript letter to "Freda."
"Reflections on the victory of the Labour Party" dated Cte St. Luc, February 25, 1950.

E/7
THE TIGHTROPE DANCER
1978.
[3] leaves; 30 cm.
In part holograph.
On leaves [1-2]:partial holograph draft of foreword to "The tightrope dancer."
On leaf [3]:partial typescript draft of foreword to "The tightrope dancer."
Published in: The tightrope dancer/Irving Layton. Toronto: McClelland and Stewart, 1978, (also in DD).

E/8
THE LOVE POEMS OF IRVING LAYTON
1978.
[2] leaves; 28 cm.
Typescript with holograph revisions.
Foreword to "The love poems of Irving Layton."
Published in: The love poems of Irving Layton. Toronto: McClelland and Stewart, 1980.

E/9
THE CHALLENGE WE FACE, OR, A POET'S VIEW OF THE WORLD
[19--].
[3] leaves; 23 cm.
Holograph.
Observations on unemployment; underdeveloped countries; the Soviet Union and China; moral weakness; challenge.
Not published to date.

E/10
WHAT IS CANADIAN CULTURE
[197-?].
[4] leaves; 28 cm.
Holograph notes on Canadian culture.
Not published to date.

E/11
FINAL RECKONING: POEMS 1982-1986 (Acknowledgements)
1987 23p., 1 leaf 22 cm., 22 leaves 28 cm.
In part holograph.
21 drafts with revisions of "Acknowledgements" to "Final reckoning: poems 1982-1986" in brown envelope labelled "21 drafts of "Final reckoning's" acknowledgements."
Published in: Final reckoning: poems 1982-1986/Irving Layton. Oakville, Ont.: Mosaic Press, 1987.

E/12
EUROPE AND OTHER BAD NEWS
1980.
[7] leaves; 28 cm.
Typescript.
On leaves [1-3]:photocopy of typescript draft of foreword to "Europe and other bad news."
On leaves [4-7]:typescript draft with revisions of foreword to "Europe and other bad news."
Cigarette burns on leaf [4].
Dated August 26, 1980.
Published in: Europe and other bad news/Irving Layton. Toronto: McClelland and Stewart, 1981.

MISC - Miscellaneous

MISC 1
POCKET ENGAGEMENT CALENDAR
1982-1983
[36] p., 16 cm.
Dominion Blueline pocket engagement calendar 1982-1983.
Includes appointments, list of names and phone numbers.

MISC 2
SYMPOSIUM
1986.
36p., 1 leaf; 28 cm.
Loose leaf photocopy script of adaptation of Plato's Symposium in which Irving Layton played the part of Socrates. Produced May 4th and 5th, 1986 at the Centaur Theatre, Montreal, Quebec, directed by Maurice Podbrey.
Includes rehearsal schedule with holograph of 6 lines of Socrates' speech.

MS - Manuscripts

MS/1
BALLS FOR A ONE-ARMED JUGGLER
[1963].
[71] leaves; 28 cm.
Typescript with holograph revisions.
Incomplete ms.
Leaves unbound in Duo-tang folder.
Holograph inscription "Balls" on cover.
Published as: Balls for a one-armed juggler/Irving Layton. Toronto: McClelland and Stewart, 1963.

MS/2
BALLS FOR A ONE-ARMED JUGGLER
[1963].
[77] leaves; 28 cm.
Typescript with holograph revisions.
Incomplete ms.
Leaves unbound in Duo-tang folder.
Holograph inscription on cover "Balls for a one-armed juggler. Poems by Irving Layton."
Published as: Balls for a one-armed juggler/Irving Layton. Toronto: McClelland and Stewart, 1963.

MS/3
BALLS FOR A ONE-ARMED JUGGLER
[1963].
116p.; 28 cm.
Typescript.
Leaves unbound between 2 leaves of cardboard.
Holograph title on cover.

...con't

MS/3...con't

Marginalia and hand drawn sketch on back cover.
Published as: Balls for a one-armed juggler/Irving Layton. Toronto: McClelland and Stewart, 1963.

MS/4
THE GUCCI BAG
1983.
[104] leaves; 28 cm.
Typescript.
Leaves inserted in pocket made from "Harbourfront Author's Festival" poster.
Inscription on cover:"The Gucci bag as revised September 22 Layton."
Published as: The Gucci bag/Irving Layton. Oakville, Ont.: Mosaic Press/Valley Editions, 1983.

MS/5
THE IMPROVED BINOCULARS
1956.
Typescript.
Revised and corrected partial typescript for 1st edition containing 89 poems.
Draft consists mainly of pages cut from earlier Layton collections; poems not intended for inclusion are crossed out.
Leaves are unbound between two pieces of cardboard.
Notation on front cover:"Dummy for The improved binoculars by Irving Layton. November, 1956."
Published as: The improved binoculars/Irving Layton. Highlands,N.C.: Jonathan Williams, 1956.

MS/6
THE LAUGHING ROOSTER
[1964].
[105] leaves; 28 cm.
Typescript.
Leaves unbound in cardboard file folder.
Published as: The laughing rooster/Irving Layton. Toronto: McClelland and Stewart, 1964.

MS/7
THE LAUGHING ROOSTER
[1964].
[31] leaves; 28 cm.
Holograph.

...con't

MS/7...con't

Drafts of selected poems from "The laughing rooster."
Accompanied by note bearing inscription "Poems in poor taste by Irving Layton" and "The laughing rooster."
Cover leaf from McGill University examination booklet.
Published in: The laughing rooster/Irving Layton. Toronto: McClelland and Stewart, 1964.

MS/8
[LOVE WHERE THE NIGHTS ARE LONG]
[1962].
[58] leaves; 28 cm.
Typescript.
Marginalia on leaf [1].
Typescript draft of: Love where the nights are long: an anthology of Canadian love poems/selected by Irving Layton; drawings by Harold Town. Toronto: McClelland and Stewart, 1962.

MS/9
[EUROPE AND OTHER BAD NEWS]
[1980].
80p., [3] leaves; 28 cm.
Typescript with holograph corrections.
Leaves loose between cardboard covers.
Title on leaf [1] "Beginnings."
Published as: Europe and other bad news/Irving Layton. Toronto: McClelland and Stewart, 1981.

MS/10
FOR MY NEIGHBOURS IN HELL
[1980].
[95] leaves; 28 cm.
Typescript.
Leaves between 2 sheets of cardboard.
On leaf [1]:"For my neighbours in hell. Irving Layton" and holograph note concerning number and order of poems.
Holograph list of 4 poems by [Irving Layton] with notes on verso of front sheet of cardboard.
Published as: For my neighbours in hell/Irving Layton. Oakville, Ont.: Mosaic Press/Valley Editions, [1980].

MS/11
FINAL RECKONING: POEMS 1982-1986
1987.
[72] leaves; 28 cm.
Typescript (photocopy).
Draft of manuscript of "Final reckoning: poems 1982-1986" in brown envelope with holograph title.
Marginalia on leaf [1].
Holograph revisions of "Acknowledgements."
Published as: Final reckoning: poems 1982-1986/Irving Layton. Oakville, Ont.: Mosaic Press, 1987.

MS/12
FINAL RECKONING: POEMS 1982-1986
1987.
[82] leaves; 28 cm.
Typescript.
Working draft of "Final reckoning: poems 1982-1986" in green folder labeled "Typing in progress" and brown envelope labeled "Final reckoning...."
Published in: Final reckoning: poems 1982-1986/Irving Layton. Oakville, Ont.: Mosaic Press, 1987.

MS/13
DANCE WITH DESIRE: LOVE POEMS
1987.
[151] leaves; 28 cm.
Typescript (photocopy).
Working manuscript of "Dance with desire: love poems" in brown envelope labeled "Working draft of Dance with desire."
Leaves [8-138, 143] are photocopies from previously published volumes.
Published as: Dance with desire: love poems/Irving Layton. Toronto, Ont.: McClelland and Stewart, 1986.

MS/14
DANCE WITH DESIRE: LOVE POEMS
1987.
159 leaves; 28 cm.
Typescript.
159 leaves of page proofs of "Dance with desire: love poems" in brown envelope addressed to Irving Layton.
Leaves numbered 10,12,15-164.
Published as: Dance with desire: love poems/Irving Layton. Oakville, Ont., Mosaic Press, 1987.

MS/15
WAITING FOR THE MESSIAH: A MEMOIR
1985.
3,000 leaves; 28 cm.
Typescript and ms.
Approximately 3,000 leaves of typescript and ms. drafts with holograph revisions.
Published as: Waiting for the Messiah: a memoir/Irving Layton.
Toronto, Ont.: McClelland and Stewart, 1985.

NB - Notebooks

NB [196-?]
[NOTEBOOK]
[196-?].
[96]p.; 21 cm.
Holograph.
Pale green notebook containing drafts of published and unpublished poems, observations and marginalia.
Pages 20-96 blank.
Reproduction of Napoleon [?] and inscription "Massena" printed on front cover.

NB 1960-68
[NOTEBOOK]
[1960-1968].
[138]p.; 20 cm.
Holograph Black "record" notebook with burgundy binding containing drafts of published and unpublished poems, essays, observations, lists and marginalia.
Holograph signature on fly leaf.
Pages [14,16,22,27,46,50-53,58,71-75,116-124] blank.

NB 1962
[NOTEBOOK]
1962.
[160]p.;21 cm.
Holograph.
Black cardboard covered notebook containing drafts of published and unpublished poems, observations, lists, and marginalia.
Pages [18,20-23,32,34,42,46-150,157] blank.
Holograph signature on fly leaf.
Dated Montreal, Quebec, September 5th, 1962.

NB 1963
[NOTEBOOK]
1963.
[78]p.; 21 cm. x 16 cm.
Holograph.
Pale blue notebook containing drafts of published and unpublished poems, lists and marginalia.
Pages [4,44-67,72-77] blank.
On front cover:"Cauderno"; "Drafts of poems"; marginalia.
Dated Spain 1963.

NB 1966
[NOTEBOOK]
1966
[36] p.; 28 cm.
Holograph Red Duo-tang folder containing drafts of poems, observations, itinerary, and names of people [Irving Layton] met with while travelling in Germany.
Dated May 10-30, 1966.
Pages [2,4,10,18,20,28,30,32,34] blank.

NB 1967
[NOTEBOOK]
1967.
[96]p.; 19 cm.
Holograph.
Blue notebook with black binding containing drafts of published and unpublished poems, observations and marginalia.
Pages [41-96] blank.
Dated Nice, France, June 1, 1967.

NB 1968/1
[NOTEBOOK]
1968.
191p.; 22 cm.
Holograph.
Blue cardboard covered notebook containing drafts of published and unpublished poems, random notes, and marginalia.
Pages [19-21, 46-191] blank.
Ms. of "[Elegy written in a country churchyard]" including stanzas from Gray's commonplace book.
Receipt for TV repair between leaves [124-125].
Letter from Aviva [Layton] to Irving [Layton] between leaves [138-139].

NB 1968/2
[NOTEBOOK]
1968
[110]p.; 20 cm.
Holograph.
Buff coloured notebook titled "Mythyma" containing personal observations, drafts of published and unpublished poems and marginalia, including sketches.
Dated Mithyma, Greece, August 1968.

NB 1968/3
[NOTEBOOK]
1968.
160p.; 19 cm.
Holograph.
Brown and beige patterned notebook with blue binding containing drafts of poems and letters, and observations.
Pages [140-160] blank.
Two unidentifiable receipts [?] in Hebrew script between p.[40- 41].
Label on front cover bears holograph inscription "Journal of Irving Layton. Piraeus Greece, February 5, 1968."

NB 1969
[NOTEBOOK]
[1969].
[108]p.; 21 cm.
Holograph.
Pale green notebook containing personal observations, drafts of published and unpublished poems, and marginalia.
Cover inscription:"The original standard exercise book."
Pages [12-30,34-107] blank.

NB 1971
[NOTEBOOK]
1971.
[100]p.; 20 cm.
Holograph.
Buff coloured notebook containing drafts of published and unpublished poems, and marginalia.
Holograph signature and title "Briefer fiction" on cover.
On p.[35]:draft of letter to "Bob" [Robert Fulford?] concerning publication in Saturday Night.
Dated Molibos, Greece, Summer 1971.
Pages [96-99] blank.

NB 1972-73
[NOTEBOOK]
[1972-1973].
[144]p.; 20 cm.
Holograph.
Black "record" notebook with burgundy binding containing drafts of published and unpublished poems, observations, lists and marginalia.
Draft of letter to "Desmond" and "George" on p.[7].
Holograph signature on flyleaf.
Pages [53-130] blank.

NB 1972/1
[NOTEBOOK]
1972.
[200]p.; 17 cm.
Holograph.
Dark green, plastic covered notebook containing drafts of published and unpublished poems, marginalia and various lists.
Flyleaf dated Piraeus, Greece, September 5, 1972.
Holograph signature on flyleaf.

NB 1972/2
[NOTEBOOK]
1972.
[298]p.; 17 cm. x 11 cm.
Holograph.
Dark green, simulated leather covered notebook containing drafts of published and unpublished poems, observations, lists, and marginalia.
Holograph signature on flyleaf.
Pages 153-298 blank.
Dated Piraeus, Greece, September 5th, 1971.

NB 1973/1
[NOTEBOOK]
1973.
[32]p.; 20 cm.
Holograph.
Notebook containing drafts of published and unpublished poems, and marginalia.
Reproduction of "The last supper" on front cover; phoenix emblem and inscription in Greek characters printed on back cover.
No."3" in upper right corner of cover.
Page [15] dated Patmos, August 25-31, 1973.
Pages [19-32] blank.

NB 193/2
[NOTEBOOK]
1973.
[108]p.; 20 cm.
Holograph.
Buff coloured notebook containing drafts of unpublished poems, segment of one untitled short story and marginalia.
Numbers "2," "149," "125" on cover.
Pages [20-21] dated Molibos, Lesbos, September 15, 1973.
Pages [22-108] blank.

NB 1976
[NOTEBOOK]
1976.
[252]p.; 21 cm. x 14 cm.
Holograph.
Black cardboard covered notebook containing drafts of published and unpublished poems, observations, lists and marginalia.
Holograph signature on fly leaf.
Dated November 24, 1976.

PR - Prose

PR/1
THE AMBASSADOR: A POLITICAL FARCE
[196-?].
[50] leaves; 28 cm.
Typescript.
Ms. of play in 3 acts by Irving Layton and Louis Dudek.
Leaf [50] blank.

PR/2
THE OLD AND QUIET ONES
[196-?].
[27] leaves; 28 cm.
Typescript.
Draft of play in 2 acts by Irving Layton and Louis Dudek.

PR/3
OSMECK
[196-?].
[9] leaves; 28 cm.
Typescript with holograph revisions.
Draft of short story by [Irving Layton].
Published in Engagements: The prose of Irving Layton/ed. by Seymour Mayne. Toronto: McClelland and Stewart, 1972.

PR/4
UP WITH NOTHING
1961.
[65]p.; 35 cm.
Carbon copy of typescript.
Script of a play in 3 acts by Irving Layton and Leonard Cohen.
Dated March 1961.

PR/5
[UP WITH NOTHING]
[1961]
[125] leaves; 28 cm.
Photocopy of manuscript.
Title on leaf [1] "Enough of fallen leaves."
Draft of play in 3 acts by [Irving Layton] and [Leonard Cohen].

PR/6
'PARASITE; UNEMPLOYED
[196-?].
[7] leaves; 28 cm.
Typescript.
Short story.
Holograph revisions throughout text.
"Unemployed" published as "A parasite" in "First Statement" vol.I, no.14, [196-?] pp.3-9.
Title "Parasite" crossed out and replaced with holograph title "Unemployed."
"Unemployed" published in: Great Canadian short stories/comp. [by] Alec Lucas. New York: Dell, 1971.

THE INDEX

The index has been created as a means of limiting the size of the catalogue. Every title found in the catalogue, i.e., both main entries and titles that have been catalogued with a main entry, has been included in the index.

Each title is followed by a location symbol, or symbols, which refer the reader to the main body of the work. These symbols, which are derived from the titles of Layton's monograph publications, have been used for both the physical arrangement of the manuscripts and as a means of ordering the entries in the catalogue. For example, the title "Gay sunshine anthology," which is followed by locations symbols EBN 21/1 and TD 20/1 will be found in the catalogue in the EBN and the TD sections. This same location symbol can then be used to retrieve the manuscript from the collection.

A single asterisk (*) placed before a *location symbol* means that the title of the poem has been changed between manuscript and publication. In other words the index title is the title as it appeared in a published monograph.

A double asterisk (**) placed before a *title* means that this is a title as it appeared on the manuscript.

EXAMPLE: Goodnight sweet lady *TD 8/2
     **Where's my damn hat TD 8/2

TITLE INDEX

Poems

2028 see Two thousand and twenty eight
**A plus, An GB 4/1, GB 12/1, GB 34/1
Absurd animal, The *DFH 9/1
Abyss, The FMNH 4/1
Accident, The TD 1/1, TD 28/1
Acquired courage DFH 3/1
Act of creation *FMBJ 3/1
Adam FMBJ 1/1
Adam and Eve PV 2/1, PV 38/1
Advice for old maids GB 24/1
Advice to a friend on his 60th birthday UN 4/1
Advice to old maids GB 14/1, GB 33/2
Aesthetic cruelty FR 10/1, FR 18/1, FR 19/1
After a sleepless night TD 2/1, TD 7/1
After Auschwitz SP 1/1
After the battle of Sinai SP 17/1
Aftermath LR 3/2
Aging Greek poet, An TD 15/1
**Aging poet reflects, An FMBJ 18/1, FMBJ 23/1
Ah, nuts GB 7/1
Alas, too noiseless GP 1/1, GP 1/2, GP 2/1, GP 4/1, GP 11/2
Alcaeus reflects on a chance encounter PV 51/1
Alison Parrott 1975-1986 FR 13/1
Alive and still kicking FMNH 10/1
American young woman in Patmos PV 3/1
And it came to pass GB 27/1
And they all fall down FR 10/1
Animal across the street, The PV 4/1
Approaching doomsday FR 20/1
Arab Harikiri TD 3/1
Arch, The FMBJ 4/1, FMBJ 20/1
Aristocrats MSGB 3/1
**Armageddon EBN 17/1
**Art SP 3/1
As seen through a glass darkly NP 1/1, NP 1/2, *NP 4/1
As you wish sir SP 5/3

---

  *   published title
 **   manuscript title

Asian suite PV 5/1
Asshole in residence FR 18/1
Asylums FMBJ 21/2
**At Tangier - a meditation upon the future FMBJ 24/1
At the Barcelona zoo FMBJ 5/1, FMBJ 21/1
At the Belsen memorial POM 9/1
At the chill centre *TD 2/1, *TD 4/1
August Strindberg MSGB 4/1
Australian bush PV 6/1
Autopsy on Aberfan SP 14/1
Autumn seen as my lady DFH 1/1
Aviva COV 5/1
Bacillus prodigiosus COV 1/1, COV 4/1**Ballad GB 28/1
Ballad of the Holstein bull GB 33/2
Balloon, The EBN 3/1
Banff poem for Harriet FMNH 11/1
Basin, The PV 7/1, PV 7/2
Baudelaire in a summer cottage BFOJ 1/1, BFOJ 1/2, BFOJ 1/3, BFOJ 1/4
Bawdy bawdy LIM 3/1
Beard, The GP 2/1, GP 6/1
Beatitude *TD 15/1
Beauty and genius FMBJ 20/1, FMBJ 25/1
Bedbugs *PV 8/1
**Bedbugs and other vermin PV 8/1
Being *EBN 2/1
Being there EBN 1/1, BFOJ 1/4
Belle France, La FMBJ 4/1
Biggest show in town, The UN 5/1
**Black moths, The SF 2/1
Black queen, The PV 51/1
Black tourist in Tinos FR 2/1, FR 3/1, FR 34/1
Blackout GP 4/1
Blind man's bluff GB 6/1
**Blood of Christ, The FMBJ 26/1
Blossom GB 23/1
Bodhidharma PV 12/1
Bonded GB 5/1, GB 7/1
Boris Pasternak GB 5/1
Boschka Layton 1921-1984 GB2 2/1, GB2 4/1, GB2 5/1, UN 22/1
Boys in October *CGE 1/1

---

*   published title
** manuscript title

**Boys, The CGE 1/1
Bravo, death, I love you TD 4/1
Breast stroke, The *GB 1/1
**Breaststroke, The GB 1/1
Bridegroom FMNH 6/1
Bring on the skinheads GB 32/1
Budapest PV 13/1
Bull, more and less GB 11/1, GB 24/1
Burning remnant, The *FMNH 1/2, *FMNH 11/1
Burnt offering FR 41/1
By ecstasies perplexed IB 1/1, *IB 1/2
Byron exhibition at the Benaki museum GP 5/1, GP 5/2
Byron in Venice FR 38/1, FR 48/1, UN 19/1
C'est fini *FMBJ 4/1
Caged bird, The SF 1/1
Cain POM 1/5
Calibrations DFH 2/1
Canadian spring LP 1/1
Canucky shmuckism UN 15/1
Captive, The *GB 28/1
Carillon, The GB 9/1
Carmen GB2 3/1, GB2 3/2
Carved nakedness, The GB 8/1
Casa Cacciatore FR 21/1
Castle, The GP 6/1
Cat dying in autumn LIM 1/1
Central heating GB 10/1
Chariot for Harriet, A GB 10/1, GB 21/1, UN 10/1
Checkmate TD 1/1, TD 28/1
**Chilean chill PV 24/1
**Chosen people, The FMNH 1/1, FMNH 1/2, FMNH 1/3
**Christmas eve 1971, Zihuatanejo LLM 2/4
Claws UN 9/1
Cleavages SP 16/1
Clio's favourites UN 17/1
Coastal mind, The PV 14/1, PV 14/2, PV 14/3, PV 14/4
Cold green element, The POM 1/1, POM 1/2
Collaboration POM 8/1
**Comb and bird DFH 11/1
Comedia, La GB 8/1

---

* published title
** manuscript title

Comrade TD 25/1, TD 26/1
Comrade Undershaftsky GB 35/1, MSGB 1/1
Context UN 12/1
Counsel for my stung love SP 14/2
Courage to be, The *GB 4/1, *GB 12/1, *GB 34/1
Cracked crystal ball, The GB 13/1, GB 16/1, GB 24/1, GB 33/2
Cracked mirror, The *FMNH 1/2, *TD 14/1
Cracks in the acropolis FR 46/1
**Cross, The FMNH 13/1
Cuisine Canadienne *DFH 1/1
**Cuisine Canadienne the real thing DFH 1/1
**Culture FMNH 1/2
Cyst, The FR 28/1, GB2 6/1
Dancing man GB 12/1
Daphnis and Chloe FMBJ 7/1, FMBJ 18/1, FMBJ 20/1, UN 21/1
Dark lady NP 4/2
**Das nichts NP 15/4
Dazed fly, The GB 11/1
Dead mothwings UN 14/1
Dead souls GB 14/1
**Deadalive WBB 2/1
Death where is your sting-a-ling *EBN 13/1
Definitions EBN 4/1
Demon, The LPIL2 1/1
**Denouement LIM 2/1
Departed PV 10/1
Descent from Eden GB 13/1
Devotion FR 48/1
Dialectical leap *TD 20/1
Dionysian reveller NP 14/3
Dionysians in a bad time GB2 4/1
Dionysus in Hampstead NP 2/1, NP 2/2, NP 2/3, NP 2/4, NP 2/5, NP 2/6
Dirty old man FMNH 4/1
Discotheque FMBJ 23/1
Displaced person PV 11/1
Diverse pleasures FR 25/1
Divine touch, The GB 2/1
Divorce DFH 9/1
Don't blame the apple TD 15/1
Dream in Pangrati, A GP 3/1

---

* published title
** manuscript title

Dysphasiac, The *FMNH 13/1
Early morning sounds *EBN 18/1
Egalitarian *FMNH 10/1
Eine kleine Nachtmusik EBN 5/1, *EBN 6/1
El Caudillo LR 1/1
Election, The *FMNH 1/1, *FMNH 1/2, *FMNH 1/3, FMNH 1/4
Elephant WBB 1/1
Empty words MSGB 4/1
End of the white mouse NP 3/1, NP 3/2, NP 3/3, NP 3/4, NP 11/1
Endangered species EBN 16/1
Enemies CGE 2/1
Entry *NP 2/3, *NP 2/5, *NP 2/6
**Envy FMBJ 30/1
Epigram for Roy Daniells BFOJ 7/1
Epistle to Catullus GB 5/1, GB 39/1, GB2 1/1
Epitaphs LIM 2/1
Eternal recurrence *EBN 17/1
Etruscan tombs FR 45/1
Excelsior FMBJ 14/1, FMBJ 28/1, *FMBJ 30/1
**F. Nietzsche GP 8/1
Fanatic in San Feliu NP 4/1, NP 4/2, NP 4/3
Fantasia in black SP 1/1
Fantasies of a stone UN 18/1
Fata Morgana DFH 3/1, DFH 3/2
Fellini FR 38/1
Fill in the blank UN 7/1
Final irony, The SP 13/1
Final reckoning: after Theognis FR 33/1
Final solution, The PV 15/1, PV 20/1, PV 32/1
Finally, the final solution FMNH 12/1
Flies TD 5/1
Florence FMBJ 8/1, FMBJ 8/2, FMBJ 8/3
Flowers he'll never smell TD 6/1
Flytrap *GP 7/1, GP 7/2
**Flytrap, The GP 7/1
**For a girl with wide apart eyes SP 2/1, SP 2/2, SP 2/3
For a young poet who hanged himself PV 18/1, *PV 18/2, PV 40/1
For Alexander Trocchi novelist BFOJ 2/1, BFOJ 2/2, BFOJ 2/3, BFOJ 2/4, BFOJ 2/5, BFOJ 2/6, BFOJ 2/7
For Andrei Amalrik PV 16/1

* published title
** manuscript title

For Anne Frank PV 17/1, PV 17/2
**For Aviva IB 1/2
For Edda FMBJ 2/1
For Ettore with love and admiration GB2 7/1
**For F.W. GP 12/1
For Francesca FMBJ 9/1
For Hans, maybe Klaus or Tadeusz EBN 5/1, *EBN 6/1
**For Hans, maybe Klaus or Pyotyr EBN 6/1
For Jesus Christ FMBJ 10/1
For Mao-Tse-Tung LIM2 1/1
For Musia's grandchildren POM 1/1, POM 1/2, POM 1/3, POM 1/4, POM 1/5, POM 1/6, POM 1/7, POM 1/8
For my brother Jesus FMBJ 11/1
For my green old age LR 2/1
For my incomparable gypsy *FMBJ 23/1, GB 8/1
**For my Old Forest Hill gypsy FMBJ 23/1
For Nadezhda Mandelstam PV 1/1, PV 1/2, PV 47/1
For Natalya Correia NP 5/1
For Priscilla *IMF 1/1
For Sandra DFH 12/1
For some of my best friends *FMBJ 4/1
For the cause SP 6/1
For the Fraulein from Hamburg PV 19/1, PV 19/2
For the girl with wide apart eyes *SP 2/1, *SP 2/2, *SP 2/3
For the wife of Mr. Milton *GB 15/1
**For the wife of John Milton GB 15/1
**For the young couple at Lum Fong Hotel PV 45/1
Fragments DFH 3/1, DFH 9/1, EBN 18/1, FMBJ 9/1, FMBJ 11/1, FMBJ 18/1, FR 1/1, FR 9/1, FR 27/1, GB 7/1, GB 14/1, GB 26/1, GB 27/1, GB 39/1, GP 2/1, GP 7/1, NP 4/1, NP 10/1, NP 11/1, PV 8/1, PV 20/1, PV 25/1, PV 38/1, PV 39/1, SP 1/1, SP 8/1, SP 14/1, TD 15/1, TD 26/1, TD 29/1
Freedom POM 2/1
**Fried fish UN 1/1
Fried fish my love *UN 1/1
From the nether world GB 5/1, GB 39/1
Frost and fences NP 6/1, NP 8/1
Functional illiterates FR 35/1
Furrow, The GB 16/1
Galim FMBJ 12/1, FMBJ 22/1
Gannymede PV 20/1

---

* published title
** manuscript title

Garden, The GB 17/1, GB 28/1
Gay sunshine anthology EBN 21/1, TD 20/1
Gelded lion, The FR 9/1, FR 16/1
Glass dancer, The COV 6/1
Goat, The TD 4/1, TD 7/1
God and John Dewey TD 4/1
God is love NP 7/1, NP 11/1, NP 14/1, NP 14/2
Gods speak out, The BFOJ 3/1, BFOJ 3/2
Goodnight sweet lady TD 8/1, *TD 8/2
Graveyard, The *SP 3/1
**Greatness of Shakespeare, The NP 14/3
Greek dancers TD 9/1
Greek epigram PV 21/1
Greek fisherman FMNH 6/1
Greek fly PV 22/1
Greek light, The TD 4/1
Greeks FMBJ 7/1, FMBJ 22/1
Grey morning in Lisbon NP 5/1, NP 8/1
**Ground for divorce PV 46/1
Guardrail, The FMNH 11/1
Gulag EBN 7/1
Haemorrhage, The FMBJ 13/1
Hag, The BFOJ 4/1
Hairy monster, The GB 36/1
Half of forever UN 20/1
Hallowing, The FMBJ 14/1, FMBJ 23/1
Happy hooker, The DFH 4/1
Harlequin romance FR 28/1
He saw them at first SP 17/1
Helios GP 9/1, GP 9/2
Hellenes GP 10/1
Herbert Vunce FR 24/1
Herzl EBN 9/1
Hex, The *DFH 3/1
High fidelity FR 7/1
Hit parade PV 23/1
Holiday Inn: Tokyo MSGB 5/1
Homage to Onassis NP 9/1
Homage to Roumania SP 13/1
Homage to Sir Mortimer FMNH 7/1, TD 28/1

---

*   published title
** manuscript title

Honeymoon PV 24/1
How many days FMBJ 15/1, FMBJ 20/1, FMBJ 23/1, FMBJ 30/1
**Human among humans NP 2/3, NP 2/5, NP 2/6
Hungry Christians NP 11/1
**Hydra FMBJ 3/1
I know the dark and hovering moth *SF 2/1, SF 2/2
**Ideal among vacationers, The PV 25/1, PV 25/2
Ideal among vacationists, The *PV 25/1, *PV 25/2, PV 50/1
Ideal husband, an GB 18/1
Immortelles for a literary strumpet FR 9/1
**Impartiality SP 13/1
In an ice age EBN 8/1, EBN 10/1
In praise of older men FMBJ 16/1, FMBJ 16/2, FMBJ 16/3
In revenge for Olga and BP GB 5/1, GB 21/1
Initiates, The UN 22/1, UN 22/2
Insect repellant FR 28/1, GB 4/1, GB 16/1
Insomnia POM 3/1
Inter-view FR 32/1, FR 36/1
Intimations TD 10/1
Investiture, The FR 2/1
Iroquois in Nice SP 4/1
Isla Mujeres EBN 10/1
Island Circe FMBJ 3/1
Ithaca GP 11/1, GP 11/2Jamsmear UN 21/1
**Jeremiah EBN 14/1
Jeshua FMBJ 30/1
Jesus and St Paul FMBJ 4/1
**Jewish ditty FMBJ 4/1
Jijimuge PV 26/1
Judea eterna FMBJ 17/1, FMBJ 22/1, FMBJ 25/1
Judgement at Murray's FR 37/1
July 21, 1969 NP 17/1
June bug FMBJ 4/1
Junk EBN 2/1
Juvenal redivivus GB2 9/1
Kakania UN 7/1
Kazantzakis: God's athlete GP 8/1, GP 8/2
Keep dying TD 11/1
Keine Lazarovitch: 1870-1959 SF 3/1
Kilmurvey strand NP 16/1

---

  *   published title
  **   manuscript title

**King David FMBJ 29/1
Kitch FR 39/1
Lady Aurora GB2 5/1, GB2 5/2
Lady Macbeth MSGB 4/1
Lake Selby NP 10/1
Last survivor, The DFH 3/1, DFH 3/2, FMNH 3/1
Latest wrinkle, The TD 17/1
Leopardi in Montreal FR 27/1
Let gentility cry out SP 17/1
Letter to a lost love DFH 5/1
Letting go GB 18/1
**Lifebuoy TD 2/1
**Lifebuoy, The TD 4/1
Like a mother demented SP 5/1, SP 5/2, SP 5/3, SP 5/4
Like once I lost COV 3/1
Lillian Roxon PV 27/1
Lines for my grandchildren PV 51/1
Lobsters NP 4/1
Los Americanos GB 23/1
Love is an irrefutable fire LIM2 1/1
Love poem with an odd twist *SP 3/1
Lullaby PV 28/1
Lures PV 13/1
Madonna and Dionysos PV 29/1
Madrigal for Anna, A LPIL2 1/1
Mahogany red *POM 4/1
Maimonidian perplexity FR 11/1, FR 17/1
Make room William Blake GB 18/1, UN 12/1
Man and woman DFH 3/1
Man going up and down BFOJ 5/1
Marche Municipale SP 6/1, SP 6/2, SP 6/3
Marriage PV 30/1
Mary PV 24/1, PV 31/1
Massacre, The FR 44/1
Me, the P.M., and the stars IBM 1/1
Meditations of an aging Lebanese poet COV 4/1
Mediterranean cemetery SP 7/1
Medusas TD 4/1
Meeting MOK 1/1
Memo to a literary pimp FR 22/1

---

 * published title
** manuscript title

Memo to Sir Mortimer TD 5/1, TD 13/1
**Mercenaries TD 14/1
Michal EBN 20/1
Mid East crisis SP 6/1, SP 9/1
Midsummer's dream in the Vienna stadpark, A PV 32/1
Mildewed maple, The *DFH 3/1
Mishnah and the eternal shmuck TD 15/1
Misunderstanding POM 2/1
Mithymna cemetery PV 34/1, PV 34/2
**Mitt a bang DFH 10/1
Modern Greek poet SP 5/2
Modern miracle *WBB 2/1
Molibos DFH 13/1, TD 21/1
Moment, The DFH 10/1
Monster, The TD 16/1
Monsters GB2 8/1, UN 7/1
Montgo LR 3/1
Mount Royal cemetery FMNH 2/1
Mountain playhouse FMNH 11/1
Mustering all his wit FR 14/1
My fair lady from Bremen PV 33/1
My flesh comfortless LIM2 2/1
Nail polish NP 11/1
Nausicaa IB 2/1
Neighbour love GB 19/1
Neolithic brain, The FMBJ 7/1, *FMBJ 18/1, *FMBJ 23/1
Nepalese woman and child WBB 3/1
Newer critics, The MOK 2/1
Nightmare in the annex FR 29/1, FR 32/1, FR 36/1
No bird but lighter than one FR 19/1
No curtain calls NP 11/1, NP 12/1
No cynic FMNH 10/1
No exit POM 8/1
No wild dog POM 1/3, POM 1/4
Nostalgia when the leaves begin to fall GB 38/1
Not all canucks are shmucks DFH 6/1
**Not all poets are liars FMNH 10/1
Not with a whimper *DFH 10/1
O Canada FMNH 6/1
O Jerusalem FMBJ 19/1, GP 8/1

---

 * published title
 ** manuscript title

Odd couple TD 14/1
Odd love poem, An SP 3/1
Odd obsession GB 14/1, GB 20/1, *GB 30/1
**Of flies and morning glories EBN 18/1
Of leaves and loves GB 22/1
Of one fairy and three Godesses MSGB 1/1
Of the man who sits in the garden FMBJ 20/1
Oil slick on the riviera SP 8/1, SP 10/1
Old and young FMNH 4/1, FMNH 5/1
Old man's wet dream, An GB 8/1, GB 24/1, GB2 3/2
Omnipresence FR 12/1
On the assassination of President Kennedy POM 3/1
On this far shore SP 3/1, SP 9/1
Once a single hair POM 4/1
One last try at a final solution SP 16/1
Opiums FR 47/1
Oracle, The TD 2/1, TD 4/1
Orpheus in Old Forest Hill GB 23/1
Overman FR 6/1
Paddler, The FR 2/1, FR 4/1
Papal election, The TD 18/1, TD 18/2
Paradox TD 30/1
Pardon me lady TD 8/2
Parque de Montjuich FMBJ 21/1, FMBJ 21/2, FMBJ 21/3, FMBJ 21/4
Parting LIM 3/1
Passing through the rockies FMNH 11/1
Peacemonger SP 17/1
Perfection GB 24/1, GB 25/1, GB 35/1
Piles of Greece, piles of Greece, The FR 23/1
Plaka, The FMBJ 22/1
Plato was an asshole FMNH 5/1, TD 15/1, UN 20/1
Poem that says it all FR 8/1
Poet *EBN 14/1
Poet at Sinai SP 5/1
Poet on Cos PV 9/1
Poet's bust PV 35/1
Poet's lament NP 14/2, NP 17/1
Poet's plea for justice, The MSGB 4/1
Poetess *SP 13/1
Poetry and the class war *PV 24/1, PV 36/1

---

* published title
** manuscript title

Poetry seminar FMNH 11/1
Pole-vaulter *PV 39/1
**Pole vaulter, The PV 39/1
Political dream, A GP 10/1
Popcorn FR 43/1
Poros *POM 5/1, UN 18/1
Portrait of a modern woman GB 26/1
Portrait of a genius BFOJ 2/1, BFOJ 2/2, BFOJ 2/7
Portraits drawn from life NP 7/1, NP 13/1
Postcard PV 38/1
Potatoes FR 45/1, UN 8/1
Prayer for a long life GB 35/1
Prayer for my old age DFH 8/1, DFH 10/1
Prelude SP 7/1, SP 10/1
Principessa Anna FR 40/1
Private enterprise TD 15/1
Prize, The TD 27/1
Professional, The TD 19/1
Proteus and Nymph PV 19/1, PV 37/1
Prototype IMF 1/1
**Prussian schoolmaster, The TD 20/1
Quay scene POM 9/1
Queen of hearts, The EBN 15/1
Queer hate poem SP 11/1
Queer mammal DFH 9/1
Question, The GB 32/1
Quidnunc DFH 5/1, UN 3/1
**Quo vadis FMBJ 25/1
Recovery, The GB 27/1
Red chamberpot, The TD 2/1
Red geranium, The FMBJ 23/1
Red moujhik, The SP 12/1
Release FMBJ 15/1, FMBJ 20/1, FMBJ 28/1, FMBJ 30/1
**Religious poet PV 50/1
Religious poet 1973 AD *PV 50/1
Reply to a rhyming notary POM 6/1
Requiem for A.M. Klein PV 40/1
Retribution for Ferdinand and Isabella FMNH 4/1
Reunion at the Hilton *GP 12/1
Revenge I'd take, The GB 33/2

---

* published title
** manuscript title

Revolution PV 35/1, PV 45/1
Ruina maya EBN 11/1
Runts FMBJ 3/1
Saint Pinchas FMBJ 12/1, FMBJ 16/3, FMBJ 25/1
Samantha Clara Layton GB 3/1
Saratoga beach CGE 3/1
Saturday night farticle FR 13/1, FR 26/1, FR 31/1
Saved FMBJ 22/1, *FMBJ 25/1, *FMBJ 26/1
Say cheese please FR 1/1
Schadenfreude TD 23/1
**Scorecard FMNH 1/2
**Script, The EBN 12/1
Self overcoming GB 29/1
Self therapy UN 2/1
September woman PV 41/1
Sex appeal FR 33/1
Shadow, The PV 42/1
Shakespeare NP 14/1, NP 14/2, *NP 14/3, NP 14/4
Shark, The GP 13/1
Shining, The UN 23/1
Shit DFH 3/1, FMNH 3/1
Shlemihl DFH 7/1
Short sermon on God and nature by the Rabbi who survived Auschwitz NP 14/1
Shrinking General, The WBB 4/1, WBB 4/2
Simpson FR 36/1
Sir TD 24/1
Sir Mortimer FMNH 5/1, TD 19/1, TD 22/1
**Smile, The GB 30/1
Smoke TD 21/1
Socrates at the Centaur FR 11/1, FR 15/1
Soft porn FR 11/1, FR 17/1, FR 33/1
Solitary, The *PV 46/1
Some Canadian birds in October LLM 1/1
**Some of my best friends are goyim FMBJ 4/1
Song for Naomi POM 1/6, POM 1/7
Sort of after dinner speech, A SP 17/1
Southern comfort *FMNH 1/2
Spaghetti western UN 24/1
Specter, The FMNH 6/1
Spectre, The FMNH 7/1

---

  * published title
** manuscript title

Spurt, The UN 25/1
Squint, The TD 2/1, TD 7/1
Star trek *TD 7/1
**Startrek TD 7/1
Stillness *DFH 11/1
Straight man, The *NP 14/2, NP 14/3, *NP 15/1, NP 15/2, *NP 15/3, *NP 15/4
Stripping telegram GB 14/1
Sunbather FMNH 8/1
Sunflowers EBN 19/1
**Swamp, The GB 33/1, GB 33/2, GB 38/1, MSGB 1/1
Sweet light strikes my eyes, The SP 13/1
Tabletalk *FMBJ 24/1, *FMBJ 24/2
Tailor's view of history, A PV 21/1, PV 49/1
Talisman, The GB 31/1
Talk at twilight SP/1
Tall man executes a jig, A BFOJ 6/1, BFOJ 6/2
Tamed birds SP 14/1, SP 14/2
**Tangiers - a meditation on the future FMBJ 24/2
Tell it to Peggy *FMNH 7/1, TD 30/1
**Tell it to Maggie FMNH 7/1, TD 30/1
**Ten year old cynic EBN 13/1
Terrorists PV 48/1
Terry Fox FR 26/1, FR 28/1, GB 28/1, UN 16/1
Theatre of Dionysos, The FR 2/1, FR 3/1, FR 34/1
There's always Job GB 25/1, GB 32/1
They also serve GB 21/1, GB 28/1
This machine age BFOJ 6/1
Thou shalt not kill EBN 13/1
Thoughts on titling my next book "Bravo Layton" COV 2/1
Three sisters, The PV 47/1
**Tic toc MSGB 5/1
Tick tock *MSGB 5/1
Tightrope dancer, The TD 12/1
To a generation of poets SP 13/1
To a schmuck with talent *EBN 12/1
**To a young poet who hanged himself PV 18/2
To Irving sans love UN 6/1
To R.E. LIM 2/1
To the Russians at the U.N. SP 17/1
To the woman with the speaking eyes PV 43/1

---

　*　published title
　**　manuscript title

To write an old fashioned poem SP 15/1
Tragedy GB 37/1
Tragedy of old age, The UN 26/1
Trees in late autumn *GB 21/1
**Trees in rain GB 21/1
Trench mouth FR 28/1, GB2 6/1
Tristezza FR 5/1
True love NP 10/1
Twentieth century gothic FR 1/1, FR 15/1, FR 36/1
Two for the road FR 42/1
Two solitudes *DFH 3/1
Two songs for sweet voices *LIM 2/1
Two thousand and twenty eight FMNH 12/1
Undeserved UN 13/1
United Church signboard FMNH 11/1
Unwavering eye, The *GP 8/1, GP 14/1, GP 14/2
Vacuum, The GB 30/1
**Vertical man NP 14/2, NP 15/1, NP 15/3
Victory LIM 3/1
Village funeral SP 6/1
Violent life, The FMBJ 27/1
Wagschal exhibition FR 30/1
Warrior poet *FMBJ 29/1
Wasp song DFH 3/1, DFH 9/1, FMNH 3/1
Watch out for his left FMNH 9/1, TD 25/1, TD 29/1
**Water skier POM 5/1
Way Keats never would have told it, The *SP 1/1
**Way Keats would not have told it, The SP 1/1
Weirdo FR 40/1, UN 11/1
Westminister Abbey POM 7/1
**What an old poet told me DFH 10/1
What another old poet told me DFH 10/1
What crazy Jenny sings in her golden ghetto DFH 9/1
What I told the ghost of Harold Laski PV 44/1
What should be done GB 28/1
Whatever else poetry is freedom LIM 3/1
When death comes for you TD 11/1
When death says come FMNH 9/1, TD 25/1
Where has the glory fled GB 34/1, UN 12/1
Where was your shit detector, Pablo? DFH 8/1

---

 *   published title
** manuscript title

**Where's my damned hat TD 8/2
Whitehern MSGB 2/1
**Who's seen de Gaulle WWB 4/2
**Why the Austrians opted for Auschwitz FMNH 11/1
Winged horse, The GB 13/1, GB 35/1
Woman MOK 3/1
Word from Diogenes, A FMBJ 2/1
Words from an old Greek poet *DFH 10/1
Wraith, The GB 8/1, UN 16/1
Xmas eve 1971, Zihuatanejo LLM 1/5, LLM 2/1, LLM 2/2, LLM 2/3, *LLM 2/4, LLM 2/5
Yeats at sixty five MSGB 4/1
Yet what if the survivors SP 16/1
Yids GB 14/1, GB 16/1, GB 33/2
You allowed the generalissimo TD 24/1, TD 29/1
You come to me TD 30/1
Young couple at Lum Fong hotel *PV 45/1
Young girls dancing LIM2 3/1, LIM2 3/2
Young girls dancing at Camp Lajoie LIM2 3/1, LIM2 3/2
Zucchini GB 39/1

OTHER ITEMS
Essays, Manuscripts & Notebooks

Ambassador: a political farce, The PR/1
Balls for a one-armed juggler MS/1, MS/2, MS/3
Canadian poems 1850-1952 E/1
Challenge we face, or, a poet's view of the world, The E/9
Collected poems of Irving Layton, The E/2
Dance with desire: love poems MS/13, MS/14
Europe and other bad news E/12, MS/9
Final reckoning: poems 1982-1986 E/11, MS/11, MS/12
For my neighbours in Hell MS/10
Gucci bag, The MS/4
Improved binoculars, The MS/5
Laughing rooster, The MS/6, MS/7
Love poems of Irving Layton, The E/8
Love where the nights are long E/3, MS/8

---

* published title
** manuscript title

Notebook NB 196?, NB 1960-68, NB 1962, NB 1963, NB 1966, NB 1967, NB 1968/1, NB 1968/2, NB 1968/3, NB 1969, NB 1971, NB 1972-73, NB 1972/1, NB 1972/2, NB 1973/1, NB 1973/2, NB 1976
Old and the quiet ones, The PR/2
Osmeck PR/3
Parasite PR/6
Pocket engagement calendar MISC 1
Poems to color E/4
Pole vaulter, The E/5
Reflections on the victory of the Labour Party E/6
Symposium MISC 2
Tightrope dancer, The E/7
Unemployed PR/6
Up with nothing PR/4, PR/5
Waiting for the Messiah: a memoir MS/15
What is Canadian culture E/10

---

* published title
** manuscript title

CHRONOLOGICAL INDEX

1942

Epitaphs LIM 2/1
To R.E. LIM 2/1
Two songs for sweet voices *LIM 2/1

1950

Reflections on the victory of the Labour Party E/6

1953

Canadian poems 1850-1952 E/1
For Priscilla *IMF 1/1
Misunderstanding POM 2/1
Prototype IMF 1/1

1954

Boys in October *CGE 1/1
Canadian spring LP 1/1
Cold green element, The POM 1/1, POM 1/2
Enemies CGE 2/1
Saratoga beach CGE 3/1

1955

Me, the P.M., and the stars IBM 1/1
Song for Naomi POM 1/6, POM 1/7
Woman MOK 3/1

1956

By ecstasies perplexed IB 1/1, *IB 1/2
Improved binoculars, The MS/5
Meeting MOK 1/1
Nausicaa IB 2/1
Newer critics, The MOK 2/1

1957

Bawdy bawdy LIM 3/1
Cain POM 1/5

---

  * published title
 ** manuscript title

1957... con't

Cat dying in autumn LIM 1/1
Parting LIM 3/1
Victory LIM 3/1
Whatever else poetry is freedom LIM 3/1

1958

For Mao-Tse-Tung LIM2 1/1
Love is an irrefutable fire LIM2 1/1
My flesh comfortless LIM2 2/1
Word from Diogenes,A FMBJ 2/1
Young girls dancing LIM2 3/1, LIM2 3/2
Young girls dancing at Camp Lajoie LIM2 3/1, LIM2 3/

196?

Ambassador: a political farce, The PR/1
Old and the quiet ones, The PR/2
Osmeck PR/3
Parasite PR/6
Unemployed PR/6

1960

Caged bird, The SF 1/1
I know the dark and hovering moth *SF 2/1, SF 2/2
Keine Lazarovitch: 1870-1959 SF 3/1

1961

Up with nothing PR/4, PR/5

1962

Baudelaire in a summer cottage BFOJ 1/1, BFOJ 1/2, BFOJ 1/3, BFOJ 1/4
Epigram for Roy Daniells BFOJ 7/1
For Alexander Trocchi novelist BFOJ 2/1, BFOJ 2/2, BFOJ 2/3, BFOJ 2/4, BFOJ 2/5, BFOJ 2/6, BFOJ 2/7
Gods speak out, The BFOJ 3/1, BFOJ 3/2
Hag, the BFOJ 4/1
Love where the nights are long E/3, MS/8
Man going up and down BFOJ 5/1

---

* published title
** manuscript title

1962... con't

No wild dog POM 1/3, POM 1/4
Portrait of a genius BFOJ 2/1, BFOJ 2/2, BFOJ 2/7
Tall man executes a jig, A BFOJ 6/1, BFOJ 6/2
This machine age BFOJ 6/1

1963

Aftermath LR 3/2
Balls for a one armed juggler MS/1, MS/2, MS/3
El Caudillo LR 1/1
For my green old age LR 2/1
Montgo LR 3/1
On the assassination of President Kennedy POM 3/1

1964

Laughing rooster, The MS/6, MS/7

1966

At the Belsen memorial POM 9/1
For Musia's grandchildren POM 1/1, POM 1/2, POM 1/3, POM 1/4, POM 1/5, POM 1/6, POM 1/7, POM 1/8
Freedom POM 2/1
Fried fish my love *UN 1/1
Insomnia POM 3/1
Mahogany red *POM 4/1
Once a single hair POM 4/1
Poros *POM 5/1, UN 18/1
Quay scene POM 9/1
Reply to a rhyming notary POM 6/1
Westminister Abbey POM 7/1

1967

After the battle of Sinai SP 17/1
As you wish sir SP 5/3
Autopsy on Aberfan SP 14/1
Cleavages SP 16/1
Collaboration POM 8/1
Counsel for my stung love SP 14/2

---

* published title
** manuscript title

1967... con't

Fantasia in black SP 1/1
Final irony, The SP 13/1
For the girl with wide apart eyes *SP 2/1, *SP 2/2, *SP 2/3
For the cause SP 6/1
Graveyard, The *SP 3/1
He saw them at first SP 17/1
Homage to Roumania SP 13/1
Iroquois in Nice SP 4/1
Let gentility cry out SP 17/1
Like a mother demented SP 5/1, SP 5/2, SP 5/3, SP 5/4
Love poem with an odd twist *SP 3/1
Marche Municipale SP 6/1, SP 6/2, SP 6/3
Mediterranean cemetery SP 7/1
Mid East crisis SP 6/1, SP 9/1
Modern Greek poet SP 5/2
Modern miracle *WBB 2/1
No exit POM 8/1
Odd love poem, An SP 3/1
Oil slick on the riviera SP 8/1, SP 10/1
On this far shore SP 3/1, SP 9/1
One last try at a final solution SP 16/1
Peacemonger SP 17/1
Poet at Sinai SP 5/1
Poetess *SP 13/1
Prelude SP 7/1, SP 10/1
Queer hate poem SP 11/1
Red moujhik, The SP 12/1
Sort of after dinner speech, A SP 17/1
Sweet light strikes my eyes, The SP 13/1
Talk at twilight SP/1
Tamed birds SP 14/1, SP 14/2
To a generation of poets SP 13/1
To the Russians at the U.N. SP 17/1
To write an old fashioned poem SP 15/1
Village funeral SP 6/1
Way Keats never would have told it, The *SP 1/1
Yet what if the survivors SP 16/

---

* published title
** manuscript title

1968

After Auschwitz SP 1/1
Elephant WBB 1/1
Nepalese woman and child WBB 3/1
Shrinking General, The WBB 4/1, WBB 4/2
Frost and fences NP 6/1, NP 8/1
To Irving sans love UN 6/1

197?

Advice to a friend on his 60th birthday UN 4/1
Clio's favourites UN 17/1
Fantasies of a stone UN 18/1
Half of forever UN 20/1
Jamsmear UN 21/1
Spaghetti western UN 24/1
Spurt, The UN 25/1
Tragedy of old age, The UN 26/1
Undeserved UN 13/1
What is Canadian culture E/10
Wraith, The GB 8/1, UN 16/1

1970

As seen through a glass darkly NP 1/1, NP 1/2, *NP 4/1
Dark lady NP 4/2
Dionysian reveller NP 14/3
Dionysus in Hampstead NP 2/1, NP 2/2, NP 2/3, NP 2/4, NP 2/5, NP 2/6
End of the white mouse NP 3/1, NP 3/2, NP 3/3, NP 3/4, NP 11/1
Entry *NP 2/3, *NP 2/5, *NP 2/6
Fanatic in San Feliu NP 4/1, NP 4/2, NP 4/3
For Natalya Correia NP 5/1
God is love NP 7/1, NP 11/1, NP 14/1, NP 14/2
Grey morning in Lisbon NP 5/1, NP 8/1
Homage to Onassis NP 9/1
Hungry Christians NP 11/1
July 21, 1969 NP 17/1
Kilmurvey strand NP 16/1
Lake Selby NP 10/1
Lobsters NP 4/1
Nail polish NP 11/1
No curtain calls NP 11/1, NP 12/1

---

* published title
** manuscript title

1970... con't

Poems to color E/4
Poet's lament NP 14/2, NP 17/1
Portraits drawn from life NP 7/1, NP 13/1
Shakespeare NP 14/1, NP 14/2, *NP 14/3, NP 14/4
Short sermon on God and nature by the Rabbi who survived Auschwitz NP 14/1
Straight man, The *NP 14/2, NP 14/3, *NP 15/1, NP 15/2, *NP 15/3, *NP 15/4
True love NP 10/

1971

Collected poems of Irving Layton, The E/2
Goat, The TD 4/1, TD 7/1
Xmas eve 1971, Zihuatanejo LLM 1/5, LLM 2/1, LLM 2/2, LLM 2/3, *LLM 2/4, LLM 2/5
Political dream, A GP 10/1
Some Canadian birds in October LLM 1/1

1973

Adam and Eve PV 2/1, PV 38/1
Alcaeus reflects on a chance encounter PV 51/1
American young woman in Patmos PV 3/1
Animal across the street, The PV 4/1
Asian suite PV 5/1
Basin, the PV 7/1, PV 7/2
Bedbugs *PV 8/1
Black queen, The PV 51/1
Bodhidharma PV 12/1
Budapest PV 13/1
Departed PV 10/1
Displaced person PV 11/1
Final solution, The PV 15/1, PV 20/1, PV 32/1
Flytrap *GP 7/1, GP 7/2
For a young poet who hanged himself PV 18/1, *PV 18/2, PV 40/1
For Andrei Amalrik PV 16/1
For Anne Frank PV 17/1, PV 17/2
For Nadezhda Mandelstam PV 1/1, PV 1/2, PV 47/1
For the Fraulein from Hamburg PV 19/1, PV 19/2
Gannymede PV 20/1
Greek epigram PV 21/1
Greek fly PV 22/1

---

* published title
** manuscript title

1973... con't

Hit parade PV 23/1
Honeymoon PV 24/1
Ideal among vacationists, The *PV 25/1, *PV 25/2, PV 50/1
Jijimuge PV 26/1
Lillian Roxon PV 27/1
Lines for my grandchildren PV 51/1
Lullaby PV 28/1
Lures PV 13/1
Madonna and Dionysos PV 29/1
Marriage PV 30/1
Mary PV 24/1, PV 31/1
Midsummer's dream in the Vienna stadpark, A PV 32/1
Mithymna cemetery PV 34/1, PV 34/2
My fair lady from Bremen PV 33/1
Poet on Cos PV 9/1
Poet's bust PV 35/1
Poetry and the class war *PV 24/1, PV 36/1
Pole-vaulter *PV 39/1
Postcard PV 38/1
Proteus and Nymph PV 19/1, PV 37/1
Religious poet 1973 AD *PV 50/1
Requiem for A.M. Klein PV 40/1
Reunion at the Hilton *GP 12/1
Revolution PV 35/1, PV 45/1
September woman PV 41/1
Shadow, The PV 42/1
Solitary, The *PV 46/1
Tailor's view of history, A PV 21/1, PV 49/1
Terrorists PV 48/1
To the woman with the speaking eyes PV 43/1
What I told the ghost of Harold Laski PV 44/1
Young couple at Lum Fong hotel *PV 45/1

1974

Adam FMBJ 1/1
Alas, too noiseless GP 1/1, GP 1/2, GP 2/1, GP 4/1, GP 11/2
Australian bush PV 6/1
Beard, The GP 2/1, GP 6/1

---

* published title
** manuscript title

1974... con't

Blackout GP 4/1
Byron exhibition at the Benaki museum GP 5/1, GP 5/2
Castle, The GP 6/1
Coastal mind, The PV 14/1, PV 14/2, PV 14/3, PV 14/4
Dream in Pangrati, A GP 3/1
For Edda FMBJ 2/1
For Francesca FMBJ 9/1
Helios GP 9/1, GP 9/2
Hellenes GP 10/1
Ithaca GP 11/1, GP 11/2
Kazantzakis: God's athlete GP 8/1, GP 8/2
O Jerusalem FMBJ 19/1, GP 8/1
Pole vaulter, The E/5
Shark, The GP 13/1
Three sisters, The PV 47/1
Unwavering eye, The *GP 8/1, GP 14/1, GP 14/2

1975

Act of creation *FMBJ 3/1
Arch, The FMBJ 4/1, FMBJ 20/1
Asylums FMBJ 21/2
At the Barcelona zoo FMBJ 5/1, FMBJ 21/1
Beauty and genius FMBJ 20/1, FMBJ 25/1
Belle France, La FMBJ 4/1
C'est fini *FMBJ 4/1
Daphnis and Chloe FMBJ 7/1, FMBJ 18/1, FMBJ 20/1, UN 21/1
Discotheque FMBJ 23/1
Excelsior FMBJ 14/1, FMBJ 28/1, *FMBJ 30/1
Florence FMBJ 8/1, FMBJ 8/2, FMBJ 8/3
For Jesus Christ FMBJ 10/1
For my incomparable gypsy *FMBJ 23/1, GB 8/1
For my brother Jesus FMBJ 11/1
For some of my best friends *FMBJ 4/1
Galim FMBJ 12/1, FMBJ 22/1
Glass dancer, The COV 6/1
Greeks FMBJ 7/1, FMBJ 22/1
Haemorrhage, The FMBJ 13/1
Hallowing, The FMBJ 14/1, FMBJ 23/1

---

* published title
** manuscript title

1975... con't

How many days FMBJ 15/1, FMBJ 20/1, FMBJ 23/1, FMBJ 30/1
In praise of older men FMBJ 16/1, FMBJ 16/2, FMBJ 16/3
Island Circe FMBJ 3/1
Jeshua FMBJ 30/1
Jesus and St Paul FMBJ 4/1
Judea eterna FMBJ 17/1, FMBJ 22/1, FMBJ 25/1
June bug FMBJ 4/1
Neolithic brain, The FMBJ 7/1, *FMBJ 18/1, *FMBJ 23/1
Of the man who sits in the garden FMBJ 20/1
Parque de Montjuich FMBJ 21/1, FMBJ 21/2, FMBJ 21/3, FMBJ 21/4
Plaka, The FMBJ 22/1
Red geranium, The FMBJ 23/1
Release FMBJ 15/1, FMBJ 20/1, FMBJ 28/1, FMBJ 30/1
Runts FMBJ 3/1
Saint Pinchas FMBJ 12/1, FMBJ 16/3, FMBJ 25/1
Saved FMBJ 22/1, *FMBJ 25/1, *FMBJ 26/1
Tabletalk *FMBJ 24/1, *FMBJ 24/2
Violent life, The FMBJ 27/1
Warrior poet *FMBJ 29/1

1976

Aviva COV 5/1
Bacillus prodigiosus COV 1/1, COV 4/1
Letting go GB 18/1
Like once I lost COV 3/1
Meditations of an aging Lebanese poet COV 4/1
Thoughts on titling my next book "Bravo Layton" COV 2/1

1977

Abyss, The FMNH 4/1
Accident, The TD 1/1, TD 28/1
After a sleepless night TD 2/1, TD 7/1
Aging Greek poet, An TD 15/1
Arab Harikiri TD 3/1
At the chill centre *TD 2/1, *TD 4/1
Beatitude *TD 15/1
Bravo, death, I love you TD 4/1
Bridegroom FMNH 6/1
Checkmate TD 1/1, TD 28/1

---

* published title
** manuscript title

1977... con't

Comrade TD 25/1, TD 26/1
Dialectical leap *TD 20/1
Dirty old man FMNH 4/1
Don't blame the apple TD 15/1
Flies TD 5/1
Flowers he'll never smell TD 6/1
Gay sunshine anthology EBN 21/1, TD 20/1
Goodnight sweet lady TD 8/1, *TD 8/2
Greek dancers TD 9/1
Greek fisherman FMNH 6/1
Greek light, The TD 4/1
Intimations TD 10/1
Keep dying TD 11/1
Latest wrinkle, The TD 17/1
Medusas TD 4/1
Memo to Sir Mortimer TD 5/1, TD 13/1
Mishnah and the eternal shmuck TD 15/1
Molibos DFH 13/1, TD 21/1
Monster, The TD 16/1
O Canada FMNH 6/1
Odd couple TD 14/1
Old and young FMNH 4/1, FMNH 5/1
Oracle, The TD 2/1, TD 4/1
Papal election, The TD 18/1, TD 18/2
Private enterprise TD 15/1
Prize, The TD 27/1
Professional, The TD 19/1
Retribution for Ferdinand and Isabella FMNH 4/1
Schadenfreude TD 23/1
Sir Mortimer FMNH 5/1, TD 19/1, TD 22/1
Sir TD 24/1
Smoke TD 21/1
Specter, The FMNH 6/1
Spectre, The FMNH 7/1
Squint, The TD 2/1, TD 7/1
Star trek *TD 7/1
Tell it to Peggy *FMNH 7/1, TD 30/1
Tightrope dancer, The TD 12/1

---

* published title
** manuscript title

1977... con't

Watch out for his left FMNH 9/1, TD 25/1, TD 29/1
When death comes for you TD 11/1
You allowed the generalissimo TD 24/1, TD 29/1
You come to me TD 30/1

1978
Absurb animal, The *DFH 9/1
Acquired courage DFH 3/1
Autumn seen as my lady DFH 1/1
Calibrations DFH 2/1
Cuisine Canadienne *DFH 1/1
Divorce DFH 9/1
Fata Morgana DFH 3/1, DFH 3/2
For Sandra DFH 12/1
Hex, The *DFH 3/1
Letter to a lost love DFH 5/1
Love poems of Irving Layton, tTe E/8
Man and woman DFH 3/1
Mildewed maple, The *DFH 3/1
Moment, The DFH 10/1
Not all canucks are shmucks DFH 6/1
Not with a whimper *DFH 10/1
Prayer for my old age DFH 8/1, DFH 10/1
Queer mammal DFH 9/1
Quidnunc DFH 5/1, UN 3/1
Shit DFH 3/1, FMNH 3/1
Shlemihl DFH 7/1
Stillness *DFH 11/1
Tightrope dancer, The E/7
Two solitudes *DFH 3/1
Two thousand and twenty-eight FMNH 12/1
Wasp song DFH 3/1, DFH 9/1, FMNH 3/1
What another old poet told me DFH 10/1
What crazy Jenny sings in her golden ghetto DFH 9/1
Where was your shit detector, Pablo? DFH 8/1
Words from an old Greek poet *DFH 10/1

---

* published title
** manuscript title

1979
Alive and still kicking FMNH 10/1
Banff poem for Harriet FMNH 11/1
Burning remnant, The *FMNH 1/2, *FMNH 11/1
Cracked mirror, The *FMNH 1/2, *TD 14/1
Dysphasiac, The *FMNH 13/1
Egalitarian *FMNH 10/1
Election, The *FMNH 1/1, *FMNH 1/2, *FMNH 1/3, FMNH 1/4
Finally, The final solution FMNH 12/1
God and John Dewey TD 4/1
Guardrail, The FMNH 11/1
Happy hooker, the DFH 4/1
Homage to Sir Mortimer FMNH 7/1, TD 28/1
Last survivor, The DFH 3/1, DFH 3/2, FMNH 3/1
Mount Royal cemetery FMNH 2/1
Mountain playhouse FMNH 11/1
No cynic FMNH 10/1
Paradox TD 30/1
Pardon me lady TD 8/2
Passing through the rockies FMNH 11/1
Plato was an asshole FMNH 5/1, TD 15/1, UN 20/1
Poetry seminar FMNH 11/1
Red chamberpot, The TD 2/1
Southern comfort *FMNH 1/2
Sunbather FMNH 8/1
United Church signboard FMNH 11/1
When death says come FMNH 9/1, TD 25/1

1980
Balloon, The EBN 3/1
Being *EBN 2/1
Being there EBN 1/1, BFOJ 1/4
Death where is your sting-a-ling *EBN 13/1
Definitions EBN 4/1
Early morning sounds *EBN 18/1
Eine kleine Nachtmusik EBN 5/1, *EBN 6/1
Endangered species EBN 16/1
Eternal recurrence *EBN 17/1
Europe and other bad news MS/9
For Hans, maybe Klaus or Tadeusz EBN 5/1, *EBN 6/1

---

* published title
** manuscript title

1980... con't

For my neighbours in Hell MS/10
Gulag EBN 7/1
Herzl EBN 9/1
In an ice age EBN 8/1, EBN 10/1
Isla Mujeres EBN 10/1
Junk EBN 2/1
Michal EBN 20/1
Poet *EBN 14/1
Queen of hearts, The EBN 15/1
Ruina maya EBN 11/1
Sunflowers EBN 19/1
Thou shalt not kill EBN 13/1
To a schmuck with talent *EBN 12/1

1981

Advice to old maids GB 14/1, GB 33/2
And it came to pass GB 27/1
Biggest show in town, The UN 5/1
Boris Pasternak GB 5/1
Breast stroke, The *GB 1/1
Bring on the skinheads GB 32/1
Captive, The *GB 28/1
Cracked crystal ball, The GB 13/1, GB 16/1, GB 24/1, GB 33/2
Dead souls GB 14/1
Furrow, The GB 16/1
Garden, The GB 17/1, GB 28/1
Ideal husband, an GB 18/1
Insect repellant FR 28/1, GB 4/1, GB 16/1
Make room William Blake GB 18/1, UN 12/1
Odd obsession GB 14/1, GB 20/1, *GB 30/1
Prayer for a long life GB 35/1
Question, The GB 32/1
Recovery, The GB 27/1
Samantha Clara Layton GB 3/1
Self overcoming GB 29/1
Shining, The UN 23/1
Stripping telegram GB 14/1
They also serve GB 21/1, GB 28/1

---

* published title
** manuscript title

1981... con't

Vacuum, the GB 30/1
What should be done GB 28/1
Yids GB 14/1, GB 16/1, GB 33/

1982
Advice for old maids GB 24/1
Ah, nuts GB 7/1
Aristocrats MSGB 3/1
August Strindberg MSGB 4/1
Ballad of the Holstein bull GB 33/2
Blind man's bluff GB 6/1
Blossom GB 23/1
Bonded GB 5/1, GB 7/1
Bull, more and less GB 11/1, GB 24/1
Carillon, The GB 9/1
Carved nakedness, the GB 8/1
Central heating GB 10/1
Chariot for Harriet,A GB 10/1, GB 21/1, UN 10/1
Comedia, La GB 8/1
Comrade Undershaftsky GB 35/1, MSGB 1/1
Courage to be, The *GB 4/1, *GB 12/1, *GB 34/1
Dancing man GB 12/1
Dazed fly, The GB 11/1
Descent from Eden GB 13/1
Divine touch, The GB 2/1
Empty words MSGB 4/1
For the wife of Mr. Milton *GB 15/1
From the nether world GB 5/1, GB 39/1
Hairy monster, The GB 36/1
In revenge for Olga and BP GB 5/1, GB 21/1
Lady Macbeth MSGB 4/1
Los Americanos GB 23/1
Neighbour love GB 19/1
Nostalgia when the leaves begin to fall GB 38/1
Of leaves and loves GB 22/1
Of one fairy and three Godesses MSGB 1/1
Old man's wet dream, An GB 8/1, GB 24/1, GB2 3/2
Orpheus in Old Forest Hill GB 23/1

---

* published title
** manuscript title

1982... con't

Perfection GB 24/1, GB 25/1, GB 35/1
Poet's plea for justice, The MSGB 4/1
Portrait of a modern woman GB 26/1
Revenge I'd take, The GB 33/2
Sex appeal FR 33/1
Talisman, The GB 31/1
There's always Job GB 25/1, GB 32/1
Tragedy GB 37/1
Trees in late autumn *GB 21/1
Where has the glory fled GB 34/1, UN 12/1
Winged horse, The GB 13/1, GB 35/1
Yeats at sixty-five MSGB 4/1
Zucchini GB 39/

1983

Carmen GB2 3/1, GB2 3/2
Cyst, The FR 28/1, GB2 6/1
Demon, The LPIL2 1/1
Epistle to Catullus GB 5/1, GB 39/1, GB2 1/1
For Ettore with love and admiration GB2 7/1
Gucci bag, The MS/4
Holiday Inn: Tokyo MSGB 5/1
Juvenal redivivus GB2 9/1
Madrigal for Anna, A LPIL2 1/1
Monsters GB2 8/1, UN 71
Tick tock *MSGB 5/1
Trench mouth FR 28/1, GB2 6/1
Whitehern MSGB 2/1

1984

Boschka Layton 1921-1984 GB2 2/1, GB2 4/1, GB2 5/1, UN 22/1
Byron in Venice FR 38/1, FR 48/1, UN 19/1
Cracks in the acropolis FR 46/1
Dionysians in a bad time GB2 4/1
Etruscan tombs FR 45/1
Fellini FR 38/1
Initiates, The UN 22/1, UN 22/2
Lady Aurora GB2 5/1, GB2 5/2
Leopardi in Montreal FR 27/1

---

 * published title
 ** manuscript title

1984... con't

Massacre, The FR 44/1
Opiums FR 47/1
Popcorn FR 43/1
Potatoes FR 45/1, UN 8/1
Wagschal exhibition FR 30/1
Weirdo FR 40/1, UN 11/1

1985

Black tourist in Tinos FR 2/1, FR 3/1, FR 34/1
Burnt offering FR 41/1
Investiture, The FR 2/1
Judgement at Murray's FR 37/1
Omnipresence FR 12/1
Paddler, The FR 2/1, FR 4/1
Theatre of Dionysos, The FR 2/1, FR 3/1, FR 34/1
Two for the road FR 42/1
Waiting for the Messiah: a memoir MS/15

1986

Aesthetic cruelty FR 10/1, FR 18/1, FR 19/1
Alison Parrott 1975-1986 FR 13/1
And they all fall down FR 10/1
Approaching doomsday FR 20/1
Asshole in residence FR 18/1
Casa Cacciatore FR 21/1
Devotion FR 48/1
Diverse pleasures FR 25/1
Final reckoning: after Theognis FR 33/1
Functional illiterates FR 35/1
Gelded lion, The FR 9/1, FR 16/1
Harlequin romance FR 28/1
Herbert Vunce FR 24/1
High fidelity FR 7/1
Immortelles for a literary strumpet FR 9/1
Inter-view FR 32/1, FR 36/1
Kitch FR 39/1
Maimonidian perplexity FR 11/1, FR 17/1
Memo to a literary pimp FR 22/1
Mustering all his wit FR 14/1

---

* published title
** manuscript title

1986... con't

Nightmare in the annex FR 29/1, FR 32/1, FR 36/1
No bird but lighter than one FR 19/1
Overman FR 6/1
Piles of Greece, piles of Greece, The FR 23/1
Poem that says it all FR 8/1
Principessa Anna FR 40/1
Saturday night farticle FR 13/1, FR 26/1, FR 31/1
Say cheese please FR 1/1
Simpson FR 36/1
Socrates at the Centaur FR 11/1, FR 15/1
Soft porn FR 11/1, FR 17/1, FR 33/1
Terry Fox FR 26/1, FR 28/1, GB 28/1, UN 16/1
Tristezza FR 5/1
Twentieth century gothic FR 1/1, FR 15/1, FR 36/1

1987
Dance with desire: love poems MS/13, MS/14
Final reckoning: poems 1982-1986 E/11, MS/11, MS/12
Self therapy UN 2/1
Date unknown
Canucky shmuckism UN 15/1
Challenge we face, or, a poet's view of the world, The E/9

---

* published title
** manuscript title